"If the statistics are right, the Jews constitute but one percent of the human race. It suggests a nebulous dim puff of star dust, lost in the blaze of the Milky Way. Properly, the Jew ought hardly to be heard of; but he is heard of; has always been heard of. He is as prominent on the planet as any other people... His contributions to the world's list of great names in literature, science, art, music, finance, medicine and asbstract learning are also way out of proportion to the weakness of his numbers."

Mark Twain, Harper's Magazine
September, 1899

THE
JEWISH
Contribution
TO THE
Modern World

researched and written by
JOE KING

Edited by
ELEANOR LONDON

With an introduction by
PROFESSOR MORTON WEINFELD

A publication of
Canadian Friends of Haifa University

in collaboration with
The Montreal Jewish Publication Society

First edition – March, 2004
Second edition – October, 2004

© Copyright Joe King 2003

Page design and layout by Renée-Maryse L'Italien
Proof-reading by Proof of the Pudding
Cover by JAM Design

Canadian Friends of Haifa University
4950 Queen Mary Road #360
Montreal, Quebec H3W 1X3
Tel. (514) 735-8500 - Fax (514) 735-8212
E-mail cfhumtl@hotmail.com

Printed in Canada

Contents

The following contributors helped make this publication possible, and we thank them for their support:

Grand Patrons
Donna and Hy Adelman
Lawrence M. Bessner, F.C.A.

Patrons
Aldo Group
CIBC Wood Gundy
Sam Luft

Sponsors
Dr. Charles Bedzow
Sheva and David Honig Foundation
Hon. Lawrence Bergman,
  Government of Quebec
Howard B. Ripstein, SBStJ, CEM
Herschel Segal
Janice and Mark Sherman
Norman Spector

Benefactors
Rosemarie and Robert Asch
Bernice and Morty Brownstein
Aaron M. Fish
Libero Rossini
Arnold and Murray Steinberg/
Nathan Steinberg Family Foundation
Sara and Irwin Tauben

Contributors
Terry Allister
A. Bram Appel
Phil Bell
Saidie Auerback
Bazz Inc.
Monty Berger
Marilyn and Dr. Herb Blumer
Robert Bornstein
Freda and Irwin Browns
Mitzi & Mel Dobrin Family Foundation
Elaine Dubrovsky
Hon. Sheila Finestone, C.P.
Beverly Horwitz
Sheila and Marvin Kussner
Irene Lande
Boris G. Levine, C.M., F.C.A.
Paperman and Sons Inc.
David Schachter
Sam Smolkin
Fannie and Louis Solomon
Tall-J Investments Ltd.

Introduction

As Dorothy Parker, poet but no great lover of Jews, once wrote:
How odd of God
To choose the Jews.
But choose them for what? In this highly-informative and readable volume, Joe King chooses them for their astounding achievements. He presents us with just a sampling of Jewish talent and creativity in the modern world.

Jews have long known that they have been statistically over-represented among lists of great innovators, thinkers, reformers, writers, artists, scientists, entrepreneurs, and the like. Jews scour annual lists of Nobel Prize winners hoping to *kvell* about any Jewish winners. Even if the winners have mixed Jewish ancestry, many forgiving Jews will turn a blind eye. For a group that today numbers barely thirteen million, the record is impressive indeed. This book provides the facts to support this intuitive sense of Jewish accomplishment.

This book offers a record of Jewish achievement in many different domains of endeavor. But one question remains: Why? Why have Jews been able to achieve? Three sorts of explanations have emerged. Since education and intelligence are seen as the key to so much of this achievement, it is natural that this should be the basis of any inquiry. The first is genetic, or biological. Jews are not a race, but they are a population group, with certain sorts of traits. Jewish diseases like Tay-Sachs are one outcome of the historic segregation of Jews. But perhaps Jews also have higher intelligence than other population groups? Historically, the best and brightest among Catholics, priests and nuns, were (in theory) lost from the gene pool. Among Jews, the brightest yeshiva students were often matched with the daughters of the wealthy, a good genetic prognosis. In fact, American studies have shown Jews with above average scores on IQ tests—whatever those things measure. So maybe some of those above average scores would translate into a greater proportion of really talented individuals, with outstanding abilities?

One has to be careful here. Recent scientific studies have found that humans regardless of origin group share well over 99% of the common genetic makeup. As anyone who has been to Israel knows, Jews come in every shade and color, and have clearly experienced an enormous amount of genetic mixing over the years. Much of the Jewish IQ advantage reflects the advantages of being middle class and perhaps of having certain cultural traits. In general one should be wary of assigning to groups biologically rooted traits. Not too long ago it was obvious that Jews could never be farmers or soldiers (though people forgot that among the immigrant Jews of North America at the turn of the century there were a great many boxers and wrestlers...)

A second explanation has to do with social structure. According to this argument, Jews have always been a kind of "middle class" people, or middle class in waiting. They had early exposure to commerce, to urban life, to trade. As a minority and often victimized, they were always predisposed to question basic values and common assumptions. They were "in" societies but never "of" them. Without a state, and without armies, Jews had to survive by their wits. As Jews in Christian societies, they had the required marginality to see things "differently." Fearful of anti-Semitism, they were socialized by their parents to do better in their schooling, to study hard. So it is these social pressures that account for Jewish achievement.

The third explanation is cultural, and rooted in the traditional Jewish cultural sources. Accordingly, Jews have always valued learning and have always revered learning. A rabbi is a learned teacher, not a holy man. Jews were perhaps the first group to espouse and achieve near universal (male) literacy. This ancient religious value then gets transformed into a secular version, from Talmud, as it were, to physics or history. Even the nature of Judaism would offer cultural support for achievement. Judaism has no Pope, and thus many rabbinic schools would compete for influence. The Talmud, perhaps the basic text of traditional Judaic learning, reflects a culture which values debate and analysis and the use of rationality over power as a way of solving disputes.

At the end of the day, no one is really sure. As you read the brief biographies of these outstanding men and women, it is hard to find a common thread that can link them all. They represent the most diverse backgrounds imaginable, from minimal Jewish ancestry and identity to the devout. But they are certainly an impressive group. Their efforts have made the world a better place in every conceivable way. The message to anti-Semites is also clear. Those who attack Jews, whether in the Diaspora or in Israel, risk impoverishing the world. This book is the evidence.

Morton Weinfeld

Morton Weinfeld is Professor of Sociology and holds the Chair in Canadian Ethnic Studies at McGill University. His most recent book is *Like Everyone Else But Different: The Paradoxical Success of Canadian Jews.*

Preface

In this immense world of six billion people, only 12,900,000 are Jews. This is a small number—less than two-tenths of one per cent of the global population. Yet this tiny group of people, with an unbroken, unmatched history of 4,000 years has made a disproportionately large contribution to humanity. In fact, Western civilization has been largely shaped by the thinking of four people—Albert Einstein, Sigmund Freud, Karl Marx, and Charles Darwin. All but Darwin were Jewish. Furthermore, any authoritative study of outstanding people—whether it is in science or technology, cultural matters or business— verifies that Jews —*where there is freedom*—are highly productive citizens. Confined for centuries in ghettos throughout western Europe, Jews were prevented from participating in the growth and development of society.

When the French Revolution freed the Jews in that country, and as Emancipation spelled freedom in nation after nation, Jews broke out of their ghettos and quickly made exceptional contributions to the well-being of the countries in which they lived.

In the *Jewish Mind*, Raphael Patai wrote:

"The suddenness with which Jews began to appear and make a mark in numerous areas of whose very existence their fathers had in most cases no idea at all, is nothing short of astounding. It seemed as if a huge reservoir of Jewish talent, hitherto dammed up behind the wall of Talmudic learning, was suddenly released to spill over into all fields of Gentile cultural activity."

Why did this happen? Patai, in his study, suggests:

"The Jewish home...is a place in which learning is highly valued. This single factor underlies all the other differences."

Historian Ernest van den Haag, in *The Jewish Mystique* (1969) wrote:

"There is no new industry, or science, no new movement in art or literature, no new theory in psychology or physics, no new movement in politics or religion in which Jews do not play a prominent part."

Discovery of the New World, together with the American Revolution, created a golden opportunity for Jews. They fled oppression in Europe and built new lives for themselves and their families in the United States —the Golden Land.

Dr. Carl Wittke, in his *We Who Built America*, wrote:

"The evolution of many a prominent Jewish family of today can be described in terms of the peddler who became a second-hand clothing merchant and then the owner of a large store, and whose descendents became the merchant princes of the department store era."

When anti-Semitic corporations denied them opportunities, they established entirely new industries. Jews, for example, were largely responsible for the creation of the American moving picture industry.

Their children and grandchildren flooded into the universities and emerged as scientists, educators, businessmen, lawyers, composers—all eager to be productive members of the American Mosaic.

When the murderous dictator, Adolf Hitler, led the Germans into a Second World War that claimed 30,000,000 lives (including 6,000,000 Jews in the Holocaust), he drove Jews out or slaughtered them. While Jews made up less than 1% of Germany's population, they had formed 12% of her university professors.

Blinded by anti-Semitism, the Nazi leader killed or expelled scores of some of Germany's most brilliant citizens.

An American named Abraham Flexner convinced two Jews (Louis Bamberger and his sister, Mrs. Felix Fuld) to fund creation of the Institute for Advanced Study at Princeton University; one of the first people accepted was Albert Einstein.

Ruth Gay, writing of this period in her *Jews of America*, stated:

"The immigration of the thirties brought not just human raw material, but people whose accomplishments won them international fame.

Twelve of the refugees won Nobel Prizes after their arrival in the United States; over a hundred were listed in *Who's Who*, and more than two hundred were represented in *American Men of Science*.

Ms. Gay adds:

"Released from the constraints of the ghetto, the Jews took fire in America."

Silvano Arieti, in his *Creativity: the Magic Synthesis*, notes:

"As a result of Fascist persecution, approximately 1,500 Italian Jews of both sexes and all ages emigrated to the United States in 1939 and subsequent years. Two of them won Nobel Prizes while residing in the United States: Emilio Segre (in physics, 1959) and Salvador Luria (in medicine, 1969)."

Jews have been awarded 157 Nobel Prizes (through 2002)—far out of proportion to their small numbers. Silvano Arieti (writing in 1976) declares: "the ratio of the Jewish winners (of Nobel Prizes) is 28 times greater than that of the rest of the world population."

Yet, despite the lessons of history, anti-Semitism is rearing its ugly head again—in the Middle East where hatred of Jews is taught in schools, and now, once more, in Europe.

Onetime British Prime Minister David Lloyd-George (1863-1945), in a newspaper interview in 1923, declared:

"Of all the bigotries that ravage the human temper, there is none so stupid as the anti-Semitic. It has no basis in reason, it is not rooted in faith, it aspires to no ideal."

This new anti-Semitism emanates, in large measure, from an effort by Arab Muslims to destroy the Jewish state of Israel. There are 22 Arab nations with 280,000,000 people. They outnumber the 5,000,000 Jews of Israel fifty-six to one and they have 690 times the land of the Jewish State.

Their stated goal is to replace Israel, the one democracy in the entire Middle East, with a "democratic Palestinian state," which is not likely to occur because, to date, there is no fully democratic Arab state. Meanwhile, with nine wars in little more than half a century, and a propaganda machine based on deliberate distortion of history, Muslim Arabs are doing immense damage to a small nation—a nation, that in a remarkably short period created seven great universities, and is engaged in world class scientific, technological, and medical research of benefit to all humanity.

History establishes that Jews are prepared to play their part, and more, in shaping civilization. When they are denied freedom, all people suffer.

The English political scientist Harold J. Laski put it this way (*New Statesman and Nation*, Feb. 13, 1943):

"The burden of history is unmistakable: the enemy of the Jew is the enemy of freedom. Those who organize the pogrom of today will tomorrow undermine the general foundation of freedom. That is why the moral stature of the nation is set by its recognition that the claim of the Jew to freedom is the claim of its own people to strike off its chains. When it is silent before the Agony of the Jew, it collaborates in the organization of its future servitude."

This book, therefore, was researched and written to identify, for the public, a selection of Jews who have made exceptional contributions to humanity. Thousands more could have been selected, but the author—with great difficulty—narrowed the list to some 350 truly remarkable individuals. They range from some of the greatest scientists the world has ever known, to composers and poets who have thrilled us with their work, to actors and comics who have entertained us.

Many of these people don't advertise that they are Jews. In fact, to many if not most, what they do, rather than what they are, is important.

So herewith a bevy of outstanding personalities, who happen to be Jewish, and who—in many cases—have affected, in a positive way, the way in which we live.

Joe King - Montreal - 2003

Acknowledgements

The inspiration for this book came from Hy Adelman, who wanted an appropriate profile made of the exceptional Jewish contribution to the development of Western civilization. I hope he is not disappointed. I was also strongly supported by Professor Lawrence M. Bessner, F.C.A.

In addition to the resources acknowledged in the bibliography, I wish to make special mention of the facilities of the Eleanor London Public Library of Côte Saint-Luc, Quebec, where I was able to tap their immense resources and received outstanding cooperation from a capable staff. The many other libraries, archives, websites and publications consulted are listed in the bibliography.

Appreciation must go to Eleanor London who was most helpful in countless ways, and my son, Howard King, whose computer knowledge and facilities were very valuable. Finally, I want to express deep appreciation to my wife, Shandle Lipkus King, who has seen little of me over the long period of researching and writing this book. In the past 55 years, she has had to share me with many challenging projects. She has encouraged and assisted me, and been an inspiration.

Joe King

CHAPTER ONE

CELEBRATED FIGURES IN SCIENCE, TECHNOLOGY, AND THE HUMANITIES

"Einstein established the most fundamental scientific premises of the century. It is worth noting, however, that other Jewish scientists played a disproportionately large role in laying the foundation for Einstein's theory of relativity. It was Hermann Minkowski who first devised the concept of a four-dimensional time continuum. Tullio Levi-Cita developed the absolute calculus, the mathematical instrument with which Einstein reached his own conclusions."

Howard M. Sacher, *The Course of Modern Jewish History*, 1990

Albert Einstein at the height of his career – regarded as the greatest mind of the 20th century.

Albert Einstein (1879-1955) had one of the greatest minds of the 20th century. His Theory of Relativity, written when he was only 26, opened the door to the atomic age and caused a revolution in science. His landmark theory superseded Newton's theory of gravitation.

Science writer James Glieck said of him:

"In this busy century, dominated like no other by science—and exalting the idea of pure intelligence—he stands alone as our emblem of intellectual power."

Albert Einstein was born in Ulm, Germany, but the family moved to Munich when he was a boy. His father set up a small factory in the City. Young Albert found himself the only Jew in his class, and a frequent target of anti-Semites. Einstein senior, disgusted by German prejudice, moved to Zurich, Switzerland where his son, after several unsuccessful attempts, was admitted to the Technical school.

Einstein was a poor student! His memory was spotty, and he spoke slowly. One of his teachers told him: "You'll never amount to anything."

Yet the man accepted as the greatest scientist since Newton, won the Nobel Prize in Physics in 1921 for his contribution to theoretical physics. During the day, he worked in the Swiss Patent Office. In the evening, he developed his imaginative theories. His theories were outlawed by the Nazis, and in 1933 Einstein renounced his German citizenship and moved to the United States—warmly welcomed at the newly-created Princeton Institute for Advanced Study.

In 1939, scientists learned that the Germans were working towards construction of an atomic bomb. American authorities refused to listen to their warnings, until Albert Einstein—now a towering figure in the scientific world— wrote President Franklin Delano Roosevelt in August of that year, warning the American leader that the Germans were engaged in research which could "lead to the construction of an ... extremely powerful bomb."

As a result of the letter, the Western allies went to work on developing their own bomb through the Manhattan Project.

Later, after the Second World War, Einstein chaired the Emergency Committee of Atomic Scientists which called for outlawing atomic and hydrogen bombs. It was held that perhaps a dozen people in the world could understand Einstein's Theory of Relativity. Even brilliant people could not grasp it.

Chaim Weizmann, for example, journeyed by ocean liner with Einstein on one occasion. "What did you talk about?," someone asked. "Throughout the voyage, the learned professor kept talking to me about his theory of relativity." "And what is your opinion of it?" Weizmann responded: "It seems to me that Professor Einstein understands it very well."

In 1919, at a meeting of the Royal Society in London, the results of an expedition to the Gulf of Guinea to observe the solar eclipse, broadly supported Einstein's theories. The President of the prestigious Society told the meeting:

> "This is not the discovery of an outlying island but of a whole continent of new scientific ideas—it is the greatest discovery in connection with gravitation since Newton enumerated his principles."

On December 31, 1999, *Time* Magazine named Albert Einstein "Person of the Century."

Albert Einstein writing the equation for the density of the Milky Way, at the Mount Wilson observatory, Pasadena. (Archives–California Institute of Technology)

———

Rosalind Franklin, (1920-1958) provided the X-ray data vital to discovery in 1953 of the double helical structure of DNA, labelled "the most important discovery in 20th century biology" but she wasn't even mentioned in the citation for the 1962 Nobel Prize.

James Watson and Francis Crick shared the Nobel Prize that recognized the importance of the discovery, but it was Franklin's preparatory work with X-ray photography that led to the discovery.

Watson, writing about the discovery in his 1968 book *The Double Helix*, referred, patronizingly, to his colleague only as "Rosy" and stated, arrogantly, "the best home for a feminist is in another person's lab."

Two books were written, in the early 21st century, telling Franklin's side of the story—*Rosalind Franklin and DNA* by Anne Sayre, and *Rosalind Franklin: The Dark Lady of DNA*.

Pioneer molecular biologist Rosalind Elsie Franklin.

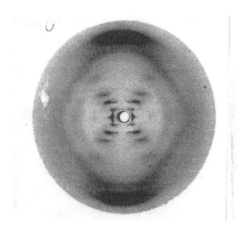

The famous photo 51 taken by Rosalind Franklin that helped determine the DNA was a double helix. 1952.
(Oregon State University)

Rosalind Franklin attended Cambridge where she earned a Ph.D. in physical chemistry despite the fact that the university was not granting women undergraduate degrees. At that time, only men were permitted in the university dining rooms!

She undertook research in Paris and at Birkbeck College in London, but in between, she spent two years in the biophysics unit at King's College London. Franklin theorized that DNA existed in two distinct forms, A and B, and then proved it with clear X-ray photos.

J.D. Bernal described her work in these words: "The most beautiful X-ray photographs of any substances ever taken."

Her "photograph 51" became famous; it clearly showed the structure of DNA. Why was Franklin denied her proper share of recognition? It likely stemmed primarily from male prejudice; anti-Semitism may have also played a part.

She died at age 37—four years before the Nobel Prize was announced for the discovery of the double helix model of DNA.

Arno A. Penzias developed the "Big Bang" theory of creation.

ARNO A. PENZIAS (1933-   ) won the 1978 Nobel Prize for research on the "big bang" theory of creation.

He shared the 1978 Nobel Prize in Physics with R. Wilson and P. Kapitza for detecting cosmic microwave background radiation, thereby supporting the Big Bang theory of the origin of the universe.

Many feel that that discovery, made in 1964 while probing the Milky Way with a radio telescope, is the most important cosmological discovery of the 20th century. Penzias was born in Munich—the year the Nazis came to power.

His family managed to escape to the United States, reaching the US when Penzias was seven. His parents had sent the boy out of Germany first. Penzias describes the experience in these words:

"One night, shortly after my sixth birthday, my parents put their two boys on a train for England; we each had a suitcase with our initials painted on it and a bag of candy. They told me to be sure to take care of my younger brother."

The family was reunited in England and sailed for the New World on the Cunard liner "Georgic". Penzias recalls:

"The gray three-inch gun on the aft deck was a great attraction for us boys."

The father went to work as a carpenter; the mother sewed coats in a factory. Penzias worked in communications with the A.T. & T Bell Labs and was vice-president in charge of research from 1981 on.

In addition to the Nobel Prize, he received the Herschel Medal in 1977; the Henry Draper Medal of the National Academy of Sciences, 1977; the Townsend Harris Medal, 1979; the Newman Award, 1983; the Joseph Handleman Prize, 1983; and the Scientific Achievement Award of Big Brothers, N.Y.C., 1985.

Jews make up only 2% of the American population, but make up 40% of American Nobel Prize winners in science/economics; 17% of the Nobels in physiology/medicine, and 11% in physics.

NATHANIEL KLEITMAN (1895-1999) discovered rapid eye movement (REM) in the sleep cycle.

Born in Kishinev, Russia, he came to the United States in 1915. He was a pioneer in research on the physical aspects of sleep. His two books were *Sleep Characteristics* (1937) and *Sleep and Wakefulness* (1939).

He found, for example, that dreams often last a long time—10 to 30 minutes per dream — and occupy, in total, about two hours of each night's sleep.

He studied sleep patterns everywhere—from Bali to northern Norway, and in such unusual places as caves and submarines. He was the first scholar in the world to specialize entirely in sleep.

The Director of the Sleep Disorders Clinic at Stanford, William Dement, says of his work:

"Kleitman put sleep on the map. He never really got the spotlight because he chose to specialize in an area that was seen as a backwater at the time, but there are now nearly six billion people on earth, they all spend one-third of their lives asleep, and for that rather substantial side of humanity, he stands alone as the major figure. Without Kleitman getting the rest of us interested in sleep research, millions of lives would have been adversely affected."

Nathaniel Kleitman discovered REM.

Abraham Flexner founded the Institute for Advanced Study at Princeton.

"Nations...borrow billions for war; no nation has ever borrowed largely for education. Probably no nation is rich enough to pay for both war and civilization. We must make our choice; we cannot have both."

Abraham Flexner, 1930

Isidor Isaac Rabi's research made possible the invention of the laser. (Courtesy of Columbia University)

THE FLEXNER BROTHERS: Abraham (1866-1959) founded the Institute for Advanced Study at Princeton University, and orchestrated the rescue of imperiled academics in Hitler's Germany (including Albert Einstein).

He is also known as the "father of modern medical education." Abraham Flexner undertook a survey of medical schools, and his report, published in 1910, caused a sensation. He found conditions in medical schools to be "sordid, hideous, unintelligent." As a result, the system was reformed and Flexner is credited with making the American medical school a world leader both in medical education and research.

Simon Flexner, a pioneer in the study of pathology.

His brother, Simon (1863-1946) was Director of the Rockefeller Institute for Medical Research 1920-1935. His research included development of a serum for cerebrospinal meningitis. And he directed poliomyelitis research which led to the identification of the virus causing the disease. In 1900, he discovered the dysentry bacillus, which is named after him. Simon Flexner was also a pioneer in the study of pathology.

ISIDOR ISAAC RABI (1898-1988) won the Nobel Prize for research which made possible the invention of the laser, the atomic clock, and medical diagnostic techniques using resonance imaging.

His research led to Magnetic Resonance Imaging (MRI), whereby doctors can make internal examinations without using harmful X-rays or dye injections. When he was a year old, his parents brought him to the United States from Austria. He attended Cornell University and then Columbia where he obtained a Ph.D.

He was the founder of a major physics research center at Columbia. His research led to discovery of the "maser" (microwave amplification by stimulated emission radiation). Rabi began studies in the late 1930s that led to the discovery of MRI, one of modern medicine's most important diagnostic tools enabling physicians to examine the body's tissues and organs without radiation or intrusion into the body. Other scientists followed Rabi's lead in developing the process.

During World War Two, which delayed research on what would be called MRI, Rabi did important work on radar technology, which helped the allies win the War. And he also worked on the atomic bomb.

He was awarded a Nobel Prize in 1944. In addition, he received the United States Medal of Merit in 1948, and the British King's Medal in the same year.

———

FRANZ BOAS (1858-1942) was the father of anthropology in the United States.

Born in Germany, he was an anthropologist, explorer, archaeologist, and linguist. He collected a vast amount of cultural, linguistic, and archaeological data—much of it firsthand. For example, he explored remote Baffin Island 1883-1884. He probed a large number of Indian languages, in both the United States and Mexico.

Ethnologist Franz Boas demonstrating the position of a Kwakuitl Winter Ceremonal dancer. The picture was taken about 1900.

He provided the first specific proof of the cultural relationship between the Siberians, Inuit (Eskimos), and Indians. His teaching career took him from the Royal Ethnography Museum in Berlin to Columbia University in the US (where he was their first professor of anthropology) and to the Museum of Archaeology in Mexico. His work was recognized internationally. And his many books influenced anthropologists everywhere. In his *The Mind of Primitive Man*, he stated he could find no inborn mental difference between blacks and whites.

Historian Daniel Boorstin wrote of Boas, in his *The Seekers*:

"Franz Boas—a Seeker of the meaning of life to primitive peoples—did more than any other single thinker to liberate Western social scientists from simplistic dogmas of racial superiority and from absolute hierarchies of cultural achievement."

"What the world needs is a fusion of the sciences and the humanities. The humanities express the symbolic, poetic, and prophetic qualities of the human spirit. Without them we would not be conscious of our history; we would lose our aspirations and the graces of expression that move men's hearts. The sciences express the creative urge in man to construct a universe which is comprehensible in terms of the human intellect. Without them, mankind would find itself bewildered in a world of natural forces beyond comprehension, victims of ignorance, superstition and fear."

Isidore Rabi,
Commencement address, 1954
California Institute of Technology

Franz Boas was the father of anthropology in the US

Einstein with Leo Szilard, who conceived the idea of the nuclear chain reaction. (Archives – California Institute of Technology)

"Learning—learning—learning: that is the secret of Jewish survival."

Ahad HaAm in letter to J.L. Magnes, 1910

LEO SZILARD (1898-1964) conceived the idea of the nuclear chain reaction. His impact on science was so significant that, in 1970, a crater on the moon was named "Szilard."

Szilard, a physicist educated at the University of Berlin, was the son of a Jewish engineer, so when Adolf Hitler came to power, the family left for England.

The scientist entered the field of nuclear physics and, in 1934, suggested the idea of the nuclear chain reaction. He kept his discovery secret and applied for a patent. He saw how the chain could be used to create a nuclear bomb. This was a decade before an atomic bomb had been created!

Moving to the United States in 1937, he convinced American physicists that they should not publish their work, thereby denying the Germans additional, important information.

Szilard, with Wigner and Teller, encouraged Einstein to send his famous letter to President Roosevelt, which convinced FDR that the US should construct an atomic bomb. Szilard actually wrote the letter for Einstein.

Once the bomb was a reality, Szilard was one of the scientists who urged that its use be only in the form of a demonstration of its power in an uninhabited area. But President Truman's advisers thought otherwise, and bombs were dropped on two Japanese cities.

Szilard—having served in the Hungarian army in World War One—had become a pacifist, but he was, reluctantly, one of the fathers of the atomic bomb. In 1948, with Hitler defeated, he organized the "Council to Abolish War."

The scientist had many other ideas including the linear accelerator, the cyclotron, the electronic microscope as well as the nuclear chain reaction. Szilard was also the first, in a 1929 paper on "Maxwell's Demon," to refer to a unit of information as a "bit."

WILLIAM STERN (1871-1938) originated the modern intelligence quotient (I.Q.) test.

His studies led to the development of Gestalt psychology. Stern was born in Berlin. His father was a failure in business so the son had to care for an ailing mother and earn money for university tuition.

His career as an academic was hampered by the fact that he was a Jew. He was offered a full professorship at Breslau—if he converted to Christianity. Two years after Stern was unanimously elected President of the German Psychological Society, the Nazis expelled him.

He joined thousands of Jewish and other scholars who left Nazi Germany for America. He spent the last five years of his life as a professor at Duke University. Stern improved on the existing (Binet) technique for testing intelligence by devising an Intelligence Quotient (I.Q.) test whereby a child's mental age was divided by their chronological age. He also conceived the "convergence theory", suggesting a role for heredity and environment. This theory was picked up and expanded by theorists in developing Gestalt psychology.

William Stern, who originated the modern I.Q. test, with his wife.

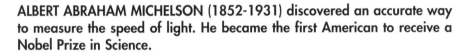

ALBERT ABRAHAM MICHELSON (1852-1931) discovered an accurate way to measure the speed of light. He became the first American to receive a Nobel Prize in Science.

Furthermore, he developed a new standard of length, adopted in 1925 by the entire world; determined that the interior of the earth is molten; and calculated the size of stars.

Michelson's interferometer, the instrument he designed to measure the speed of light. Variations are still in use.

Michelson's parents fled Prussia after the political unrest of 1848; Albert was two years old. His brilliance was quickly noted. In high school, although still a student, he was placed in charge of the school's scientific instruments. When he sought admission to the United States Naval Academy, an unprecedented special appointment was arranged for him.

He designed an instrument, called the interferometer, to help in his research. Alexander Graham Bell helped fund his studies. His team determined the velocity of light, in a vacuum, as 299,774 kilometers (186,264 miles) per second. His work led the way to Albert Einstein's

A.A. Michelson accurately measured the speed of light. (Archives – California Institute of Technology)

development of the theory of relativity. Michelson's interferometer is still widely used in spectroscopy, chemistry, and meterology.

In 1907, the year he received the Nobel Prize, he was also awarded the Copley Medal of Britain's Royal Society. His Nobel laurels were in recognition of his "dedication to the design of precise scientific equipment."

"The ignorant man always adores what he cannot understand."
Cesare Lombroso
in The Man of Genius

CESARE LOMBROSO (1836-1909) founded the modern school of criminology, and was the first person to use a scientific form of lie detector.

He was a native of Verona, Italy, and he came from a family of rabbis and Hebrew scholars. His parents belonged to the Jewish aristocracy of Cheri and Verona. He lived the first years of his life in the elegant Palazzo del Greco in Verona. By age 15, he had published two essays on Roman history. In university, before studying medicine, he was interested in literature, linguistics, and archaeology. In post-graduate studies in Padua, Paris, and Vienna, he became increasingly interested in studying insanity. He worked, for a time, as a military physician and director of an insane asylum, but then became a professor of forensic medicine at the University of Turin in 1876.

In 1895, Lombroso was the first person to employ a scientific instrument to indicate whether a person was telling the truth. The scientist used a "hydrosphygmograph," to indicate physiological responses to questioning. He made modifications to the device so that changes in pulse and blood pressure indicated guilt or innocence.

He switched to psychology 21 years later and then, in 1905, was appointed professor of criminal anthropology.

He is known as the founder of the science of criminology, and believed there was a "criminal type." His theory was that a person who broke the law was characterized by physical, mental, and nervous deviations from the norm. He changed the focus of study from the crime to the criminal. He argued that, from his studies, it was clear that criminals are born with a criminal instinct. He also believed that genius was close to madness.

In 1906, the Sixth International Congress of Anthropologists, meeting in London, presented him with a testimonial recognizing his contribution to science and medicine. On his return to Italy, the 70-

Cesare Lombroso founded the modern school of criminology.

year-old physician received a similar tribute from the Italian Congress of Criminal Anthropology.

LUDOVIC LAZARUS ZAMENHOF (1859-1917) created the Esperanto language.

Ludovic L. Zamenhof created the Esperanto language.

He felt that by creating one international language he would help lead the world to greater understanding and, in the long run, to peace. Esperanto means "One Who Hopes."

Zamenhof was born in Bialystok. His father was a Hebrew scholar and teacher of languages. By the time he was 15, and studying in a Warsaw High School, he could speak five languages—Polish, French, German, Yiddish, and Hebrew. At 14, he made his first attempt at creating an international language. He had to work in secret because of the repressive regime in Poland.

When he was 19, his work on the new language had gone far enough for him to start instructing a handful of people. And on December 17, 1878, he had a lively party to celebrate the creation of Esperanto.

He labored for 15 years over a book on the proposed language-without-borders and published a slim volume of 40 pages—the fruits of all his work. Among those who welcomed Esperanto was Count Leo Tolstoy, who declared that, by consulting Zamenhof's book, he learned to speak the language in only two hours. Zamenhof became an oculist but was widely known as "Dr. Esperanto" because of his earnest efforts to further the brotherhood of man by developing the new, international language.

The first national Esperanto association was formed in 1898 in France, and a British association was launched in 1902. But, to date, little progress has been made in achieving wide acceptance of this proposed world language.

85% of college age Jews in the United States are enrolled in universities. The Hillel Guide found that Jews make up 30% of the student body at Yale, 14% at Princeton, 32% at Columbia, 27% at Harvard, 16% at Cornell, Chicago, and Duke, 14% at Stanford and 23% at Brown.

Esperanto	English
Tra densa mallumo briletas la celo,	Through a thick darkness the objective glows
Al kiu kuraĝe ni iras	To which we go bravely
Simile al stelo en nokta ĉielo	The same as stars in the night sky
Al ni la dirketon ĝi diras.	They show us direction.
Kaj nin ne timigas la noktaj fantomoj,	And the night ghosts do not make us afraid
Nek batoj de l' sorto, nek mokoj de l' homoj,	Nor the strikes of fortune, nor men's mockery,
Ĉar klara kaj rekta kaj tre difinita	Because clear and straight and very definite
Ĝi estas la voj' elektita.	It is the elected Way.
Nur rekte, kuraĝe kaj ne flankiĝante	Only even, brave and non diverting
Ni iru la vojon celitan!	Let's go on the meant way!
Eĉ guto malgranda, konstante frapante,	Even a little drop, striking constantly
Tralaboras la monton granitan	Makes a hole through the granite mountain.
L' espero, l' obstino kaj la *patienco*	Hope, stubbornness, and Patience.
Jen estas la signoj, per kies potenco	There are the signs by which power
Ni paŝo post paŝo, post longa laboro,	We step by step, after a long work,
Atingos la celon en gloro.	Will reach our aim in glory.
Ni semas kaj semas, neniam lacigas,	We sow and sow, never getting tired

Some passages in Esperanto.

A.A. Baginsky was the founder of modern pediatrics.

ADOLF ARON BAGINSKY (1843-1918) was the founder of modern pediatrics.

His *Textbook of Pediatrics* was the accepted international authority in the field for years. Eight editions were printed, and it was translated into many languages.

He was born in Ratibor, Silesia, and studied medicine at the University of Berlin. He specialized in children's infectious diseases and, with Rudolf Virchow, founded the Kaiser und Kaiserin Children's Hospital and became its director.

Hans Albrecht Bethe discovered how the sun and other stars burn by nuclear fission. (Archives – California Institute of Technology)

HANS ALBRECHT BETHE (1906-   ) discovered how the sun and other stars burn by nuclear fission. *Time* magazine once declared that Bethe was "one of Nazi Germany's greatest gifts to the United States."

He was educated at the Universities of Frankfurt and Munich but, when the Nazis came to power in 1933, moved to England and undertook research in Manchester and Bristol.

In 1935, he joined Cornell University in the United States. In his research, Bethe concluded that stellar energy was the result of the condensation of four hydrogen nuclei to form one helium nucleus, with a consequent emission of fusion energy. In effect, he had discovered what makes the sun shine!

His discovery, known as the "Bethe carbon cycle" was an explanation of solar and stellar energy, and he estimated that the "cycle" took 5,000,000 years to complete.

In presenting him with the Nobel Prize for physics in 1967, he was cited "for his contributions to the theory of nuclear reactions, especially his discoveries concerning the energy production of stars."

EMILE DURKHEIM (1858-1917) founded modern sociology.

He suggested that the "collective mind of society", through constraint of the individual, is the "wellspring of religion and morality."

After earning a doctorate at the Sorbonne, he taught at the Universities of Bordeaux and Paris.

He was born in Epinal, France, and his Orthodox family presumed he would follow tradition and become a rabbi. However, as a youth, he turned away from religion.

In 1892 he became a teacher of philosophy. Five years later, reports on his cleverness earned him an invitation to teach at the University of Bordeaux. He held the University's first chair in sociology. Ten years later, the Sorbonne invited him to join their faculty to teach sociology and education, and he spent the rest of his working life there. Durkheim felt that sociology was a method for "investigating social phenomena" and that research in the field depended on a team representing related social sciences—such as history, geography, and child psychology.

Emile Durkheim founded modern sociology. (The Emile Durkheim Archive)

LEON M. (MAX) LEDERMAN (1922-   ) shared the Nobel Prize in Physics for his role in detecting a subatomic particle so small, he wrote it is "barely a fact." He detected the muon neutrino which in turn led to a number of spectacular advances in research in particle physics.

Lederman was born in New York City, son of two Russian-Jewish immigrants who operated a laundry.

After receiving a science degree from City College in 1943, he served for the next two years in the United States Army Signal Corps. After the war he enrolled in Columbia University, earning his master's degree in physics in 1948, and his Ph.D. in 1951.

Remaining with Columbia, he worked in the physics department's center for experimental research in high energy physics. Lederman states he was "handed the finest equipment to do the work I most wanted to do." Facilities at the center included a particle accelerator capable of boosting particles to energies of several hundred million electron volts. He also had access to the 33 billion electronic volt Cosmotron accelerator at Brookhaven National Laboratory on Long Island.

Working in collaboration with Melvin Schwartz and Jack Steinberger, he carried out experiments that detected the muon neutrino.

In 1988, he shared the Nobel Prize in physics.

Leon Lederman detected tiny subatomic particles. (Archives – California Institute of Technology)

Leon Lederman with his bubble chamber.

In an interview with *Discover* magazine he stated:

"Part of being a scientist is compulsive dedication, the insistence on working without rest until you get what you're after ... the best discoveries always seem to be made in the small hours of the morning."

MAX PERUTZ (1914-2002) is known as the "father of molecular biology" and was co-winner of the 1962 Nobel Prize in chemistry.

Born in Austria, he became fascinated by reports on research underway at Cambridge University's Cavendish Laboratory. He joined the lab's staff and won the Nobel Prize for his "elucidation of the structure of the hemoglobin molecule."

During the war, he suspended his work to study the possibility of using ice floes as aircraft carriers. It never worked out. Perutz published two collections of essays on science, scientists, and medicine—*Is Science Necessary*? in 1989 and *I Wish I'd Made You Angry Earlier* in 1998.

Max Perutz is known as "the father of molecular biology."

MURRAY GELL-MANN (1929-   ) entered Yale University at age 15 and discovered and named the "quark."

He earned his Ph.D. from the Massachusetts Institute of Technology, and was professor of physics and theoretical physics at the California Institute of Technology for most of his teaching career.

In the 1950s scientists were discovering a variety of new subatomic particles. Gell-Mann, in studying particles, suggested that an undiscovered one could best explain the theoretical complexity. He called the particle a "quark" after the passage in James Joyce's *Finnegan's Wake*, reading "Three quarks for Muster Mark." Proof of the existence of quarks came in 1974.

Five years earlier he had been awarded the Nobel Prize in physics.

Murray Gell-Mann discovered and named "quarks".

LEO GRAETZ (1856-1941) pioneered in the study of the dispersal of electrical waves, and therefore the telephone, radio, and television are all based on his discoveries.

Graetz was born at Breslau, Germany—son of the famous Jewish historian Heinrich Graetz.

He studied in Breslau, Berlin, and Strassburg, and become a professor at the University of Munchen. Initially, he studied heat conduction, radiation, friction, and elasticity. But, beginning in 1890, he focused on electromagnetic waves and cathode rays.

The study of electricity was in its infancy when he began his research and his book *Electricity and its Applications* was printed in 23 editions. He also wrote the five-volume *Handbook of Electricity and Magnetism*.

Leo Graetz was a pioneer in the study of electricity. His research led to the development of the telephone, radio, and television.

CHAPTER TWO

MAJOR MEDICAL ACHIEVEMENTS

"In medicine, as early as 1850, Jewish scientists argued for the existence of micro-organisms which cause contagious disease, laid the foundations for modern heart therapy, bacteriology, and clinical pathology. They first advanced theories that chemical processes within the cell were responsible for glandular activity, proposed serum immunity for contagious diseases, discovered phagocytes, pioneered in the chemistry of muscles, and made blood transfusions possible through discovery of the different blood types."

Max I. Dimont, *Jews, God and History*, 1962

Paul Ehrlich was the father of chemotherapy.

PAUL EHRLICH (1854-1915) was the bacteriologist who developed a treatment for syphilis; he was the father of chemotherapy, and a pioneer of hematology and immunology.

Ehrlich received the Nobel Prize in 1908 for his identification of a treatment for syphilis. He called his discovery "606" because it was his 606th experiment. He used arsenic to destroy the microbe responsible for the deadly disease.

A happy-go-lucky scientist, he smoked 25 cigars a day and was fond of downing seidels of beer. Referring to his discovery, he declared "we must learn to shoot microbes with magic bullets."

Ehrlich was not a good student; he moved from medical school to medical school, disliking the emphasis on memorizing long tracts. The medical faculties knew that he was a special student, but they insisted that he learn medicine their way. Nevertheless, while still a student he made an important discovery—-he used amline dyes to determine the different kinds of white blood cells.

Docteur EHRLICH

Max Lieberman's cartoon of Paul Ehrlich's search for a drug effective against syphillis.

ALBERT LUDWIG SIGESMUND NEISSER (1855-1916) discovered the bacterium that causes gonorrhea; he was a classmate of Paul Ehrlich.

Neisser was born in Schweidnitz, in Silesia—son of a well-known Jewish physician. Most of his studies and research were done in Breslau. He was not a great student. He had to take the chemistry test twice.

When there were no openings in an internal medicine clinic, Neisser turned to dermatology and after two years of work discovered the gonococcus. Ehrlich named the microorganism. Neisser was only 24 when he made the discovery, and his students affectionately called him "father of gonococcus."

His discoveries, and those of Ehrlich, were part of substantial progress made in the diagnosis and treatment of venereal diseases in the late 19th and early 20th centuries. But it was only when penicillin was discovered that this deadly disease could be controlled.

Albert Neisser discovered the bacterium that caused gonorrhea.

SIR ERNEST B. CHAIN (1906-1979) received the 1945 Nobel Prize, with Fleming and Florey, for their work on penicillin.

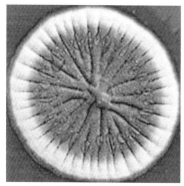

A penicillin mold. Alexander Fleming contaminated the contents of a petrie dish. But he didn't recognize what he had discovered. Ernest B. Chain and an associate later showed that penicillin killed bacteria or inhibited their growth. (Andrew McClenaghan / Science Source.)

Chain was another one of the many German-born scientists who fled to England in the tragic year of 1933 when Hitler became the head of government.

Chain worked with Florey in Oxford on a study of the antagonisms between microorganisms. This included penicillin, which had been discovered by Fleming, who did nothing with it.

Chain, Florey, and Fleming shared the 1945 Nobel Prize for the discovery but it was Chain and Florey who isolated the drug, tested it on humans and marketed this first antibiotic. But Fleming got the lion's share of the credit because of the unusual way he discovered penicillin—he accidentally contaminated a bacteria sample.

Sir Ernest B. Chain was a co-discoverer of penicillin.

Gregory Goodwin Pincus (center) led the team that developed the birth control pill.

GREGORY GOODWIN PINCUS (1903-1967) played the principal role in developing the birth control pill.

Pincus, in collaboration with Dr. M. Chiang, developed the first practical oral contraceptive birth control pill.

A leader in the American birth control movement, Margaret Sanger, had persuaded Pincus to undertake the task. His team was given a research grant in 1951 by the Planned Parenthood Federation.

Pincus and Chiang experimented with more than 200 substances before they derived effective steroid compounds from the roots of the wild Mexican yam. After field tests in 1956, the United States Food and Drug Administration (FDA) authorized their use the following year.

Pincus was born in Woodbine, New Jersey, and received his doctorate of science from Harvard in 1927.

The pill became an instrument for population control and caused a revolution in sexual attitudes.

Pincus was elected to the National Academy of Sciences in 1965.

Marshall Nirenberg's research efforts led to the solution of the genetic code. (National Library of Science)

MARSHALL W. NIRENBERG (1927-   ) laid the groundwork for solution of the genetic code, and won the Nobel Prize in 1968.

Nirenberg was born in New York but the family moved to Orlando, Florida in 1939. He received his Ph.D. degree from the University of Michigan's Department of Biological Chemistry.

In 1959, he began to study the steps that relate DNA, RNA, and protein. He determined that "synthetic messenger RNA preparations can be used to decipher various aspects of the genetic code."

In 1962, Nirenberg (who is married to Perola Zaltzman, a biochemist) became head of the Biochemical Genetics Section of the National Institutes of Health.

ARTHUR EICHENGRUN discovered aspirin, but the Nazis altered the lab records to give the credit to one of his assistants.

A Scottish scientist, Dr. Walter Sneader of the University of Strathclyde, states that the Nazis gave credit for the discovery to Felix Hoffman, but Sneader's studies of Hoffman's laboratory notes, made during a visit to the Bayer Corporation in 1999, showed that Eichengrun actually made the discovery. The Scottish scientist presented his conclusions to the Royal Society of Chemistry, and published his findings in both the *British Medical Journal* (2000) and *The Biochemist* (2001) .

Acetylsalicylic acid ("Aspirin" is a trade-name) had been synthesized in 1853, but it was only in 1897 that it was produced in a pure enough form to be used therapeutically.

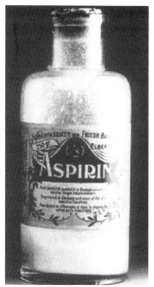

Arthur Eichengrun discovered aspirin. This was an aspirin bottle a century ago.

SELMAN ABRAHAM WAKSMAN, (1888-1973) who had been a yeshiva student in his native Russia, discovered the antibiotic streptomycin in 1943.

Streptomycin successfully combats infections resistant to penicillin and sulfa drugs. The antibiotic represented the first breakthrough in drug treatment of tuberculosis.

He was awarded the Nobel Prize in 1952.

Selman Waksman was a member of the Rutgers University faculty for more than 40 years, and he directed the Rutgers Institute of Microbiology from its founding in 1949 until his retirement in 1958.

Waksman was the first person to use the term "antibiotics." It comes from the Greek words meaning "against (microscopic) life."

Selman A. Waksman discovered the antibiotic streptomycin.

Karl Landsteiner discovered there are different kinds of blood.

Baruch S. Blumberg identified the virus that caused hepatitis.

KARL LANDSTEINER (1868-1943) made blood transfusions safe by his discovery, in 1900, that there were different kinds of blood.

By 1902, his research team had determined there were four blood groups which he labeled A, B, AB, and O. He identified four blood groupings for safe transfusions—A could accept blood from A and O donors; B from A and O; O only from O; and AB from all donors.

His discoveries meant that blood banks could be established, allowing major surgery to take place.

In 1919 however, Landsteiner was so poor that he had to take a basic lab job in a hospital. But he was later invited to head the research laboratory at the Rockefeller Institute in New York. There, he and a young assistant identified three more blood factors—M, N, and P.

The scientist's additional blood classifications may be used to help determine paternity and are helpful in the investigation of blood stains at a crime scene. Landsteiner had studied medicine in Vienna but his work on immunology was undertaken at the Rockefeller Institute.

Illa Vij, writing about Landsteiner in the *Tribune* (March 25, 2000), commented that his "work has touched and benefited nearly every human being." He was totally devoted to his work, putting in 12-hour days. His research on microbes set the stage for the discovery of vaccines that prevent typhus.

He was awarded a Nobel Prize in 1930.

Moreover, in 1940, he, with A. Wiener and P. Levine, announced the discovery of the rhesus (rh) factor in the red blood cells of certain individuals.

BARUCH SAMUEL BLUMBURG (1925-   ) identified the virus that caused the hepatitis infection, thereby giving biochemists a way to identify the infection in blood before it is used for transfusions.

He won the 1976 Nobel Prize for his research on the origin of infectious diseases. And he was co-developer of the vaccine for hepatitis "B." Blumberg's identification of the "Australia antigen" in 1963 made possible a test to identify hepatitis "B" carriers among prospective blood donors.

Born in New York City, he dedicated his life to determining why people of different racial, ethnic, and family backgrounds react differently to diseases. His field trips took him everywhere from Surinam in South America, to the Basque area of northern Spain.

"You can't get too far away from people and diseases," he stated, "if you're going to understand people and the diseases they get."

AUGUST VON WASSERMAN (1866-1925) , a physician and bacteriologist, developed the "Wasserman Test", with Reuben Kahn in 1906; this helped physicians to diagnose syphilis. He also did revealing and important research on immunology.

Wasserman was born in Bamberg, Germany, and took his medical degree at the University of Strasbourg in 1888.

In addition to his famous test for syphilis, he also developed inoculations against cholera and typhoid. And he discovered diagnostic tests for tuberculosis.

August von Wasserman developed the test to diagnose syphilis. (etching by Bedrich Feigl)

JONAS EDWARD SALK (1914-1995) and ALBERT BRUCE SABIN (1906-1993) created the vaccines which ended the scourge of infantile paralysis.

During the 1940s and 1950s, millions of children were infected by polio and, in the United States alone, 640,000 children were paralyzed. Salk developed a polio vaccine, and children in 44 states were inoculated with it (after Salk had tried it out on himself.) Unfortunately, one batch of the vaccine was flawed and 250 people were infected with polio.

Albert Sabin originated the oral polio vaccine. Here is at the National Institute of Health in the Mid 1980s.

Jonas E. Salk developed a polio vaccine. (The Salk Institute)

At this time, Sabin came forward with a vaccine which could be given orally, eliminating the use of needles. The new vaccine was given to children on a lump of sugar. There is still a very small chance that someone taking the Sabin vaccine can be infected. In the 80s, the rate of infection was four per million.

Novelist Wilfred Sheed stated: "Salk's career stands out in at least two respects: the sheer speed with which he outraced all the tortoises in the field and the honors he did not receive for doing so."

Rita Levi-Montalcini won the Nobel Prize for her discovery of the Nerve Growth Factor in collaboration with Stanley Cohen.

RITA LEVI-MONTALCINI (1909-   ) was only the fourth woman to be awarded the Nobel Prize for physiology or medicine. The Italian-born research scientist and neurobiologist won the award for her discovery of the Nerve Growth Factor.

The discovery, made jointly with her colleague, biochemist Stanley Cohen, has helped scientists understand such disorders as cancers, birth defects, and Alzheimer's Disease.

Dr. Levi-Montalcini had to defy her father when she decided on a career in medicine. Then, after graduating from the University of Turin in 1936, she had to hide from the authorities because she was Jewish. She set up a homemade research lab in the countryside.

In 1947, she moved to the United States and worked with Dr. Viktor Hamburger at Washington University. She remained there for 30 years, and then returned to Italy to direct the Laboratory of Cell Biology of the National Council of Research in Rome.

Despite her father's efforts to dominate her, she wrote in her autobiography, "it was he rather than she (her mother) who had a decisive influence on the course of my life."

Stanley Cohen.

BURRILL B. CROHN'S (1884-1983) research achievements are recognized by the fact that Crohn's Disease (granulomatous colitis) bears his name.

Crohn was one of 12 children in a German-Jewish immigrant family. His stockbroker father and his mother just made ends meet with their large family. Burrill Crohn was 23 before he could enter the City University of New York; the year was 1907.

He interned at the Mount Sinai Hospital for two years, and then — after passing a challenging examination—began working in the hospital's clinical laboratory.

His name was attached to the disease when he identified it in the lab.

Burril B. Crohn identified Crohn's disease.

Casimir Funk discovered and named vitamins. He spelled it "vitamines".

CASIMIR FUNK (1884-1967) discovered and named "vitamins."

This Polish-born biochemist studied in Berne and London before joining the Pasteur Institute in Paris.

Eventually, he founded the Funk Foundation for Medical Research in New York in 1953.

Noting that all food factors associated with deficiency diseases belonged to the chemical group "amines," he tacked on a "v" and suggested the word "vitamine." The "e" was lopped off in 1920.

Casimir Funk identified vitamins and sought to verify how they could contribute to good health.

WALDEMAR MORDECAI HAFFKINE's (1860-1930) vaccine checked the spread of cholera. He inoculated himself with the cholera serum to demonstrate that it was safe.

The Haffkine Institute in India is named for him.

He was educated in Russia but when an offer of a lectureship was made conditional on his becoming a Christian, he left the country.

Waldemar Mordecai Haffkine created the vaccine to check the spread of cholera. (Institut Pasteur – Archives Haffkine)

Haffkine became an associate of Pasteur, Ehrlich, and Ethnikoff in Paris. When a cholera epidemic hit India in 1893, he developed the vaccine which checked the outbreak. He also developed a new technique of inoculation against the bubonic plague, reducing the death rate from that disease by 80-90%. The Indian people called him the "White Magician," because he saved so many lives.

He was born in Odessa. His mother died when he was very young and he was a lonely child.

Queen Victoria presented him with the Order of the Indian Empire in 1897.

Haffkine left a bequest of 45,000 pounds with the Banque Cantonale Vaudoise in Lausanne, with instructions that the income was to be used "to benefit traditional Jewish learning."

ADRIAN KANTROWITZ (1918-   ) developed the Kantrowitz-General Electric pacemaker, and, with his brother, invented the lifesaving intra-aortic balloon. He pioneered in the use of bioengineering for the heart.

Kantrowitz received his medical degree from Western Reserve University in 1943, and after World War Two began studying cardiovascular physiology under Carl John Wiggins. In 1954, working with Alan Lerrick, he devised a plastic heart valve. Four years later, he designed and built a heart-lung machine. During the years 1961-1962, he developed an internal pacemaker, and in 1964, with Tetsuzo Akutsu, he built an auxiliary left ventricle. In 1966 he performed the first implantation of a partial mechanical heart in a human.

On December 6, 1987, he performed the second human cardiac transplant (the first in the United States).

Kantrowitz owns more than 15 patents for cardiovascular devices and implantation methods. These include the revolutionary intra-aortic balloon pump. The pump is called the most practical heart assist device in use today and is claimed to save more than 100,000 lives annually. He also was a pioneer in taking motion pictures inside a living heart.

Adrian Kantrowitz pioneered bio-engineering for the heart.

BERNARD SACHS (1858-1944) identified Tay-Sachs Disease.

"Barney" Sachs was born in Baltimore, Maryland, and studied at Harvard Medical College. His interest in the study of mental disorders was aroused when one of his teachers, the famous psychologist and philosopher, William James, was having trouble with his eyes and asked Sachs to read from Wilhelm Wundt's *Psychology*.

Graduating from Harvard with honors, he went to Europe to study with eminent medical personalities in Strassburg, Vienna, Paris, London, and Berlin.

Tay-Sachs, the genetic disorder he recognized, is marked by mental and motor deterioration. Death generally occurs before age three.

Sachs published almost 200 articles on his research, and wrote several books.

Bernard Sachs identified Tay-Sachs Disease.

BELA SCHICK's (1877-1967) test identified vulnerability to diphtheria.

He was born in Bolgary, Hungary, and became associate professor of pediatrics at Vienna University.

He moved to the United States in 1923 and became pediatrician in chief at the Mount Sinai Hospital in New York. In 1936, he was named clinical professor of pediatrics at Columbia University.

He was most famous for his discovery of a skin test determining susceptibility to diphtheria. It became known as the Schick test. Use of this test to identify vulnerability to the disease enabled physicians to make an early diagnosis and treatment, thereby saving many lives.

Joseph Goldberger found that lack of vitamin B caused pellagra.

DR. JOSEPH GOLDBERGER (1874 -1929) found that the lack of vitamin B caused the disease pellagra. He is credited with laying the foundation for the science of nutrition.

Goldberger often used himself as a guinea pig in doing research into other diseases.

The World Book Encyclopedia states Goldberger "added to the knowledge of yellow fever, typhoid, typhus, Rocky Mountain spotted fever, straw-mite itch, measles, diphtheria, and influenza."

Here is Dr. Goldberger working at the Hygienic Laboratory c. 1926. (US National Library of Medicine)

Abraham Jacobi established America's first medical clinic for children.

DR. ABRAHAM JACOBI (1830-1919) was America's first pediatrics professor. He established the first medical clinic for children in the United States.

Jacobi was born in Germany and became involved in revolutionary activities. He was charged with high treason and jailed from 1851 to 1853 in Berlin and Cologne.

On his release, he emigrated to America where he became professor of children's diseases at New York Medical College, 1861-1864. Subsequently he took a similar position at the University of the City of New York, 1865-1870 and then at the College of Physicians and Surgeons, 1870-1892.

L.H. Garrison, in his *Dictionary of American Medical Biography*, 1928, said of Jacobi "his whole person being dominated by a large splendid head—leonine, magisterial with a crown of bushy hair; he was the living embodiment of an ancient high-priest of Knowledge."

DR. SIMON BARUCH (1840-1921) was the first doctor to diagnose appendicitis. He was the first surgeon to remove a diseased appendix.

He served in the Confederate army for three years during the American Civil War, and was taken prisoner twice.

In civilian practice, in South Carolina and New York, he diagnosed the first case of a perforated appendix and operated successfully. He is credited with development of the appendectomy.

Simon Baruch was the first doctor to diagnose appendicitis.

————

GEORGE WALD (1906-1997) discovered vitamin A in the retina; he showed that retinene is a light-sensitive pigment. He was awarded the Nobel prize in 1967.

He was born of immigrant parents (they came from what was then Austrian Poland) in New York City. He received the degree of Bachelor of Science from New York University and earned his Ph.D. from Columbia in 1932.

While on a National Research Council Fellowship, 1932-1934, he first identified vitamin A in the retina.

His research in the field of vision won him a multitude of awards, the most important—other than the Nobel Prize—being the Lasker Award of the American Public Health Association "in recognition of his outstanding discoveries in biochemistry with special reference to the changes associated with vision and the function of vitamin A" (1953); The Proctor Medal of the Association for Research in Ophthalmology (1955); The Rumford Medal by the American Academy of Arts and Sciences (1959); The Ives Medal of the Optical Society (1966); the Paul Karrer Medal, with his wife Ruth, of the University of Zurich (1967); and the Whitney Foundation's T. Duckett Jones Memorial Award (also in 1967).

George Wald discovered vitamin A in the retina.

Tadeus Reichstein isolated cortisone.

TADEUS REICHSTEIN (1897-1996) succeeded in isolating the hormone now known as cortisone. Earlier, he had succeeding in synthesizing Vitamin C. He was a joint winner of the Nobel Prize in Medicine in 1950.

Reichstein was born in Wloclawek, Poland, but he spent the first eight years of his life in Kiev, in the Ukraine, where his father worked as an engineer The family ultimately moved to Zurich, Switzerland, where Reichstein earned a degree in chemical engineering (1920) and went to work in a factory manufacturing flashlights. He went back to university and received his doctorate in organic chemistry in 1922.

His first big success was the synthesis of ascorbic acid—the anti-scurvy vitamin C. Later he derived cortisone from ox bile.

GERALD M. EDELMAN (1929-   ) established the structure of gamma globulin that carries the body's defense mechanism against disease. It won him the 1972 Nobel Prize in medicine and physiology.

Born in New York, the son of a physician, and educated at the University of Pennsylvania, Edelman became a professor at Rockefeller University in 1966, a position he held for more than three decades.

Edelman, whose research continued into the field of proteins, is a member of the National Academy of Sciences and the American Academy of Arts and sciences.

Gerald Edelman established the structure of gamma globulin.

GERTRUDE BELLE ELION (1918-1999) spent 60 years researching, and often defeating some of humankind's deadliest diseases.

In 1988, Gertrude Elion shared the Nobel Prize in Physiology/Medicine with Dr. George Hitchings and Sir James Black. She was only the fifth female Nobel Laureate in Medicine.

Elion was born in New York City of immigrant parents from eastern Europe. She wrote in her autobiography: "I was born in New York City on a cold January night when the water pipes in our apartment froze and burst."

She was inspired to seek a career in medical research when, at 15, her beloved grandfather wasted away from cancer and died. "In the hope that I could do something to combat disease, I decided to become a scientist."`

Because she was a woman, she could not find work in a laboratory, but after a search of a year and a half she was hired for $20 a week as an assistant in a biochemistry laboratory.

Simultaneously, she studied for a Master's Degree in chemistry and graduated in 1941 with the highest honors.

She still found it difficult to find an appropriate position because of her gender, but World War Two drew away large numbers of men and opened positions for women previously denied them.

Her career of serious medical research began in 1944 when a pharmaceutical company hired her for $50 a week.

She and her research partners learned how to block the replication of cancerous cells and infectious microbes without doing damage to normal cells. They developed "target specific" drugs.

Her team developed cancer treatments, achieving remission in 40% of children with leukemia. In 1957, the team developed a drug that suppressed the immune system, helping the body to accept transplanted organs.

Drugs developed by Drs. Elion and Hitchings include Acyclovir for herpes, Azathioprine to help prevent rejection of transplanted organs, and to treat severe rheumatoid arthritis, Allopurinol to treat gout, Pyrimethamine to fight malaria, and Trimethoprim to combat bacterial infections.

In 1991, she received two exceptional honors: President George Bush presented her with a National Medal of Science, and she became the first woman to be inducted into the Inventors Hall of Fame.

Gertrude Elion has helped defeat some of humankind's deadliest diseases.

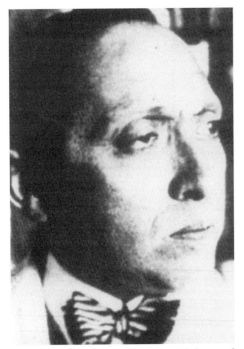

Bernhard Zondek devised a widely-used pregnancy test.

Max Tishler's contribution to health was described by President Reagan as that of "a giant".

BERNHARD ZONDEK (1891-1966) helped develop the classic test for pregnancy. Zondek obtained his doctorate in Berlin in 1919. He worked and did research in the University Women's Clinic in the Berlin Charite, and the municipal hospital of Berlin-Spandau.

When the Nazis came to power in 1933, he was dismissed from his position. He went first to Sweden, and then in 1940 he moved to Jerusalem where he was named professor of obstetrics and gynecology at the Hebrew University and head of these two departments at the Hadassah Hospital.

He was co-discoverer of the Aschheim-Zondek test for pregnancy in which the patient's urine is injected into female mice.

MAX TISHLER (1906-1989) was described by President Reagan as a "giant on the chemical scene these past fifty years."

He was born in Boston—the fifth of six children. His father was a shoemaker who abandoned the family when Max was five years old. The youngster helped support the family by delivering bread for a bakery, selling newspapers, and doing other odd jobs.

He got a job as assistant to a pharmacist—working at the soda fountain, dishing out ice cream when he wasn't packing and delivering drugs. Some of his deliveries were to victims of the influenza epidemic of 1918 and that experience convinced the lad that he should go into health care.

His marks in high school were outstanding—good enough to earn him a full scholarship and, in 1928 he graduated from Tufts College with a B.S., magna cum laude in chemistry. He went directly to Harvard, earning his M.A. in 1933 and his Ph.D. in organic chemistry in 1934.

With few jobs available during the depression years, Tishler was hired by Merck, then a small company in New Jersey.

In his first assignment, Tishler developed an economical, large-scale production process, greatly increasing the yield and permitting, for the first time, the use of riboflavin to enrich white bread. Later, he led a team that succeeded in synthesizing cortisone on a large scale.

Ultimately, the chemist worked out processes for synthesizing ascorbic acid, riboflavin, cortisone, miamin, pyridoxin, pantothenic acid, nicotinamide, methionine, threonine, and tryptophan.

In 1987 President Reagan—presenting Tishler with the National Medal of Science—stated: "The importance of Dr. Tishler's specific contributions to the nation's health can be scarcely be exaggerated."

Stanley N. Cohen.

STANLEY N. COHEN (1935-   ), with Herbert W. Boyer, created the first genetically engineered organism.

In 1973, Cohen and Boyer spliced DNA fragments together—from several different species of an organism—to create something entirely new. This accomplishment formed the basis for modern biotechnology. Five years later, they teamed up to synthesize human insulin.

Cohen was born in Perth Amboy, New Jersey. He studied at Rutgers and the University of Pennsylvania—interning at Mount Sinai Hospital in New York.

He undertook his research program at Stanford while Bayer was at the University of California at San Francisco.

Cohen's awards include the Albert Lasker Basic Medical Research Award in 1980, and the Wolf Prize in 1981.

PAUL MAURICE ZOLL (1911-1999) originated the idea of electrical stimulation of an ailing heart—the first and important step to creation of the pacemaker.

He graduated from Harvard Medical School summa cum laude in 1936.

Zoll remained with Boston's Beth Israel Hospital for almost his entire career other than wartime service with the 160th US Army Station Hospital overseas.

The Bostonian was deeply troubled by the death of a 60-year-old woman with Stokes-Adams disease. "This should not happen to a heart perfectly normal except for a block of conduction," the doctor stated. "It should be possible to stimulate the heart."

Maurice Zoll originated the concept of the pacemaker – using electricity to re-start ailing hearts.

In 1952, using an esophageal wire, Zoll worked to stimulate the heart of a 65-year-old man with end-stage coronary disease, and recurrent cardiac arrest. External stimulation was used and the patient lived another six months.

The prestigious *New England Medical Journal* praised the new technique, but many doctors declared they opposed the procedure because it went against the will of God! However, a Catholic newspaper *The Pilot* praised his efforts.

To ensure that the new electrical technique was used only for emergencies, Zoll, with technicians, devised a device for monitoring the beating of the heart.

Karl Koller, at the suggestion of Sigmund Freud, used cocaine as a local anesthetic for eye operations.

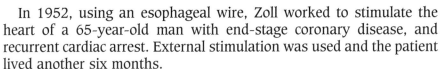

KARL KOLLER (1857-1944) , a Viennese ophthalmologist—encouraged by Sigmund Freud—used cocaine as an anesthetic during eye operations. In doing so, he originated modern local anesthesia.

Freud used cocaine to relieve his own chronic depression, and suggested that its numbing effect would make it usable as a local anesthetic during surgery. Koller found, in 1884, that cocaine hydrochloride could be used for surgery on the ear, nose and throat as well as the eyes.

Anesthesia has been called the most important invention of the past 2000 years.

BENJAMIN I. RUBIN (1917-   ) invented a needle that helped eradicate smallpox.

Rubin invented the "bifurcated vaccination needle" in 1968, and the needle has been given much of the credit for enabling the World Health Organization to wipe out smallpox in the next eleven years.

The stainless steel needles were manufactured by the Wyeth Laboratories in Philadelphia. The design of the needles enabled medical personnel to train vaccinators in minutes, and the needles could be sterilized and reused.

Using Rubin's needle, a single health worker could vaccinate as many as 1,500 in one day !

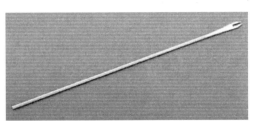

Benjamin Rubin originated a vaccination needle that helped wipe out cholera worldwide.

LEO STERNBACH (1908-   ) discovered valium—for years the world's most popular tranquilizer.

Sternbach was a Polish-Jewish chemist, who managed to escape the Nazis during World War Two. He went to work for a New Jersey pharmaceutical company, Hoffman-Laroche, and synthesized the relaxing drug called valium. The company chose the name from the Latin word valere—meaning being strong.

By 1978, annual sales approached 2.3 billion tablets. Valium was the most prescribed drug in the US in the period from 1969 to1982, earning the manufacturer, at its peak, $600-million a year. However its popularity declined when such drugs as Prozac, Paxil and other anti-depressants appeared.

When Sternbach, who patented more than 230 items, retired, the company awarded him a miserly pension of $10,000 a year for ten years !

Leo Sternbach discovered valium – the most popular tranquilizer in the United States for a dozen years.

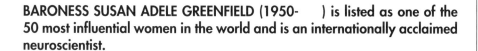

BARONESS SUSAN ADELE GREENFIELD (1950-   ) is listed as one of the 50 most influential women in the world and is an internationally acclaimed neuroscientist.

She graduated in experimental psychology from Oxford and by 1977 had completed her doctorate. Her research (she heads a team of 18 scientists) has focused on the aging brain and such problems as Parkinson's disease and Alzheimer's.

She is the first woman to be named director of the 204 year old Royal Institution of Great Britain.

She has been a popular broadcaster on both radio and television, and undertook a series on the brain for the BBC.

In 2000 she was named a Commander of the British Empire (CBE); in 2001 she was one of four women named as "People's Peers."

Baroness Susan Greenfield, the first woman named to direct the Royal Institution of Great Britain.

"Happy people are not ambitious; they do not build civilizations."

Baroness Susan Greenfield
Fullerian Professor of Physiology and
Comparative Anatomy Oxford University

O.M. SCHLOSS developed the "scratch test" to identify allergies in 1912.

CHAPTER THREE

INVENTORS AND ENGINEERS

"You can't predict the future, but you can invent it."
Dennis Gabor, Inventor of the Holograph

Emile Berliner invented the microphone and the gramophone.

EMILE BERLINER (1851-1929) invented the flat recording disc, founding the modern recording industry. He also invented the microphone. He improved the telephone so that it could be used for long-distance calls; he worked with his son Henry Adler on pioneer helicopters, and invented the acoustic tile.

Despite his important inventions, he is not well-known. In Montreal, where he invented the gramophone, there is a small museum, run by volunteers, which pays tribute to this exceptional inventor.

Berliner was born in Hanover, Germany, one of eleven children. He had to drop out of school at age 14 to help support the family. He worked in a print shop and then as a clerk in a dry goods shop. There, without any scientific training, he designed and constructed a weaving machine.

Later, hired to analyze sugar in a laboratory, he discovered a way to manufacture saccharin out of coal tar.

Moving to the US, he studied at night in the scientific library of Cooper Union. In 1876, Berliner invented two improvements to Alexander Graham Bell's telephone, an instrument which—until then—did not work well. (Bell's telephone was based on research by another Jewish inventor, Johann Philip Reis.) Bell Telephone bought Berliner's microphone, which received and transmitted voice through a wire, and his transformer, which maintained the sound level in transmissions. Berliner's undulating coil made the Bell telephone a satisfactory communications device.

For a time, the instrument was called the Bell-Berliner telephone. Next, Berliner improved on Edison's talking machine, which used soft wax cylinders to record the human voice. The Jewish inventor created the gramophone in 1887, using flat discs, offering a much higher quality of recording.

The machine, manufactured and distributed by the Victor Talking Machine Company, was sold all over the world as a modestly-priced provider of home entertainment.

Discs cost 50 cents and became increasingly popular, but their acceptance exploded when Enrico Caruso, one of the greatest tenors in history, recorded on Berliner discs. The tenor was the first performer to sell a million records.

In 1895, Berliner developed a unit to make several copies of a record from a master disc.

When his infant daughter died of an intestinal disorder, Berliner campaigned for pasteurization of milk, achieved in 1907—despite opposition from the medical profession !

In 1915, Berliner invented the first acoustic tile. Also in 1915, he designed a light internal combustion engine, and—with his son Henry Alden Berliner—designed and flew three different types of helicopters during the period from 1919 to 1926. Despite his age (he was then in his 70s), he sometimes flew the machines himself. The first helicopter flight of importance in the United States was made by Henry Berliner on June 16, 1922, at College Park, Maryland, in the presence of officials of the US Bureau of Aeronautics. The machine had two lifting propellers in front, and a third prop in the rear to provide forward motion. The early helicopter rose to a height of seven feet on three occasions.

During the Second World War, Henry Berliner was Chief of War Plans for the 8th US Air Force. He lost an arm from a wound suffered during a mission.

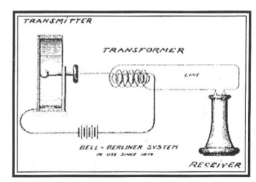

The telephone system adopted by the Bell Company, incorporating Emile Berliner's microphone and induction coil. It was referred to, for a time, as the Bell-Berliner Telephone.

SIEGFRIED MARCUS (1831-1898) designed and built the first benzine-powered automobile.

The Nazis did everything they could to destroy all records of Marcus' accomplishment. They were so efficient that Daimler and Benz are credited with creation of the first automobile.

A Seigfried Marcus car survived despite the German sweep. It was hidden by a quickly constructed wall and the vehicle is now on display in Vienna, Austria.

Siegfried Liepmann Marcus was born in Malchin, Mecklenburg—the third son of a businessman and leader of the Jewish community.

Marcus was apprenticed to a mechanic, attended a technical school and worked for some major firms before establishing his own workshop. A telegraphic relay was the first of 158 patented

Siegfried Marcus invented what probably was the first gasoline-powered automobile.

inventions. These included an instrument called the "artigraph," which allowed lithographers and engravers to transfer their designs without resorting to mirror images; electromagnetic naval mines; and a handgun capable of firing 30 shots a minute. He invented the carburetor (he called it a device to 'carburate air'), a mobile internal combustion engine (possibly the very first), and a motorcar dated 1887-1888. That date is two years earlier than the Daimler and Benz auto.

———

AL GROSS (1918-2000) invented the walkie-talkie, the pager, and is known as the "founding father of wireless communication".

Born in Toronto, he became fascinated with radio while on a steamboat trip on Lake Erie when he was nine years old. A ship's radio operator let him listen to the wireless.

Now living in Cleveland, by age 12 Gross had collected equipment from junkyards and built a crystal detector set in his basement. At 16, he obtained amateur radio license W8PAL, and to many in wireless communications, that is how he was known.

In 1938, using unexplored frequencies above 100 MHz, he invented the "walkie-talkie."

The US Office of Strategic Services (OSS) recruited Gross to design a portable two-way air-to-ground communications system. He developed two—a ground unit called "Joan" and an airborne facility, "Eleanor." His units enabled the allies to communicate with each other, using Herzian radio waves, without fear the enemy would be able to monitor their transmissions.

Gross' work resulted in creation of the "Citizens Radio Service Frequency Band", approved by the Federal Communications Commission (FCC) in 1946. And he formed a company in 1948 which produced two-way radios for personal use. In 1949, he developed the telephone pager, using a pocket-sized wireless receiver.

William E. Kennard, Chairman of the FCC, formally acknowledged Gross' achievements in 1999, noting that his "contributions included such wireless devices as the walkie-talkie, the cordless telephone, and the beeper."

President Bill Clinton joined in the tribute to the inventor, then 82, with a letter of commendation.

Al Gross who invented the walkie-talkie, the beeper and the handheld wireless telephone.

John Stanley, in an article in the Arizona Republic on January 7, 2001, wrote:

"If you've ever used a cell phone, pager or garage-door opener, thank Al Gross."

Federal Communications Commission

Wishes to Honor

AL GROSS

An American engineer, inventor and educator by acknowledging and recognizing his many contributions to portable, personal wireless communications equipment over a forty year period starting before World War II and continuing into the 1990's. These contributions include such wireless devices as the walkie-talkie, the cordless telephone and the beeper.

Al Gross' vision and groundwork into wireless telecommunications equipment, as well as, the Commission's insight into that vision have made it possible for many derivative devices, such as the cellular telephone, and a booming worldwide telecommunications industry.

William E. Kennard
Chairman

The FCC document honoring Al Gross for his achievements.

Edwin Land, inventor of the Polaroid camera.

EDWIN HERBERT LAND (1909-1991) invented the Polaroid camera—that is, instant photography.

Land attended Harvard but did not have the patience to complete his degree program. (The university awarded him an honorary degree in 1957.)

In 1932, he invented "Polaroid," which was used in a variety of ways including safety glass, sunglasses and, of course, photography.

He was responsible for other innovations but the most important was the Polaroid Land Camera, invented in 1947. His camera could develop pictures within seconds of being shot. He conceived the idea of an instant photo at a family picnic in 1943, when —after taking a snapshot—his three-year-old daughter jumped up and down, waiting to see the picture.

In all, Land held patents for well over 500 inventions. In addition to the Polaroid Company, which he headed until 1974, he established, in 1980, the Rowland Institute for Science. Institute staff created a laser instrument that could manipulate microscopic organisms.

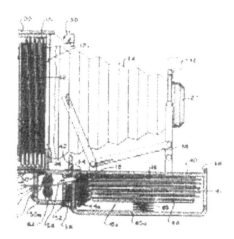

Patent No. 2435720 – "apparatus for exposing and processing photographic film." Aug. 29, 1946. E.H. Land

Johann Philip Reis.

JOHANN PHILIP REIS (1834-1874) was the unacknowledged (in the United States) inventor of the telephone.

A German schoolmaster, his device was first made public, in 1861, as a "scientific toy" displayed at Frankfurt-Am-Main. But there is no question that Reis' concept formed the basis for Alexander Graham Bell's telephone design.

(Reis' students called their teacher "the plumber' because he was always tinkering in a little shed.)

Reis is widely accepted in Europe as the originator of the telephone. That first crude instrument sought to copy the design of the human ear. Reis used a sausage skin for a diaphragm. The mouthpiece was a hollowed out bung from a beer barrel.

He improved on his device and demonstrated it before the Physical Society of Frankfurt on October 26, 1861—fifteen years before Bell patented his device. In the demonstration, he transmitted sound over a three-hundred foot line.

In 1864, he showed off an improved telephone at a scientific congress at Giessen. As a result of that demonstration, the Ries telephone was written up in several publications. This early telephone could carry a voice in only one direction.

Twelve days after Bell's first transmission of intelligible speech, the *New York Times* ran an editiorial about Philipp Reis entitled "The Telephone." The author referred to Reis' "remarkable instrument." Bell was not mentioned. Among those challenging Bell's claim that he invented the telephone was the United States government!

Bell, a native of Edinburgh, studied at the Institute of Natural Science at Edinburgh University, and it was there that he saw a Ries instrument.

The telephone Bell ultimately built was a great improvement over the Ries instrument, but even his device had to await the invention of a superior mouthpiece by Emile Berliner.

Reis died, of lung disease, in 1874. He was only 40. And he left his family impoverished. Physicists collected donations and erected a monument to his memory.

The Reis telephone – 1861.

"It is only men who are free who create the inventions and intellectual works which to us moderns make life worthwhile."
Albert Einstein, quoted in the New York Times

ELIAS E. REISS invented the device that made movies with sound possible.

In 1923, he sold his device to Lee DeForest. Reiss was an electrical engineer. And he also invented a convertor for alternating current, making the electrification of railways possible.

Elias E. Reiss' invention made the "talkies"-movies with sound possible.

DENNIS GABOR (1900-1979) invented holography, which led to creation of the laser.

The Hungarian-born physicist left for England when Hitler came to power.

Working on the electron microscope, he got the idea for holography. He developed the theory in 1947, but it was another 18 years before a technique for production was worked out. The hologram is widely used on credit cards. His technique improved imaging processes to permit creation of true three-dimensional pictures.

Gabor was born in Budapest and had a good start: his parents provided their two sons with a laboratory in their home.

The scientist, in England, worked on the electron microscope which provided poor resolution at higher magnifications. He worked out a technique of taking what he called a "bad picture," and then correcting it later—merging the two pictures to make what he called a "hologram"—that is, complete picture.

Gabor's discovery occurred in 1947, but it was 13 years later that Theodore Harold Maiman took Gabor's studies and built the first working laser.

Gabor received the 1971 Nobel Prize for Physics.

Dennis Gabor invented holography.

Zora Arkus-Duntov (centre) invented four-wheel disc brakes.

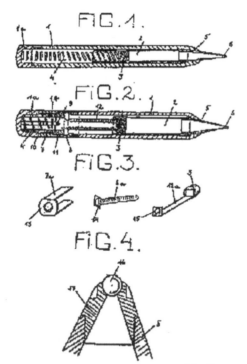

FIG.1.

FIG.2.

FIG.3.

FIG.4.

This the drawing for the original ball point pen invented by Laszlo Biro. It accompanied his submission for a patent.

Inventors' day in Argentina is celebrated on Biro's birthday.

ZORA ARKUS-DUNTOV (1909-1996) invented four-wheel disc brakes and a fuel injection system still used in many cars. Moreover he was co-designer of the Corvette.

He was born in Belgium, of Russian parents, and served in the French Air Force in World War Two. He worked for General Motors in the United States from 1953 to 1974.

——————

LASZLO BIRO (1899-1985) is known as the "father of the ball point pen." He also invented the automatic gearbox.

A Hungarian journalist, sculptor and hypnotist, Biro noticed how quickly the ink, used in printing the newspaper, dried. However, he found that thicker ink, used to print journals, would not flow from a pen nib. So he fitted his pen with a tiny ball and developed a pressurized ink cartridge.

Biro fled Fascist-dominated Hungary to Argentina where he obtained a patent in 1943. In 1944, the Royal Air Force purchased quantities of the "Biro" because the pen functioned well at high altitudes, despite the cold. The first "Biros" were manufactured in Reading, England by 17 women working in an unused aircraft hangar. The entire output of that first year—30,000 pens—was for use by airmen.

The first ballpoint pens for the public became available in 1945 and were manufactured in Buenos Aires.

A visiting American, discovering that Biro had neglected to patent the pen in the United States, began manufacturing them in the US, claiming that it was the "first pen that writes under water." Gimbel's, in New York, sold 10,000 of them for $12.50 each, the first day.

In some parts of Europe, ballpoints are still called "Biros."

Biro found the clutch mechanism on his new, red Bugatti automobile too clumsy, and, after a year of experimentation, patented his "automatic gear-box."

General Motors in Germany purchased the patent after tests verified the reliability of the automatic gear-shift. But Biro earned little from the deal. The contract gave him $200 a month (US) for five years, and he was to be paid a royalty on each gear-box sold. But GM America suppressed the patent "for commercial reasons," and the project was buried in some company file.

H. JOSEPH GERBER (1924-1996) helped perfect computer-assisted equipment, allowing opticians to produce eyeglasses in an hour.

At age 15 the Austrian-born Gerber was a prisoner in a German Labor Camp. But he escaped and, with his mother, made it to America.

In college, he invented the "Gerber Variable Scale," said to be "the most revolutionary engineering tool since the slide rule." In the 50s, he invented the first digital drafting machine, or "photoplotter." The plotter is used in three-quarters of television circuit boards.

A decade later he came up with the "GERBERcutter S-70," a fully-automated system for cutting cloth. This equipment is currently in use in some forty countries.

In addition to his inventions, Gerber set up a company to promote and market his new products.

H. Joseph Gerber made eyeglasses in an hour possible.

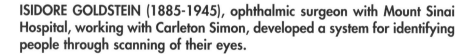

ISIDORE GOLDSTEIN (1885-1945), ophthalmic surgeon with Mount Sinai Hospital, working with Carleton Simon, developed a system for identifying people through scanning of their eyes.

The system, first demonstrated to the International Association of Chiefs of Police, on July 7, 1935, in Atlantic City, New Jersey, was based on the identification of the pattern formed by the veins and arteries of the retina.

Dr. Simon, associated in this discovery, was the former Deputy Police Commissioner of New York City.

Isidore Goldstein created a system for identifying people by scanning their eye.

CHARLES PAULSON GINSBURG (1920-1992) led the team at Ampex that invented the first practical videotape machine.

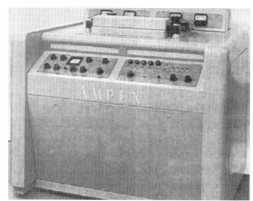

The invention revolutionized television. Until videotape came along, productions were presented live or on the more expensive film, or on such poor quality systems as kinescopes.

Videotape meant TV stations could readily and inexpensively record and edit programs. Later home videotape playback systems were built.

The first Ampex video-taping machine.

People, at home, were able to record programs off their television screens and play them back later.

Home systems meant that movies, put on videotape, could be bought or rented, and played back in the home.

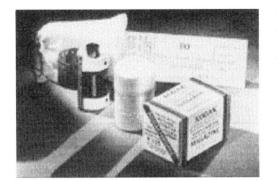

Leopold Godowsky and Leopold Damrosch invented Kodachrome film.

LEOPOLD GODOWKSY (1900-1983) and Leopold Damrosch Mannes developed the first quality color film, for Kodak.

Eastman Kodak had developed a color film "Kodachrome" but the quality was not satisfactory. Mannes, who was studying to be a concert pianist, and Godowsky who was a violinist, teamed up on this unusual assignment. They had been friends from age 16, and shared a passion for photography.

The desire to create quality film stemmed from their visit to see what was billed as a "color movie" in 1916. It was a poor reproduction, and they set out to do better. Their families gave them $800 to finance their research, which was undertaken while Godowsky was at the University of California, and Mannes was at Harvard.

By the 1920s, their work was so promising that Eastman Kodak began to provide technical support and a New York investment firm provided financial assistance.

In 1930 the company hired Mannes and Godowsky to continue and intensify their efforts. After five years of experimentation, their new film, with the old name Kodachrome, was put on the market. Kodachrome was marketed for stills, slides, and motion pictures.

Goldman's original shopping cart.

SYLVAN N. GOLDMAN (1898-1984) invented the shopping cart. It made the self-service store possible.

The oil boom in Oklahoma attracted the Goldman family in the early 1900s. The family went into the grocery business, and Sylvan Goldman gave a lot of thought to how customers could be induced to make more purchases. At the time, he owned the Standard Food Stores chain of Oklahoma City, Oklahoma.

In 1936, he devised his first shopping cart, comprised of two folding wire baskets fitted onto a wheeled frame. He improved his first design and introduced the cart into his stores on June 4, 1937. The idea was so well received that Goldman left the grocery business to manufacture shopping carts. He designed the modern cart in 1947.

Charles P. Steinmetz was an outstanding electrical engineer, with more than 200 inventions.

CHARLES PROTEUS STEINMETZ's (1865-1923) inventions included dynamos, electric motors, and devices making possible transmission of high voltage electricity over long distances.

Steinmetz, like his father and grandfather, was born a hunchback. Because he did not want to pass on this deformity, he never married.

He was an excellent student. His papers were so interesting his father, a bookbinder, bound them into folios.

In the face of German anti-Semitism in the late 1880s, he fled, first to Switzerland and then the United States. He began work in a small factory which was absorbed by the General Electric Company of Schenectady, and there he worked for the rest of his life. He was recognized as one of America's foremost electrical geniuses.

Steinmetz's first encounter with GE involved a problem they were having with a huge electrical generator. The engineer solved the problem and submitted a bill for $1,000—a considerable amount. The company asked Steinmetz for an itemized bill. He did so. His bill listed $1.00 for making a chalk mark on the generator, and $999 for knowing where to make the mark.

Major figures—from Edison to Einstein—came to visit him and study the way in which he solved electrical problems. GE catered to him. When smoking was forbidden in the labs, he declared "No smoking; no Steinmetz." So the rule was changed. No one could smoke, except Steinmetz.

His research habits were unusual. He would work out intricate problems while drifting in a canoe.

He patented more than two hundred inventions, and his textbooks influenced a generation of electrical engineers.

Thomas A. Edison in a 1922 visit to Steinmetz to study the engineer's work.

Peter Carl Goldmark invented the LP and the first color television system. Here he is making the first color television broadcast in 1940. (CBS photo Archive)

PETER CARL GOLDMARK (1906-1977) developed the first marketable long-playing record and the first color television system.

Goldmark studied physics at the University of Vienna (as an undergraduate he designed a television receiver with a postage-stamp-sized screen) and, on graduation, joined the staff of the television division of Pye Radio in Cambridge, Massachusetts.

He moved on to CBS, where, in 1950, he became vice-president in charge of engineering, research and development. In that same year, the Federal Communications Commission approved Goldmark's system for broadcasting color television.

The engineer's interest in color television stemmed from seeing the movie *Gone With The Wind*, in technicolor, during a visit to Canada. He told the *New York World Telegram* that he developed "an inferiority feeling about television in black and white."

Three months after going to work on the idea of transmitting in color, he was able to transmit motion pictures of flowers and marine scenes. He had invented the long-playing microgroove record (LP) in 1948. Apparently the idea of developing the LP occurred to Goldmark when, at a party, he was annoyed at the need to change recordings frequently. There had been LPs much earlier. RCA Victor produced a 33 1/3 rpm microgroove in 1947 but the record players were too expensive for most people. The LP record players sold for $250 to $1,000.

Goldmark's player, for Columbia, cost $29.95 and up. The inventor received no royalties from Columbia; they presented him with a copy of each LP they pressed.

Fritz Haber discovered how to convert nitrogen and hydrogen into ammonia.

FRITZ HABER (1868-1934) developed a process for converting nitrogen and hydrogen into ammonia, which then could be made into fertilizer or explosives. With the British naval blockade during World War One, Germany would have run out of explosives by 1916 if the Haber process had not been created. He received the Nobel Prize in chemistry in 1918.

Haber, a fiercely loyal German, also helped develop poison gases used in World War One. In 1915 Haber directed the first use of poison gas. Chlorine gas was released to drift over allied trenches at Ypres. By 1917, he had developed the deadlier mustard gas.

Despite his tremendous accomplishments, when the Nazis came to power, Haber felt compelled to resign. He wrote in his resignation: "I have selected my collaborators on the basis of their intelligence and their character and not on the basis of their grandmothers."

He worked for a time in England, but left for Israel, becoming fatally ill en route.

———

HEINRICH RUDOLPH HERTZ (1857-1894) opened the door to development of the radio, television, and radar with his discovery of electromagnetic waves, Hertz was born in Hamburg, Germany—son of a prominent lawyer and legislator. The family had a workshop and Hertz delighted in designing implements.

He studied at the Universities of Munich and Berlin and received his Doctor of Philosophy degree magna cum laude. He lectured at Karlsruhe Polytechnic and, later, at the University of Bonn.

He made his discovery of electromagnetic waves between 1886 and 1888, and also demonstrated that light waves and electromagnetic waves were identical.

Henrich Hertz was the first to produce and detect "Maxwell's Ways", opening the door to the development of radio, television, and radar.

———

HERMAN ARON (1845-1913) was an electrophysicist who developed the theory of condensers, perfected a type of microphone, and was a pioneer in wireless telegraphy.

He was born in Germany and taught at the University of Berlin. But, rather than teach, he wanted to, and ultimately did, devote himself entirely to practical work in the field of electricity.

He used "hertzian waves" to transmit signals. He had telephones wrapped in wire, called them "cable probes" and was able to communicate, without wires, across an impressive distance.

He lectured on his discovery at the International Electrical Exposition in Vienna in 1883.

Aron was a very quiet person and few knew of him and his work. However, he did draw attention in 1884 when he invented, the "Aron Clock Meter," which automatically measured the flow of electricity.

Joseph L. Popper was the first to formulate the idea of transmitting electric power.

JOSEF (LYNKEUS) POPPER (1838-1921) was the first to propose the concept of transmission of electrical power.

In 1862 the Austrian engineer and author explained his theories, in a written submission to the Imperial Academy of Sciences in Vienna. The Society published his paper—20 years later.

He made important innovations in the fields of aeronautics and gyroscopic motion as well as in electricity. His book *Flugtechnik*, published in 1888, discussed the mechanical adaptation of bird flight.

Later in life, he abandoned science to do what he could to correct society's problems, especially developing ideas for preventing war. He reacted to the pogroms in Russia by moving closer to Judaism and Zionism.

RALPH SCHNEIDER started the first credit card organization, "Diners Club," in 1950.

Schneider is said to have thought of the card, when he was handed the bill in an expensive restaurant and found that he had forgotten his wallet.

The first credit cards were issued to 200 subscribers. The only businesses, at first, that signed up to accept the cards were 27 New York restaurants. Customers were billed monthly by Diners Club, who in turn would reimburse the restaurants—minus a commission. However, the new "plastic money" was not popular until the magnetic strip was added in 1970.

Isaac Meritt Singer borrowed $40 to pay for materials used to make the first home sewing machine.

ISAAC MERRITT SINGER (1811-1875) borrowed $40 and manufactured the first home sewing machine.

The first sewing machine was built in 1829—thirty-one years before Singer produced his machine. Barthelemy Thimmonier built a sewing machine for his own use, but a Paris uniform manufacturer found out about it and ordered 80 for his plant. However, workers in the plant feared they would lose their jobs to the device, and destroyed all but one. Thimmonier tried to manufacture his invention again in 1845, but once more a mob destroyed the equipment.

Isaac Singer was intrigued by an early Blodgett and Lerow sewing machine brought to him for repairs. The inventor immediately recognized how he could make the machine more efficient and, at the same time, he had the marketing skills to make his machine a household word. He built the first machine for home use in 1851 in Boston.

Singer was born in Troy, New York, to a large immigrant family. He left home at 12 and for seven years worked at a variety of unskilled jobs. For a time, he worked at and for the theatre—as an actor, a stagehand, and even in the promotion of plays.

He had natural mechanical ability. And about 1850, he went to work to improve the sewing machine. He patented his new device in 1851 and began manufacturing it in Boston. The Singer sewing machine became the top seller in the field, around the world.

The machine made him a wealthy man, and the onetime laborer flaunted his riches—riding often through New York's Central Park in a bright yellow coach.

After his retirement, in 1863, he moved to England where he built a mansion in the seaside resort of Torquay. In all, he had 24 children—both legitimate and illegitimate—and he was hospitable to all of them.

His estate amounted to $13 million—a huge sum in the late 19th century.

This is the 1853 model Singer Sewing Machine. It was sold worldwide.

MORRIS MICHTOM AND HIS WIFE, who ran a candy store in Brooklyn, invented the "Teddy Bear."

Their inspiration came from the occasion, in 1902, when President Theodore "Teddy" Roosevelt refused to shoot a bear cub in Mississippi. His hosts had trapped the cub, and tied it to a stake to ensure that Roosevelt could not miss. The President refused to shoot the animal.

Clifford Berryman drew a cartoon, for the *Washington Evening Star* of November 18, showing "Teddy" with his back to the cub.

This is Rose and Morris Michtom's "Teddy's Bear," c. 1903 – now in the Smithsonian Institution.

The cartoon in the Washington Post by Clifford Berryman; it inspired the idea of the teddy bear.

Michtom, a Jewish immigrant from Russia, was so moved by the story that he and his wife created a plush brown bear with button eyes, and asked Roosevelt to grant him permission to call it "Teddy's bear." Roosevelt replied that he didn't think his name would be "worth much to the toy bear cub business," but Michtom put his Teddy's bear in the window, with a copy of Berryman's cartoon. By 1906, the Teddy bear was the best-selling toy in America and almost a million were sold in 1907.

Michtom gave up his candy store and founded what would later become the Ideal Toy Company, the world's largest manufacturer of dolls.

———

DONALD ARTHUR GLASER (1926-   ) designed the "bubble chamber"; it became an indispensable tool for research in nuclear physics. It won him the Nobel Prize for Physics in 1960.

Glaser was born in Cleveland, Ohio. He was a dreamer in school, and only the intervention of a psychologist blocked plans to transfer him to a class for backward children.

He adjusted, however, and in 1949, was awarded a Ph.D. in physics and mathematics by the California Institute of Technology.

Glaser says he studied bottles of beer, ginger ale, and soda water in working out the idea of his bubble chamber. The chamber has become one of the most important detection devices in the work of particle physicists.

———

ARTHUR KORN (1870-1945) invented the first practical photoelectric facsimile system (i.e. the Fax). By 1910, facsimile transmission over the telephone linked Paris, London, and Berlin.

Born in Germany, he taught physics at the University of Munich, 1903-1908, and was Professor of electro-physics at the Berlin Institute of Technology, 1914-1936.

Using his system, Korn sent photos over the telephone line from Munich to Nuremberg—a distance of more than 600 miles. In 1907, he sent the first wire photo from the continent to England.

On May 6, 1922, he wired a picture from near Rome to Berlin and then it was radioed across the Atlantic Ocean to the US Navy radio station in Maine.

In 1939, his family emigrated to the United States where he taught at the Stevens Institute of Technology in Hoboken, New Jersey.

Jaron Lanier is called the "father of virtual reality."

JARON LANIER (1960-   ) is a computer scientist and composer who is known as the father of "virtual reality." He also coined the term.

Lanier was the son of artist/musicians and grew up in rural New Mexico. His initiatives include the first performance animation for 3D computer graphics.

He is on the faculty of, or serves as a consultant to, a number of universities and companies. He came up with the term "virtual reality" in the early 1980s and founded the first company to sell such products—-VPL Research.

Lanier, who wears his hair long and in dreadlocks, is extremely versatile. He writes chamber and orchestral music. He is also a musician, paints and draws and is a popular author and speaker.

The Encyclopedia Britannica lists him as one of history's "greatest inventors."

Despite this extraordinary range of achievements, he has no university degrees. Yet he was the lead scientist in developing Internet 2—with about 180 universities participating.

Dr. Robert Adler invented the TV remote control.

ROBERT ADLER (1913-   ) invented the TV remote control.

Adler was born in Vienna, studied at the University of Vienna and received his doctorate in physics in 1939.

He left wartime Austria, first for England and then the United States.

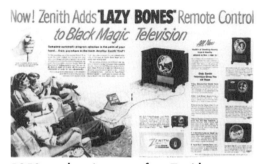

1950s advertisement for Zenith remote control.

The Research Division of the Zenith Corporation hired him. His first breakthrough on behalf of Zenith was the gated-beam tube, a new concept in receiving tubes, and he conceived other systems improving the quality of reception on television.

His remote control used sound (at frequencies higher than the human ear can pick up) to communicate with the television set. He improved his system in the 1960s, using his control to generate ultrasonic signals electronically. More than 9,000,000 TVs were sold by Zenith with Alder's remote control system before infrared light technology was introduced in the early 1980s.

Robert Alder ultimately was granted 180 US patents for electronic devices. His many awards include the Inventor of the Year Award from George Washington University, in 1967 and the Edison Medal in 1980.

EMANUEL GOLDBERG (1881-1970) was an inventive pioneer in the field of imaging technology.

Emanuel Goldberg contributed to almost all aspects of imaging technology. He was once kidnapped by the Nazis.

Born in Moscow, he became an inventor, a chemist, and industrialist, making an important contribution to almost every aspect of information technology—photographic sensitometry, reprographics, standardized film speeds, color printing, aerial photography, extreme microphotography (microdots), optics, camera design, the first hand-held movie camera, and early television technology.

Goldberg received his doctorate from Wilhelm Ostwald's Institute in Leipzig in 1906.

In 1927 he designed a "statistical machine," regarded by many as the first information retrieval system using electronics.

By 1933 he had become head of Zeiss Ikon, in Dresden, Germany—the largest camera manufacturer in the world ! Then he apparently was kidnapped by the Nazis—and disappeared for a time. German thugs are said to have tied him to a tree for three days, but fellow workers from Zeiss freed him and helped him escape.

He surfaced in Paris and then moved to Tel Aviv, where he established a workshop for crafting precision instruments. That workshop grew into a major Israeli manufacturer—El-Op.

Many of the details of his life and accomplishments have vanished. The Nazis destroyed some ... a bombing of Dresden scattered others ... and his records were damaged or destroyed by a flood in Israel.

CHAPTER FOUR

THE ATOM

"The Jewish Connection in atomic research is more likely an indication that, as much as the Jewish personality is rooted in an allegiance to the past, the Jewish mind is oriented to the future. With no vested interest in preserving the status quo, Jews, especially Jews with brilliance, may very well find it easier than others to question old assumptions. Jewish physicists could seize on the idea of atomic power as a vast new energy source precisely because it looks to the future."

M. Hirsh Goldberg, *The Jewish Connection*

Meitner was Germany's first woman physicist.

LISE MEITNER (1878-1968), with her nephew Otto Frisch and aided by Otto Hahn, published the first report on nuclear fission.

She was the first to explain how tremendous energy would be released by splitting the atom.

During the 30s, Meitner and Hahn conducted the experiments which set the stage for development of both the atomic bomb and nuclear power.

The Austrian-born physicist, despite her brilliance, had to work under extraordinarily difficult conditions—because she was Jewish and also because she was a woman. In those days, male scientists would often not allow a woman to work in their laboratories.

Meitner, the first woman physics professor in Germany, was allowed to publish articles using her last name only. When she submitted a paper with her first name, it was refused. Hahn wisely welcomed Meitner into his lab as a collaborator.

Meitner and Hahn discovered and named the process "fusion,"and first described their conclusions publicly with an article in the publication *Nature* in 1939. They set the stage for the Atomic Age.

Oddly enough, the culmination of their work came when they were far apart. Meitner was forced, like other Jewish scientists working in Germany, to flee after the Nazis took over. She went to work in Stockholm, where she continued her research. Hahn remained in Germany.

She refused an invitation to participate in the American Manhattan Project that developed the atomic bomb. And, after a bomb was dropped on Hiroshima, Japan in 1945, she told *The Saturday Evening Post*:

"You must not blame us scientists for the use to which war technicians have put our discoveries."

The 1944 Nobel Prize for Chemistry went to Hahn, and Meitner was not mentioned. The scientist, while continuing to be prominent in nuclear physics research, refused to lend her knowledge to efforts to create weapons.

In 1992, element 109 was named Meitnerium in her honor.

J. ROBERT OPPENHEIMER (1904-1967) supervised the assembly of the first atomic bomb.

He had been put in charge of the Los Alamos laboratory, and that is where the first atomic bomb was designed and constructed.

When he opposed development of the hydrogen bomb, his loyalty was questioned, and access to secret papers was denied. His status was not restored until a few years before his death.

He was born in New York City and was sent to boarding school in Los Alamos—-a rugged part of New Mexico to which he would return to work on the first atomic bomb.

He was unquestionably a genius. And during his studies at Harvard, he assumed a course load equal to seven normal undergraduate requirements. He graduated from Harvard in 1925 "summa cum laude" and received a Ph.D. degree in 1927 from the University of Gottingen.

A number of universities tried to woo him. He decided to teach at the University of Southern California, Berkeley, because of the immense collection of French Renaissance poetry in its library!

In 1942, Oppenheimer was chosen to head the ultra-secret Manhattan project—mandated to design and build an atomic bomb. He recruited many top scientists, including several Nobel laureates, to work on the bomb. Many had been driven out of Europe by Adolf Hitler and other extreme right-wingers in such countries as Italy, Austria, and Hungary.

The first bomb, code-named "Trinity" was tested July 16, 1945, and the power of the explosion shocked even the experts. Oppenheimer was heard to quote from Bhagavad Gita:

"I am become Death, the destroyer of worlds."

He was awarded the Presidential Medal of Merit for his work on the bomb.

In 1963, President Lyndon Johnson presented him with the Enrico Fermi Award including a gold medal and $50,000, the highest honor bestowed by the US Atomic Energy Commission.

Lise Meitner with associates published the first report on nuclear fission. Her nephew Otto Hahn worked closely with her.

J. Robert Oppenheimer headed the team that developed the atomic bomb. He is seen here at Princeton with Albert Einstein. (Manhattan Project Heritage Preservation Assoc. Inc.)

There must be no barriers to freedom of inquiry. There is no place for dogma in science. The scientist is free, and must be free to ask any question, to doubt any assertion, to seek for any evidence, to correct any errors.

J. Robert Oppenheimer, *Life*, October 10, 1949

Dr. Oppenheimer's work on the creation of the atomic bomb has overshadowed his other achievements.

In 1939, he demonstrated mathematically how a star, a bit bigger than our own sun, could implode—collapsing into a super dense body. He estimated that such a body would be only ten miles across and its density would be so great that a cubic inch would weigh 10 billion tons.

He was describing a neutron star, and 28 years later, in 1967, a graduate student, Joselyn Bell, at Cambridge University, discovered such a star.

Furthermore, Oppenheimer—at about the same time (1939) theorized that an immense star—-much, much larger than our own—could collapse into a black hole. This theory was verified 33 years later (in 1972), when a black hole was detected in the binary star Cygnus X-1.

Working with Oppenheimer's mathematical computations, scientists theorized that black holes are an entry point into other universes!

Edward Teller, a towering figure in atomic science.

EDWARD TELLER (1908-2003), father of the hydrogen bomb, was an admirer of the *Alice In Wonderland* story.

He was born in Budapest, and his genius in mathematics was quickly recognized. He earned a Ph.D. from Leipzig in 1930, and later studied with nuclear physicist Niels Bohr in Denmark. In 1935 he and his family moved to the United States.

He left his teaching position at Columbia to work on the atom bomb.

After the war, he pushed for development of a nuclear bomb because he feared the Soviet Union would build one first.

He was one of the people who convinced President Harry S. Truman to undertake research on the H-bomb. However, after the weapon was built, he returned to the lecture hall, and campaigned for the peaceful use of nuclear power.

NIELS HENDRIK DAVID BOHR (1885-1962) won the 1922 Nobel Prize for physics for his work on quantum theory and the atomic structure.

Niels Bohr won the 1922 Nobel Prize for his work on quantum theory.

He was Danish and worked in his native land for his entire life other than for a period of study at Cambridge and Manchester University, and his flight to America when the Nazis seized Denmark.

Carlsberg, the brewers, sponsored his trip to study in England, with J.J. Thomson at Cambridge, and Ernest Rutherford at Manchester University.

In the United States, during World War Two, he worked on the atomic bomb at Los Alamos.

It was Bohr who suggested that the isotope uranium-235 would be more fissionable than the more common uranium-238. After the war he campaigned for international control of nuclear weapons and in 1955 he organized the first Atoms for Peace Conference.

His son, Aage Bohr (1922-) also won the Nobel prize — sharing the prize for physics in 1975.

Sam T. Cohen invented the neutron bomb – a powerful weapon with a limited target area.

SAM COHEN (1921 -) invented the Neutron Bomb.

With a physics degree from UCLA, Cohen joined the US Army after the Japanese attack on Pearl Harbor.

In 1944, he was assigned to the ultra-secret Manhattan Project and filled a minor role in the development of the first atomic bomb. He stood beside the Air Force's General Jimmy Doolittle in the Nevada Desert when the first atomic explosion took place. "The little guy was blown down," Cohen says.

After the war, the physicist continued to explore the potential of nuclear weapons as a member of the staff at the Rand Corporation. In the late 50s he created the neutron bomb, a weapon that would produce a powerful explosion but a smaller one. In other words, the weapon could be used against a specific enemy target but with limited collateral damage. And, after the explosion, neutron radiation dissipated quickly.

However, it was not until President Reagan intervened, that the US manufactured and deployed the new weapon, on a limited basis.

After the collapse of the Soviet Union, and the cutback in nuclear arms, the stockpile of neutron bombs was destroyed. Sam Cohen feels the US made a terrible mistake in removing neutron bombs from its arsenals. He claims that a number of nations—including Russia, China, and Israel—have neutron bombs and that, in the event of a major conflict, these weapons could be used to destroy an advancing enemy without permanently contaminating the land.

CHAPTER FIVE

FLIGHT

"The two men who have done more than any others in America to help advance and popularize aeronautics are Daniel Guggenheim (1856-1930), and his son, Harry F.; it is as a the result of their efforts that the United States leads the world today in military and commercial aviation."

Jews in the World of Science, 1956

Emile Berliner and his son Henry designed and built an early helicopter that flew.

EMILE BERLINER AND HIS SON, HENRY ALDEN BERLINER, were pioneers in the development of aircraft, aero-engines, and helicopters.

Emile Berliner, already cited as the inventor of the microphone, the gramophone, and the flat record, teamed up with his son in developing aircraft.

The Berliner helicopter made its first successful, tethered flight in about 1909. The chopper could move forward at a speed of about 40 miles per hour, and could maneuver in all directions.

The copter, with two counter-rotating main rotors, was based on the fuselage of a French aircraft—the Neuport 23.

The Berlin helicopter was successfully demonstrated to the US Army in 1924. (One of the copters is in storage in the Smithsonian Air and Space Museum.)

Later, Henry Berliner—who continued the helicopter experiments—began manufacturing aircraft as the Berliner Company and later as the Berliner-Joyce Company.

Aircraft builder Marcel Dassault (in white coat).

MARCEL DASSAULT (1892-1986) headed one of the world's most important aircraft manufacturing concerns, designing, among other aircraft, the Mirage series of fighters.

His real name was Marcel Bloch, but he used "Dassault" as his code name in the French resistance. After the war, he formally changed his name.

He founded Dassault Aviation, one of the most important designers and manufacturers of aircraft in the world.

His firm's product line included the Mystere and Mirage fighters. And his company also manufactures jet business aircraft.

Dassault was publisher of the glossy magazine *Jours de France*, backed a number of motion picture producers, and supported housing developments. In its earliest years, Israel depended largely on

Dassault-designed fighter jets. However, in 1967—as Israel was threatened by its neighbours—French President De Gaulle refused to allow delivery of aircraft and other weapons to the Jewish state.

Ultimately, Israel—through Switzerland—obtained blueprints and manufactured Mirage fighters as well as improvements on it.

Meanwhile, Dassault Mirage jets played a major role in the Six-Day War, defeating a combination of Egypt, Syria, and Jordan.

From that time on, Israel purchased its fighters from the United States, or manufactured its own.

The Mirage Fighter – one of the Dassault's greatest designs. This one is in service with the Israeli Air Force.

HARRY HALTON (1922-2003) designed Canadair/Bombardier business jets which were developed into the company's highly successful regional jets-the "RJs".

The immigrant from Czechoslovakia was involved in the design and manufacture of virtually every new aircraft for Bombardier, from the late 1940s on. However, laid low by illness, he was surprised when the company president appeared at his hospital bedside and stated "Harry, we need you to design a new aircraft."

"I'm sorry," Halton replied. "I'm busy dying." However, he recovered, partially, and designed the Challenger business jet. From that design came the RJs—Regional Jets — and billions of dollars in orders.

Halton was born in Pilsen, Czechoslovakia, and grew up fascinated by aircraft. Whenever he could, he would visit the airport to watch the activity. "I wasn't interested in flying them. I wanted to build them."

When World War II broke out, the family shipped the 16 year old lad to London where, ultimately, he studied electrical engineering.

His income in London came from selling 24 cases of Pilsen beer his father sent him weekly.

In 1948 he moved to Montreal and joined Canadair where he became a major designer. His projects included a remote-controlled drone, then a water bomber.

He had a leg problem, and operations left him paralyzed from the waist down. Undaunted, when his bosses visited him and asked "How would you like to work on the Challenger (business jet)? Halton, in fever and in pain, began to work on the project from his hospital bed.

Harry Halton designed the Challenger Business jet, which evolved into the widely-used RJs – regional jets.

Canadair/Bombardier's Challenger Business jet, designed by Halton.

Engineers, technicians, secretaries, and others from Canadair came to the hospital to receive directions from the bed-ridden aircraft designer.

In time, Halton went back to work—in a wheelchair—and the Challenger, the world's first wide-body business jet became a reality, And from that basic design came a host of developments which made Canadair/Bombardier one of the largest manufacturers of business and regional jets in the world.

In his downtown Montreal apartment, he is surrounded by precise models of every plane he designed.

OTTO LILIENTHAL's (1848-1896) pioneer glider designs led to the Wright Brothers' first heavier-than-air flight.

Lilienthal designed eighteen different gliders, made nearly 2,000 successful flights and was about to attempt powered flight, in 1896, when he was fatally injured in a glider crash.

The Wright Brothers, who achieved the first heavier-than-air flight in 1903, acknowledged their debt to Lillienthal. They were guided by the glider designer's book *Birdflight as the Basis for Aviation*, published in 1889.

The Wright brothers, in an article in *Century* magazine, in 1908—three years after their first heavier-than-air flight—declared: "It was not till the news of the sad death of Lilienthal reached America in the summer of 1896 that we again gave more than passing attention to the subject (flight)."

One of Lilienthal's gliders is on display at the National Air and Space Museum in Washington.

Otto Lilienthal's glider designs led to the Wright Brothers' first heavier-than-air flight.

Lilienthal in flight in one of his glider designs. (Otto Lilienthal Museum)

ABE SILVERSTEIN (1908-2001) was in charge of the National Aeronautics and Space Administration full-scale wind tunnel in which advanced research led to the development of increasingly better performance in World War Two warplanes.

Furthermore, he was one of the most important personalities in the development of the US Space program. Silverstein was born in Terre Haute, Indiana, and studied mechanical engineering at Rose Polytechnic Institute.

He began his professional career at the Langley Research Center, and directed research leading to significant improvements in aircraft engines. He was responsible for development of America's first supersonic propulsion wind tunnels. His work contributed greatly and directly to development of supersonic aircraft. Silverstein structured the National Aeronautics and Space Administration (NASA) when it was created in 1958. In his new position, he supervised the Mercury unmanned space program, laid the foundation for manned flights to the moon, and was the first director of the Goddard Space Flight Center.

Abe Silverstein was a wind tunnel expert whose work spanned decades of progress in the design of military aircraft.

THEODORE VON KARMAN (1881-1963) developed rockets and rocket engines, formulating theories that led to supersonic flight.

He was born in Budapest, son of a professor of education knighted by Emperor Francis Joseph I of Austria-Hungary for his reorganization of Hungarian education. He studied at the Royal Polytechnic University and later taught there.

From 1912 until 1930, Theodore von Karman was Director of the University of Aachen, an appointment interrupted by service during World War One, in the Hungarian Aviation Corps.

After traveling widely, as a visiting professor, he accepted an invitation, in 1930, to direct the Guggenheim Aeronautical Laboratory at the California Institute of Technology.

He participated in the founding of the US Institute of Aeronautical Sciences. Von Karman developed 14 prototype rockets and rocket engines, later used in achieving supersonic flight.

President John F. Kennedy presented him with the first National Medal of Science.

The Bell X-1, using a rocket engine developed by Theodore von Karman's Reaction Motors cracked the sound barrier in what has been called "one of the most significant flights in the history of aviation." (NASA photo)

David Schwarz invented the dirigible; this is his machine on its first flight.

DAVID SCHWARZ (1845-1897) invented the dirigible; his widow sold the patents to Count von Zeppelin, who is generally credited with the achievement.

Schwarz's test airship, powered by a 12 horsepower Daimler engine, took off from Templehof Airfield on November 3, 1897, but crashed after flying only four miles. The pilot was slightly injured.

The fundamental problem with the Schwarz dirigible was that the buoyancy chamber, filled with gas, consisted of a single compartment. Later, more successful airships had compartmentalized chambers and were able to function better despite temperature changes.

Schwarz had built a prototype of his airship in Russia, in 1882, but the German government sent him a telegram stating they would back his efforts. The inventor apparently became so excited he dropped dead. However, the project went ahead with Schwarz's widow in charge. Count Zeppelin, a retired German army officer, became fascinated and bought the patents.

The contract between the Count and Mrs. Schwarz is in the archives of the Hebrew University in Jerusalem.

———

KARL ARNSTEIN (1897-1974) designed the huge American airships "The Los Angeles" and the "Macon."

He was born in Prague, Czechoslovakia, and studied a strange combination of subjects: philosophy and engineering sciences.

In 1915, Count von Zeppelin hired him to work on airships for the German Air Force. In 1924, he designed large American airships. He also designed stratospheric balloons, railway trains, prefabricated aluminum homes, ultralight helicopters, and seaplanes.

Arnstein first worked with the Zeppelin people in pre-war Germany.

Arnstein's The Macon.

DANIEL GOLDIN (1940-   ) headed the American Space program for ten years (1992-2002).

Before joining NASA, Goldin spent 25 years with TRW Space and Technology Group, in Redondo Beach, California. In that position, he directed development and production of advanced spacecraft and instruments for use in space.

He graduated as a mechanical engineer from City College of New York.

Daniel Goldin headed the US space program for 10 years.

JOHN M. GRUNSFIELD (1956-   ) has been on four shuttle missions, has walked in space, and helped upgrade the Hubbell Space telescope.

Grunsfield's family were German Jews who came to the Chicago area in the 1840s.

After graduating from the University of Chicago with a doctorate in physics, he joined the American space program in 1992. He was on shuttle missions in 1995, 1997, 1999, and 2002.

The '97 mission lasted 10 days and included docking with the Russian space station Mir and an exchange of astronauts. The journey was for 39 million miles.

In 1999, Grunsfeld undertook two of the three space walks, involving the installation of new gyroscopes and scientific instruments on the Hubble Space Telescope.

John Grunsfield's four shuttle missions included a space-walk to upgrade the Hubble space telescope.

Harry Guggenheim (1890-1971) was a World War One flyer whose family funded the first University-level school of aviation, supported Charles Lindbergh's flights in 1930 to develop new air routes, and was the main source of funding for rocket pioneer Robert Goddard.

Guggenheim (whose family is better known for its support of the arts) interested his father, Daniel, in providing funds for creation of the Daniel Guggenheim School of Aeronautics, the first such school in the United States (1925).

Harry Guggenheim's family funded the earliest university-level courses in aeronautics in the US Here he stands to the left of Charles Lindbergh in 1927.

A year later, the Daniel Guggenheim Fund for the Promotion of Aeronautics was created, stimulating serious development of the commercial and industrial aspects of flying rather than the spectacular (that is, stunt-flying).

Furthermore, the Daniel and Florence Guggenheim Foundation underwrote research in rocketry by Robert H. Goddard. Many people, at that time, regarded rockets as little more than toys, but 40 years later, rockets developed from Goddard's pioneer work took astronauts to the moon. The American scientist, with the support and encouragement of the Guggenheims, developed the essential features of the Saturn V rocket system that lifted Apollo XI off on its 1969 flight to the moon.

Harry Guggenheim, born in West End, New Jersey, studied at Yale and Cambridge. He was a pilot in World War One, rising from the rank of lieutenant in the United States Naval Aviation Forces, to become a lieutenant commander before leaving the service in December, 1918. But this experience triggered a deep and creative interest in aviation.

In addition to encouraging his father's support for aeronautics, he campaigned for public support for passenger travel by air, financed the nationwide tour of Richard E. Byrd's North Pole plane in 1926, and established schools of aeronautics, and centers, at Cornell, Princeton, Columbia, and other universities.

After Daniel Guggenheim's death, Harry continued to provide financial support for Goddard's rocket research.

Harry Guggenheim returned to active service when the US became involved in World War Two, assuming command of Mercer Field in Trenton, New Jersey. Later, he served on the aircraft carrier Nehenta Bay in the Pacific campaign. In 1945, he returned to civilian life after attaining the rank of Captain and receiving two commendation ribbons.

Edwin P. Hoyt, in his book *The Guggenheims and the American Dream*, suggested "Harry and Daniel (Guggenheim) were fathers of American aviation."

The Daniel Guggenheim Medal, was created, in 1928, to recognize "great achievements in aeronautics."

MIKHAIL GUREVICH (1892-1975) was the "G" in the MIG range of Russian fighter aircraft, teaming up with Mikoyan. He led the design team for the MIG-29 fighter.

His first aeronautical engineering work was on license-built American C-47s (Dakotas). He and A.I. Mikoyan teamed up with six other engineers to form the MIG OKB design and production groups.

Mikhail Guerivich was the "G" in the MIG range of Soviet fighter planes; he was design chief for the MIG-29 fighter, among others.

Gurevich helped design the propellor-driven MIG fighters of the Second World War. After the war, he helped design Soviet jet fighters. He became head of the design group after the death of Mikoyan.

He led the design team for the MIG-29 which flies at more than twice the speed of sound.

SEMYON LAVOCHKIN (1900-1965) designed Soviet fighter planes during World War Two, including the LA-7, the best Soviet low-and-medium altitude fighter of the War.

Semyon Lavochkin designed many of the USSR's fighter planes during World War Two including this Lagg-5.

Lavochkin's early designs were not effective against the German Messerschmidts and Focke-Wolfes. But his LA-5 and LA-7 fighters were able to match the performance of the German aircraft.

Semyon Lavochkin in his uniform as chief designer at the OKB-301 Aircraft Design Bureau.

Marsha Ivins has flown an estimated 20,000,000 miles in space. (NASA)

MARSHA IVINS (1951-   ) has been on five shuttle missions, beginning in 1990, and has flown an estimated 20 million miles in space.

Ivins has been with the space program since 1974. She became a mission specialist in 1984.

Joseph Kaplan played a key role in the launch of the US's first artificial earth satellite.

JOSEPH KAPLAN (1902-1991) was an important figure in planning America's initial ventures into space, and was a key personality in planning the launch of the USA's first artificial earth satellite.

He was born in Hungary but came to the United States with his family at age eight.

He graduated from Johns Hopkins University and joined the faculty of the University of California at Berkeley, 1928-1970. Kaplan helped initiate and directed the University's Institute of Geophysics and Planetary Physics from its inception in 1944. He chaired the United States National Committee for the International Geophysical Year.

JAY APT (1949-   ) was flight controller responsible for Shuttle payload operations at the Johnson Space Center, 1982-1985; as an astronaut, he has circled the earth 562 times.

Dr. Apt has had a multi-faceted career. Graduating from Harvard and MIT, he became a post-doctoral fellow in laser spectroscopy at MIT. Then, from 1978 to 1980, he was on staff at the Center for Earth and Planetary Physics, of Harvard University, preparing temperature maps of Venus for the NASA Pioneer Venus Mission.

Apt joined NASA itself in 1980, doing planetary research. He studied Venus, Mars, and the outer solar system. After taking over direction of Shuttle payload operations for three years, he qualified as an astronaut in 1986.

More recently, Dr. Apt served as Director of the Carnegie Museum of Natural History from 1997 to 2000.

Jay Apt, as an astronaut, circled the earth 562 times.

CHAPTER SIX

THE WARRIORS

"Their valor under the Maccabees, their exploits in the campaign which ended with Titus' destruction of Jerusalem, their desperate rebellion under Bar Kochba, and later on, their defense of Naples against Balisarius, and of the passes in the Pyranees against the Franks, place the Jews on a par with the greatest heroes known to history."

Matthias Jakob Schleiden, 1804-1881 German scientist
Importance of Jews in . . . Learning, 1876

Admiral Rickover inspecting USS Nautilus, the world's first nuclear submarine.

ADMIRAL HYMAN GEORGE RICKOVER (1900-1986) was the father of the atomic submarine; he proved that nuclear sea power was feasible.

In the wake of World War Two, Rickover was head of the Nuclear Power Division of the US Bureau of Ships. Beginning in 1947, he worked on making a reactor to power the "Nautilus," the first nuclear submarine. It was launched in 1954 —the first, to date, of more than 150 nuclear-powered vessels.

In 1980, he was awarded the Medal of Freedom.

Rickover was born in Russian Poland, but was educated in Chicago and graduated from the US Naval Academy in 1922.

After the war, he convinced Admiral Chester Nimitz, then head of naval operations, that nuclear sea power was feasible. The "Nautilus" put to sea and did not have to be refueled for three years, that is, until 1957, after sailing 62,500 miles. Nuclear power changed naval warfare, as the concept was extended from subs to aircraft carriers and other vessels.

Rickover, who had an abrasive personality, was repeatedly passed over for promotion.

A Navy Board reported "he does not have enough all-around experience to warrant his advancement to Rear Admiral." However, he was promoted to Rear Admiral in 1953, and named a Vice Admiral in 1958.

Rickover was outspoken. He once declared: "The Defense Department is already too big and if you let it grow on as it is, it soon will be controlling the country."

Nuclear-powered warships became a reality in the United States Navy only because of his refusal to accept the decisions of officers senior to him. He finally became a full Admiral in 1973 and nine years later, after a record 63 years of service, was retired.

Rickover twice received the Congressional Gold Medal. These honors included recognition of the input he gave to the development of civilian nuclear power plants.

Admiral Hyman Rickover who proved that nuclear sea power was feasible with President Carter. (US National Archives)

MORRIS ABRAHAM "TWO GUN" COHEN (1889-1970) commanded the 19th Chinese Route Army.

Cohen was born to poverty-stricken immigrants in London and stole food. He was first arrested at age ten, and placed in an "industrial school." This was the Jews' Free School in Camden Town, in London's East End. He also spent some time in a reform school.

His orthodox family, disgusted with his lawlessness, borrowed money to send him to Canada. He was 18 years old.

He didn't change his ways in western Canada. Instead, he became a gambler. His idea of a relaxed evening was to have a Chinese dinner and then gamble all night. One of his favorite haunts in Edmonton, Alberta, was a room behind a Chinese restaurant. But when Cohen dropped in one evening, he was angered to find an armed man holding up the aged proprietor of the café.

The hefty gambler was not going to have his evening interrupted, so he stunned the armed man with one blow to the head. Then, after disarming him, he hurled the would-be holdup man out the door.

The Chinese restauranteur was amazed. Never before had he known a white man to help an Asiatic. Canada at that time was very prejudiced, particularly against Asians.

"Two Gun" Cohen, who commanded the 19th Chinese Route Army.

Morris Cohen became a celebrity within the Chinese Community. And when a representative of Chinese President Sun-Yat Sen visited Canada, he hired Cohen to serve as the President's bodyguard.

He was the only foreigner ever to become a member of the Chinese ruling party, the Kuomintang. When the Japanese invaded China, in the late 30s, the new President, Chiang Kai-Shek, named Morris Abraham Cohen to command the 19th Chinese Route army. His troops had an outstanding record in encounters with invading Japanese forces.

He acquired the nickname "Two-Gun" because he packed two .45 caliber automatics and was said to be ambidextrous—capable of handling each gun with equal dexterity.

The Japanese captured him in 1943, in Hong Kong (he was trying to rescue Madame Sun Yat-Sen) and planned to execute him. But the British—for reasons never disclosed—felt he was sufficiently important to justify a prisoner exchange. The Japanese had particularly targeted Cohen because he had obtained a cylinder establishing that they had used poison gas against the Chinese.

After the war, in Montreal and Manchester, England, Cohen tried to live a normal life and make a normal living. But he never was able to make the adjustment.

Much of the Cohen story has yet to be told. He obviously worked for allied intelligence services, and the CIA has blocked attempts to access the Morris Cohen files.

Cohen is buried in a Manchester Jewish cemetery and there are Chinese characters on his tall black tombstone, written by Madame Sun Yat-Sen to record the gratitude of the Chinese people to their onetime Jewish General.

General Moshe Dayan who entered the ranks of Israeli fighting men at age 15.

GENERAL MOSHE DAYAN (1915-1981) masterminded the Israeli victory over Arab armies in the 1967 "Six Day War."

Dayan was born on a kibbutz (collective farm) on the shores of the Sea of Galilee.

At 15, he joined the "Haganah", the Jewish underground self-defense force. In 1937, he became a member of Orde Wingate's "special night squadrons," which defended Jewish settlements from Arab attackers.

In 1939, amid criticism from the League of Nations, the British Mandatory power broke its commitment to the Jewish people with a White Paper, closing the gates to Palestine to would-be Jewish immigrants at the critical moment when the Nazis were well along in their murderous campaign against Jews in Europe.

Dayan was arrested in the British crackdown (he was jailed in an old Turkish prison in Acre, and was crawling to freedom when he encountered what he thought was a snake, and turned back. The "snake" was the roots of a tree, but this courageous soldier feared vipers). Released, he joined the Western allies' attacks on the (pro-German) Vichy French in Syria, with the Jewish "Palmach", a commando force. He lost an eye during that campaign and chose to wear a distinctive eye patch thereafter . Once stopped in Israel for speeding, he said to the police officer "I have only one eye; what do you want me to watch—the speedometer or the road?"

With the rebirth of Israel, in 1948, he became an officer in the Israeli Defense Forces—ultimately serving as Chief of Staff from 1953 to 1958, a period during which Israel went to war once more, and captured the Sinai Peninsula.

Six weeks before the decisive Six Day War of 1967, he was named Minister of Defense and directed the triumphant Israeli forces which drove the Egyptians out of the Gaza Strip, the Jordanians out of the West Bank, and the Syrians out of the Golan Heights.

Out of uniform, like many Israeli generals, he entered the turbulent field of Israeli politics.

———

LEON TROTSKY (1879-1940), as Commissar for War in 1918, was the architect of the Red Army of the Soviet Union.

Born in the Ukraine, he was a fervent revolutionary. After the communists seized power, under Vladimir Lenin, Trotsky was named Commissar for War and set to work organizing the Red Army. A stirring speaker, he persuaded thousands of young men to serve the revolution in its army.

Trotsky was a candidate to head up the Government of the Union of Soviet Socialist Republics when Lenin died in 1924—only seven years after the revolution. But Joseph Stalin ruthlessly exterminated rivals and assumed dictatorial control of the nation. Trotsky, who had spent many years in exile before the revolution (including a few months when he was editor of a radical newspaper in the Bronx), fled with his wife and son—journeying from country to country, seeking sanctuary. (In his book, *My Life*, Trotsky wrote "It was the extreme expression of the mediocrity of the apparatus that Stalin himself rose to his position.")

He finally was accepted by Mexico and lived with the great muralist Diego Rivera. In the USSR, two rigged trials condemned him to death in absentia. He moved into a fortress-like building near Mexico City which on one occasion came under machine-gun fire. Trotsky's bedroom was sprayed with bullets but he was not hurt. The structure was protected by a brick wall 15-feet high, and armed guards were positioned in concrete pillboxes.

However, an agent for the Soviet Union, named Mercador visiting under the assumed name of Jacques van den Dreschd, managed to get an appointment with Trotsky. Under the agent's trench coat were a number of weapons, including a dagger, an ice pick, and a pistol. While the Russian leader was reading at his desk, Mercader attacked from behind, fatally wounding him with the pick.

The onetime Bolshevik leader survived only 24 hours. Mercader, who also called himself Frank Johnson, was convicted of murder in 1943.

Leon Trotsky in his later years. (Montreal Jewish Public Library Archives)

If the October revolution could not have taken place without Lenin, it could not have triumphed without Trotsky, who, as Minister of War, created the Red Army out of chaos and found the new men and the new talents (often Jewish) to replace the Tsarist officer corps, a large part of which had joined the White Armies or had fled into exile. Churchill called him the Carnot of the revolution.

Chaim Bermant, The Jews, 1977

Lieutenant General Sir John Monash commanded the force of nine divisions that helped end World War One by breaking through the Hindenberg Line.

LIEUTENANT GENERAL SIR JOHN MONASH (1865-1931), one of Australia's greatest soldiers, led a force of nine divisions—five Australian, two British and two American— breaking the formidable Hindenberg Line in World War One in 1918.

He was born in Melbourne of immigrant Jewish parents.

Monash graduated from Scotch College and Melbourne University, and was a construction engineer. He enlisted in the Australian Citizen Force in 1887 and was a commissioned officer. With the outbreak of World War One in 1914, he was given command of a brigade with the rank of Colonel.

He commanded the 4th Australian Brigade at Gallipoli (1914-1915), the 3rd Australian Division in France (1916), and the Australian Corps, with the rank of Lieutenant-General (1918).

He was recognized as one of the outstanding generals of the war and, in 1918, was given command of nine divisions from three countries for the final assault on the Hindenburg Line. This successful attack, coordinating tanks and infantry for the first time, so weakened the German army they were unable to mount further major offensives.

The British general staff frequently frowned on Monash's innovations. But Field Marshall Montgomery, one of the most famous British generals in World War Two (and a junior officer in World War One) called Sir John Monash "the best general on the western front in Europe."

The Australian general recognized that outdated allied tactics resulted in an immense slaughter. "The true role of infantry," he declared, "was not to expend itself upon heroic physical effort, not to wither away under merciless machine-gun fire, not to impale itself on hostile bayonets." On the contrary, Monash stated troops should "advance under the maximum possible array of mechanical resources, in the the form of guns, machine-guns, tanks, mortars, and aeroplanes."

King George V knighted Monash at the General's field headquarters—the first time in almost two centuries that a British monarch had knighted a commander in the field.

British Prime Minister David Lloyd George called Monash "the most resourceful in the British Army." And the great correspondent for *The Times* felt that, had the war continued after 1918, Monash would have been made commander-in-chief of the Combined Allied Forces. Close to 300,000 people attended his funeral.

An Australian university, a city, and a medical center are named in his honor. His portrait is on the Australian $100 note. And the most important post-graduate scholarship in Australia bears his name.

MAJOR GENERAL MAURICE ROSE (1899-1945) served in both World Wars and was decorated by France and Belgium as well as the United States. He was murdered in a chance encounter on the battlefield.

Rose joined the US Army in 1916. He was a private, and served on the Mexican border. He showed such leadership skills that he was assigned to the first officers' training course at Fort Riley, Kansas in 1917. He served overseas in the First World War and was wounded.

During World War Two, Maurice Rose served with what are regarded as the three greatest American armored Divisions:

–"Old Ironsides,"(the 1st)—in Africa and Italy.

–similarly with "Hell on Wheels,"(the 2nd)

–and finally leading his own 3rd Armored Division, called "Spearhead," in a bold offensive through Western Europe.

However, during the advance, General Rose rounded a bend with two companions to find themselves confronted by a group of Germans. A young officer demanded that the General drop his pistol. When Rose moved to do so, the German shot him in the head.

War correspondent Hal Boyle wrote:

"Rose lived and died as a professional. He would be the last to regret that he had a soldier's ending."

He was one of only two American divisional commanders killed in the European theatre.

Major-General Maurice Rose served with the three greatest World War Two American armored divisions.

Some other Jewish warriors:

Jacob Grigoryevich Kreiser.

SOVIET GENERAL JACOB GRIGORYEVICH KREISER (1905-1969), a general at 31, commanded the Russian Third Army; he was made a Hero of the Soviet Union in connection with his troops' defense of Moscow.

Indeed, he is said to have masterminded the successful defense of the Soviet capital city. On the offensive, he led his 51st army in the liberation of the Donets Basin, Sevastopol, the Crimea, and the Balkan States.

KEN (KLAUS) ADAM (1921-   ), [and his brother], were the only German-born pilots in the Royal Air Force in World War II; Ken was an ace.

He was more than a pilot. After the war, he won two Oscars for set design. He conceived the sets for seven James Bond movies. And he was also responsible for the *Dr. Strangelove* sets.

BENJAMIN R. SAMSON (1916-   ) commanded the Indian Navy in its 1965 war against Pakistan.

HERMAN BECKER, in the German air force in World War One, shot down 23 enemy planes and his decorations included the "Pour le Merite," the German equivalent of the Victoria Cross.

However when the Nazis came to power, he left the country. The government made a special concession to Becker—allowing him to take his savings with him. He moved to the United States.

Claude Bloch was Commander in chief of the United States Fleet in 1938.

ADMIRAL CLAUDE BLOCH (1878-1967) was named Commander in Chief of the US Fleet in 1938.

Bloch was born in Woodbury, Kentucky, and entered the US Naval Academy in 1895. He served in the Spanish-American War—and was decorated for saving Spaniards from a flaming warship. In 1900, he took part in the expedition to China to suppress the Boxer Rebellion.

He undertook administrative duties during World War One.

In 1923, he was promoted to Rear Admiral, and four years later he was placed in command of the battleship California.

He was Commander in Chief of the US fleet from 1938 to 1940.

HERBERT Y. SCHANDLER (1928-   ) was one of the most decorated soldiers in the Vietnam War, winning four Legions of Merit, 13 air medals, three bronze stars, and three Vietnam crosses of Gallantry.

DARIUS P. DASSAULT (1882-1969) commanded France's Fifth Army Corps in World War Two.

Born in Paris, he served with the army during World War One. He was in charge of military training for senior officers and, with the outbreak of the Second World War, commanded the Fifth Army Corps.

When the French surrendered, he joined the underground. After the Allies liberated France, Dassault was promoted to the highest rank in the French Army—general d'armée. And he was appointed Governor of Paris.

IVAN D. CHERNYAKHOVSKI (1906-1945) commanded the Third Belorussian Army and led forces to retake the cities of Vilna, Grodno, Minsk, and Kiev from the Germans.

He was the Red Army's youngest front commander when fatally wounded in the final months of the war.

Chernyakhovski, the son of a railroad worker in the Ukraine, joined the Red Army in 1924—seven years after the revolution. When Germany invaded the Soviet Union, Chernyakhovski rose rapidly to Colonel in 1940, and by 1943 he was a lieutenant general commanding the 60th army.

In the summer of 1944, he led the northern Russian offensive against the crack German Third Panzer Army. In that battle, he trapped the Germans' 53rd Corps. And then, driving into East Prussia, he retook Minsk, Vilna, and Kaunas.

He was mortally wounded while on an inspection tour near Koenigsberg. Chernyakhovski was twice named Hero of the Soviet Union (1943 and 1944).

LIEUTENANT-GENERAL MATVEY GRIGORYEVICH VAYNRUB used his tanks to break the German seige of Stalingrad.

Marshall Zhukov commended Vaynrub a number of times in his dispatches on the crucial Battle of Stalingrad. He was a key figure in the defense of the Soviet city. However, he was one of the few commanders who, although they survived the costly battle, was not promoted. Later he led Chuikov's 62nd army in the reconquest of the Donets coalfields. He commanded the forces that liberated Odessa and Krivoshein, and led the first Soviet force to burst into Berlin.

He was named a Hero of the Soviet Union in 1945.

CAPTAIN ABE BAUM of the US Army's 4th Armored Division, led a task force of 300 men, in March of 1945, 60 miles beyond the German lines in World War Two. The goal was to free General Patton's son-in-law from a German Prison of War Camp.

Baum's strike force reached the POW Camp but, en route back to the American lines, they were surrounded and forced to surrender. A month later, they were liberated by American forces. Baum received the Distinguished Service Cross.

Captain Abe Baum who led a strike force of 300 men 60 miles beyond the German lines in 1945.

VICE ADMIRAL BEN MOREELL (1892-1978) was the founder of the famous Seabees.

Moreell grew up in St. Louis, Missouri, and graduated from Washington University. He spent much of World War One stationed in the Azores, but his engineering talents were so well-known that, immediately prior to the outbreak of World War II, President Roosevelt promoted him to Rear Admiral (without having served as a Captain) and named him Chief of the Bureau of Yards and Docks, and Chief of the Civil Engineering Corps.

Admiral Moreell organized the Navy's construction battalions— known as as Seabees (from the CB in construction battalions).

President Harry S. Truman also recognized his capabilities— placing him in charge of most of the American petroleum industry

Admiral Moreell's Seabees at work cable laying on Guadalcanal in World War Two.

during a nationwide strike in 1945. He spent 29 years in the navy, retiring in 1946.

Admiral Moreell received the Navy's Distinguished Service Medal; a gold star in lieu of a second DMS; the Legion of Merit; the Order of the British Empire; and a number of decorations from other allied governments.

———

REAR-ADMIRAL EDWARD ELLSBERG (1891-1983) recovered the wreckage of the submarine, S-51, in 1926—-the first time a submarine had been raised from mid-ocean depths.

He became the US Navy's foremost salvage expert. Ellsberg developed the underwater cutting torch, pontoons for raising a sunken vessel, and a system for speedily raising a sunken submarine.

He was the son of Jewish immigrants from Russia. Ellsburg was not a robust youth, and he barely met the requirements for admission to the Naval Academy. However, he took top honors in seamanship and navigation.

When the submarine S-51 sank in September, 1925, the rescue vessel "Falcon" was sent to salvage the wreckage. Ellsberg convinced Captain (later Admiral) Ernest J. King to assign the salvage job to him. The S-51 sat in 132 feet of water; no vessel, to that time, had ever been raised from that depth.

The salvage officer started a school to train divers (including himself) and overcame challenging technical problems with his inventions.

After Pearl Harbor, in 1941, Ellsberg and a rag-tag crew raised a huge Italian floating dry dock, even though "experts" had declared it could not be salvaged. The dry dock was mostly used to repair British warships.

After the Allied invasion of French North Africa, in 1942, he became chief salvage officer for the western Mediterranean. He went from port to port, raising two more floating dry docks and several British warships. And he unblocked the port of Oran.

Despite heart problems, he was in Britain in the spring of 1944-helping prepare artificial harbors for the huge D-day landing.

Ellsberg's salvage team working at raising the US submarine S51.

MORDECHAI FRIZIS (1893-1940) was one of Greece's greatest soldiers of the 20th century.

He went from studying law to undergo military officer training in Eubea. He served in Macedonia, then in a campaign in the Ukraine. In Kishinev, site of bloody pogroms, the Greek officer was ordered to find supplies. Frizis spoke to Jewish shopkeepers in Hebrew. The stores' owners, astonished that there was a Jewish officer in the Greek Army, brought wagonloads of supplies and refused payment.

In the Greek campaigns in Turkey, 1921-1922, he was captured and held prisoner for almost a year—refusing an offer of freedom because he was the only non-Christian prisoner.

When Italy invaded Greece, his troops were among the first to take invaders prisoner. In one confrontation with Mussolini's troops, Frizis' soldiers turned back the Italians, capturing 700 and leaving hundreds of bodies strewn over the battlefield.

He led a sweeping attack against the Italians, refusing to dismount from his horse despite attacks by warplanes. He was wounded twice—the second time fatally.

The unit's priest placed his hand on the dying officer's head and declared:

"Hear, O Israel, the lord our God, the Lord is one."

King George II of Greece wrote to his widow: "On the glorious death for his country of your beloved husband, the heroic Colonel Mordechai Frizis, His Majesty has instructed me to convey to you and your family his deepest condolences."

COMMANDER SOLOMON ISQUITH was awarded the Navy Cross for saving 90% of the crew of the warship *Utah* after it was torpedoed in December 7, 1941.

Utah was one of the first warships attacked at Pearl Harbor. Two torpedoes slammed into the port side of the vessel as members of the crew were raising the Stars and Stripes on the fantail. The ship began to sink almost immediately, listing 15 degrees. The senior officer on board at that time, Lieutenant Commander Solomon Isquith ordered "all hands on deck" and then "abandon ship" as, four minutes after being torpedoed, the vessel's list had increased to 40 degrees.

Commander Solomon Isquith saved 90% of the crew of the battleship Utah when it was torpedoed by the Japanese on December 7, 1941. *(Utah Organization photo)*

Commander Isquith's quick reaction saved hundreds of lives. The *Utah* capsized at 8:12 a.m.—only 11 minutes after being hit.

Rescue boats endeavored to save men struggling in the water despite strafing by Japanese planes. Thirty officers and 431 enlisted men survived the sinking while the death toll was estimated at six officers and 52 men—some trapped in the hull of the capsized battleship and others fatally wounded by strafing.

———

LIEUTENANT JACOB BESER was the only man to serve on the crews of both aircraft that dropped atomic bombs on Japan, ending World War Two.

Beser was radar counter-measures officer aboard the Enola Gay B-29 bomber that delivered an atomic bomb against Hiroshima, and on the Bockscar for the mission against Nagasaki.

He was awarded both the Silver Star and the Distinguished Flying Cross.

Jacob Beser was the only person to serve on both crews of the aircraft that dropped atomic bombs on Japan in 1945. Beser stands in front of the Enola Gay, the plane that bombed Hiroshima.

CHAPTER SEVEN

LEADERS AND LAWYERS

"The fundamental principle of the Hebraic commonwealth was that there are great moral laws. . . not dependent on the will of monarch, oligarchy, aristocracy, or public assembly."

Abbot, Life and Literature of Ancient Hebrews, 1901

Felix Frankfurter, a Harvard law professor and advisor to US presidents.

FELIX FRANKFURTER (1882-1965) was a champion of human freedom, and helped found the American Civil Liberties Union.

Forty-six years after he landed in the United States from Austria, aged 12, President Franklin Delano Roosevelt appointed him to the Supreme Court of the United States. He was the only appointee to the high court, in history, who had no previous judicial experience.

He was a legal prodigy, graduating from Harvard Law School in 1906. In 1914 he became a Harvard law professor, and then Dean of Law for 25 years.

Frankfurter was appointed to the Supreme Court in 1939, and served until 1962. Before his appointment to the Bench, he was a close adviser to President Roosevelt and an important member of what was known as the "New Deal Brain Trust"— intellectuals who helped devise programs for FDR to assist those most affected by the Great Depression.

Max Freedman, in his *Roosevelt and Frankfurter* said of the great law professor:

"Small, quick, articulate, jaunty, Frankfurter was inexhaustible in his energy and his curiosity, giving off sparks like an overcharged electric battery. He loved people, loved conversation, loved influence, loved life."

President John F. Kennedy awarded Frankfurter the Presidential Medal of Freedom.

Certainly the affirmative pursuit of one's convictions about the ultimate mystery of the universe and man's relation to it is placed beyond the reach of law. Government may not interfere with organized or individual expressions of belief or disbelief. Propagation of belief—or even of disbelief—in the supernatural is protected, whether in church or chapel, mosque or synagogue, tabernacle or meeting house.

Felix Frankfurter: Majority decision, Jehovah's Witnesses Case, 1940. Minersville School District v. Gobitis, 310 US 586.

MILTON FRIEDMAN (1912-   ) won the 1976 Nobel Prize for his work on economics. He was awarded a scholarship to Rutgers at age 16.

Friedman was born in Brooklyn, New York, son of Eastern European immigrants. His father was repeatedly unsuccessful in his ventures, and his mother ran a store. "The family income was small." Friedman recalled, "Financial crisis was a constant companion."

After Rutgers, he continued his education until Columbia awarded him a Ph.D. in 1946. In the academic world, and in government appointments, he has been consistently opposed to anything but a minimum of government intervention in the economy. One of his earliest publications, on monopoly practices by doctors, was so controversial that its publication was delayed.

He was professor of economics at the University of Chicago for 21 years—-1945-1976. Friedman was named to the President's Economic Policy Advisory Board in 1981. He was awarded the Presidential Medal of Freedom in 1988 and received the National Medal of Science that same year.

Friedman was one of the most important figures in the shaping of American economic policies for decades.

Milton Friedman won a scholarship to Rutgers at age 16.

Alan Dershowitz was the youngest Harvard law professor ever. (Montreal Jewish Public Library Archives).

ALAN MORTON DERSHOWITZ (1938-   ) is one of the most renowned lawyers in the United States, and a defender of individual freedom.

Dershowitz was born in Brooklyn. He graduated first in his class from Yale Law School, where he was editor-in-chief of the *Yale Law Review*.

After his clerkship, he joined the faculty of Harvard Law and was promoted to full professor three years later—at 28, the youngest full professor in the school's history.

While still teaching, he appeared in court on behalf of a number of famous clients, ranging from Claus von Bulow to O.J. Simpson. Despite the fact that he was Jewish, he defended the right of American neo-Nazis to march, and speak out in Skokie, Illinois.

He is equally well-known for his books, many of which analyze his more important courtroom appearances.

"Defending the guilty and despised," he states, "even freeing some of them—is a small price to pay for our liberties."

"American Jews need more chutzpah. Notwithstanding the stereotype, we are not pushy or assertive enough for our own good and for the good of our more vulnerable brothers and sisters in other parts of the world."
Alan M. Dershowitz, Chutzpah, 1991

Jews have served as the heads of governments in the Diaspora in nine different countries: England (Benjamin Disraeli), France (Leon Blum, Pierre Mendes-France and Rene Mayer), Italy (Luigi Luzzatti and Sidney Sonnino), Austria (Bruno Kreisky), Australia (Sir Isaac Isaacs), Bavaria (Kurt Eisener), Hungary (Bela Kun), India (Marquis of Reading), and Palestine (Sir Herbert Samuel).

M. Hirsh Goldberg
The Jewish Connection, 1975

Lord Reading was Lord Chief Justice of England.

Benjamin Disraeli was the first and only Jewish Prime Minister of Britain. As a young man, he wrote novels.

THE MARQUIS OF READING (1860-1935) was, as Sir Rufus Isaacs, Lord Chief Justice of England, 1913-1921, and later, Viceroy of India.

Rufus Isaacs, the son of a fruit merchant, spent a year at sea as a ship's boy. He came from a distinguished family. His uncle was the Lord Mayor of London and his great-uncle was boxing champion Daniel Mendoza.

After a fling in the stock market, he was unable to pay his bills. He then went into law, becoming a barrister in 1887. He was brilliant at the bar, and served as leading counsel in a number of famous cases.

He became a crown attorney and won two sensational cases—particularly the Seddon murder trial where his aggressive cross examination was the key to a conviction. Now a wealthy man, he was elected to parliament in 1904, and, in 1910 was knighted and named attorney-general. He was named Lord Chief Justice, raised to the peerage and took the title Lord Reading.

During World War One, he journeyed back and forth across the Atlantic—acting as the link between British Prime Minister David Lloyd George and President Woodrow Wilson. From 1915 he was "special envoy to the United States," and in 1918 he became "special ambassador" to the United States.

In 1921, he was appointed Viceroy and Governor General of India, and he remained in that office until 1926. He was made an Earl in 1916 and a Marquis in 1926.

In many parts of the world, Jewish lawyers have formed "Lord Reading Societies," in tribute to his outstanding career in the law.

―――――――

BENJAMIN DISRAELI (1804-1881), Earl of Beaconsfield, was Prime Minister of Britain and improved working conditions in factories, strengthened public health services, and cleared slums.

Disraeli began his career as a novelist and moved into politics in 1837 when he was elected to parliament. He was leader of the House of

Commons and Chancellor of the Exchequer, in 1852 and 1858-1859, and Chancellor again in 1866.

He was Queen Victoria's Prime Minister in 1868 and again from 1874 to 1880. Disraeli was a towering figure in British history, acquiring the Suez Canal for England and glorifying the crown by having the Queen named Empress of India.

BERNARD MANNES BARUCH (1870-1965) became a millionaire at age 30, and was the legendary adviser, often from a park bench, to five American Presidents.

He was the son of a doctor who had emigrated from East Prussia. Baruch, after graduating from the College of the City of New York, started his career as an office boy in a firm selling glassware.

He next found work with stockbrokers and was so successful that he became a partner at age 26. Baruch became involved in government through his friendship with Woodrow Wilson.

Later he advised President Franklin Delano Roosevelt, and met and corresponded with Winston Churchill, whom he met at Versailles in 1919 while serving as a member of the American Peace Mission.

He donated his papers to Princeton in 1964, and the extent of his close association with world leaders is underscored by the fact that they included 1,200 letters from nine Presidents, and 700 letters from Churchill alone.

His plan for the international control of atomic energy, submitted to the United Nations Atomic Energy Commission in the late 40s, is named for him.

His family's arrival in America has been traced back to 1690, when a Spanish-Portuguese Jew, Isaac Rodrigues Marhues, arrived in New York.

He was decorated for his activities as an "elder statesman" by Belgium, Italy, France, and the United States, and was awarded seven honorary degrees.

The Wit and Wisdom of Benjamin Disraeli

Irish leader Daniel O'Connell, speaking in the British House of Commons, made a snide remark about Disraeli's Jewish ancestry. The intended victim replied:

"Yes, I am a Jew. And when the ancestors of the right Honorable gentleman were living as savages in an unknown island, mine were priests in the Temple of Solomon."

A university should be a place of light, of liberty, and of learning.
                    House of Commons, March 11, 1873

Youth is a blunder; Manhood a struggle; Old Age a regret,
                    From his book Coningsby

Every man should marry — and no woman.

Little things affect little minds.
                    Sybill, Bk III, Ch. 2

A book may be as great a thing as a battle.
                    Memoir of Isaac Disraeli

Referring, at a banquet, to his longtime political opponent Gladstone (July 27, 1878):
A sophisticated rhetorician inebriated with the exuberance of his own verbosity."

Bernard Baruch was advisor to five American Presidents.

Even when we discover basic truths about human affairs, it is another thing to overcome human failings—the greed, hatred, sloth, or whatever it is that keeps us from acting on those truths. In a laboratory, men follow truth wherever it may lead. In human relations, men have a supreme talent for ignoring truth, and denying facts that they do not like.

Bernard M. Baruch, from his Baruch:
The Public Years, 1960

Leon-Andre Blum was Premier of France in the critical years leading up to World War Two.

LEON-ANDRE BLUM (1872-1949) was Premier of France in some of the most critical years (1936-1937) leading up to World War II; he did not enter politics until he was 47.

A poet, writer, and critic, he stepped into the political fray in angry response to the Dreyfus Affair.

He was one of the leaders of the Front Populaire, a left-wing alliance formed to counter a rising tide of fascism in France. In the wake of scandals, the Front won a large majority in 1936 and Blum became the first Jew and the first socialist to become Premier of France.

He resigned in 1937 when the French parliament refused to grant him emergency powers.

After France collapsed, in 1940, the Vichy government indicted him on charges that he had helped bring on the war. But his defense was so brilliant that the trial was suspended. He was freed from a concentration camp in May 1945.

In liberated France, he became a respected elder statesman and negotiated a large credit for France from the United States. He served one more brief term as Prime Minister from 1946 to 1947. He was a man before his time, a visionary, declaring "We must create Europe. We must do it with Germany and not for her. We must do it with Great Britain and not against her."

All my life I have hoped to see an alleviation of the suffering of the world's disinherited. Should I then now, when the opportunity comes to me to assure those of France a larger measure of justice, abandon them? I accept the challenge which comes to me as a Jew and as a citizen of France.

Leon Blum, in 1936, when a Jewish delegation pressed him to refuse the office of Premier fearing a rise in anti-Semitism.

SAMUEL GOMPERS (1850-1924) was the father of the labor movement in the United States.

He was born in London to Dutch Jewish parents. His family moved to the United States when he was 13. He quickly found work—-as a journeyman cigar maker. After a long work day, he studied conscientiously and became deeply concerned about workers' living conditions.

He moved into leadership roles in the young labor movement. In 1875, he became President of the Cigarmakers' Local 144. By 1881, he had risen to become leader of the Federation of Organized Trades and Labor Unions of the United States and Canada. In 1894, he convinced the US Congress to make the first Monday in September a legal holiday, honoring the worker—Labor Day. When the American Federation of Labor (AFL) was formed, he was its first President and served in that role—with the exception of one year (1895)—until his death in 1924. During his tenure, the AFL's membership grew from 150,000 to almost 3,000,000.

The *New York Times*, in its December 14, 1924 edition, presented the story of his death on its front page, with a two-column portrait, and declared:

"Nation mourns the great labor chief."

The economist and labor historian, John R. Commons, said:

"Samuel Gompers was, in my opinion, one of the ten or twelve great Americans."

Rose Lee Guard, quoted in B. Mandel's *Samuel Gompers* said of him, "a myriad-sided nature; a creature of poetry and practical action; a dreamer, yet a doer of the world's work; a soul of storm while diffusing sunshine—-a combination of wholly opposing characteristics."

Samuel Gompers is regarded as the father of the labor movement in the US

Henry Kissinger was a US Secretary of State.

HENRY KISSINGER (1923-   ) was one of the USA's most celebrated Secretaries of State.

During the Nixon years, he helped bring about a ceasefire in Vietnam, negotiated a detente with the Soviet Union and opened China to American influence. The *New York Times*, in 1977, stated "Henry Kissinger has not been President of the United States for the past eight years; it only seemed that way."

Kissinger was born in Furth, Bavaria. The family fled the Nazis, and settled in Washington Heights in northern Manhattan—an area dubbed the "Fourth Reich." The

What does Labor want? We want more schoolhouses and less jails; more books and less arsenals; more learning and less vice; more leisure and less greed; more justice and less revenge; in fact, more of the opportunities to cultivate our better natures, to make manhood more noble, womanhood more beautiful, and childhood more happy and bright.

Samuel Gompers

The wisdom of Henry Kissinger

People think responsibility is hard to bear. It's not. I think that sometimes it is the absence of responsibility that is harder to bear. You have a great feeling of impotence.

The nice thing about being a celebrity is that when you bore people, they think it's their fault.

Kissingers had a hard time, at first. Kissinger Senior who had taught geography in Bavaria, became a clerk and bookkeeper while his mother worked as a cook in better homes.

Kissinger himself studied at George Washington High School at night, and worked in a shaving brush factory during the day. He was drafted into the army in 1943, and assigned to the 84th Infantry Division. He was sent back to Germany—as a member of the unit's Counter-Intelligence Corps.

Returning to the US, he went to Harvard and from the Law School he was invited to serve as an advisor at the highest levels of the US government.

Today, out of the political fray, Dr. Kissinger has his own consulting firm. Some of the world's largest corporations consult him, on a retainer of $250,000 a year plus $100,000 a month for actual consultations.

He once declared: "When I was a professor, I thought great forces shaped history. Now, I see what a difference personalities make."

Senator Joseph Lieberman came within a razor's edge in 2000 of becoming Vice-President of the US

SENATOR JOSEPH I. LIEBERMAN (1942-) was vice-presidential candidate in the American elections of 2000 and was, in 2004, the first Jew to seek the Presidency of the United States.

Joe Lieberman has been running for office almost from the time he could first walk and talk. He won his first election while attending public school in Stamford, Connecticut. He was chosen president of his ninth grade class.

While attending Yale, he began to think of seeking public office. He was chairman of the *Yale Daily News*, the political centrality for students. There was no formal student government.

He got his feet wet, politically, by working as an intern in Washington—first, in the office of Senator Abraham A. Ribicoff and, a year later, for the chairman of the Democratic National Committee, John M. Bailey.

In 1970, after working for a time as an attorney, he was elected to the Connecticut State Senate. One of his campaign volunteers was a 24- year- old Yale law student Bill Clinton—the future President of the United States. Lieberman was a State Senator for ten years.

He was the State's Attorney General from 1982 to1988, and in the latter year, he was elected to the US Senate. After 15 years in the chamber, and after coming within a whisper of being named Vice-President of the United States, Joe Lieberman has cast his yarmulke into the presidential ring for 2004.

Senator Lieberman makes no bones about his orthodoxy. He did not attend the Democratic Convention nominating him for the Senate in 1988 because it was held on a Saturday—the Jewish Sabbath.

When he ran with Presidential candidate Al Gore for the vice-presidency, polls showed few Americans were concerned about a candidate's religious affiliation.

MAXIM LITVINOV (1876-1951) was Foreign Minister of the Soviet Union, influencing Russian policy from 1926 to 1939, 13 critical pre-war years.

Born Meir Walach, he became interested in Marxism while serving in the Imperial Russian Army. He was arrested for "revolutionary activity" in 1901 but escaped custody and made his way to Britain.

From 1903, he was a member of the Bolshevik faction and was engaged in party activities throughout Europe.

With the Bolshevik seizure of power in 1917, Litvinov joined the Commissariat for Foreign Affairs.

He became increasingly prominent—leading the Soviet delegation to the *League of Nations* Disarmament Conference (1927-1930)—proposing sweeping disarmament to the conference.

He led the Soviet delegation to the World Economic Conference in London (1933) and conducted negotiations leading to the establishment of diplomatic relations between the USS.R. and and the United States (1934).

When Adolf Hitler and the Nazis seized power, Litvinov urged members of the *League of Nations* to engage in collective resistance against Germany (1934-1938). He negotiated anti-German treaties with France (1935) and Czechoslovakia (also in 1935).

When the western powers appeased Hitler, the Soviets dismissed Litvinov before concluding a Treaty of Nonaggression with the Germans in August, 1939—only weeks before the Nazis attacked Poland, triggering the Second World War.

After the Germans invaded the Soviet Union, Litvinov was recalled and served as Ambassador to the US 1941-1943, and then as Deputy Commissioner for Foreign Affairs.

He retired in 1946.

Maxim Litvinov was the Soviet Union's Foreign Minister in the period 1926-1939.

Pierre Mendes-France (2nd from r.) was Prime Minister of France 1954-1955.

PIERRE MENDES-FRANCE (1907-1982), who was Prime Minister of France from 1954 to 1955, joined the Free French Forces in London during the Second World War.

Mendes-France served in the French Air Force in Syria, and then returned to France. Wounded, he was imprisoned by the collaborationist Vichy Regime, but made a dramatic escape to London.

General de Gaulle ordered him to proceed to Algeria to join the provisional Free French government. After the war, he served as Director of the International Monetary Fund for eleven years.

In 1954, possibly the only cabinet officer of the Fourth Republic untouched by scandal, he was elected Prime Minister. He orchestrated an end to the Indo-Chinese war at the Geneva Conference, but his administration was overthrown by a parliamentary coalition.

He returned to power with the Guy Mollet government in 1957, but resigned when he recognized that Mollet planned to continue and intensify the war in Algeria.

His political career virtually ended when he opposed the return to power of De Gaulle in 1958, and that same year he lost his seat in parliament.

Luigi Luzzatti was Prime Minister of Italy.

LUIGI LUZZATTI (1841-1927) parlayed his success in organizing a mutual aid society for gondoliers in Venice into ultimately becoming Prime Minister of Italy.

He was born into a prominent Venetian Jewish family. He took a law degree and then studied to become a professor of economics and constitutional law. He was deeply concerned about social injustice.

After Luzzatti organized a mutual aid society for Venetian gondoliers, he was called a revolutionary and expelled from the city. However, instead of being discouraged, he journeyed from city to city in Italy, organizing mutual aid societies. These organizations, he declared, would "assure you a subsidy in case of illness, a pension fund provides for your old age, workmen's associations enable you to acquire your own homes, cooperative warehouses provide food and other necessities at a low price."

He entered the Italian parliament shortly after he turned 30. And he was in cabinet and played other leading roles during the turbulent years that led to the seizure of power by Benito Mussolini and the Fascists.

In 1910, he was named Prime Minister. He was in office for only a short time, but managed to push through legislation banning pornography, white slavery, and cruelty to animals. Even out of office, he pressed for liberal legislation including compulsory accident insurance.

In 1925, he spoke out for a Jewish state, declaring:

"The bold experience of colonization undertaken by the Jews in Palestine has a value transcending that of the problems of race and Zionism. It proves that the Jews can, after twenty centuries, be again unsurpassable cultivators, and it proves too that the Syrian land, for thousands of years a squalid, desolate, rocky desert, can become once more a smiling desert."

ALBERT BLAUSTEIN (1921-   ) was a law professor who drafted constitutions for dozens of countries, including post-Cold War Russia, Romania, Peru, and Fiji.

Blaustein was born in New York and graduated in law from Columbia. He was extremely active in human rights efforts, and is proudest of the fact that he served as official constitutional consultant for Liberia, Bangladesh, Zimbabwe, and Peru. In addition, he was consulted on framing the constitutions of Cambodia, the Republic of Korea, Uruguay, and Niger.

DAVID BEN-GURION (1886-1973) was the founding Prime Minister of Israel.

Born David Gruen in Plonsk, at that time in Russian Poland, Ben Gurion was a lifelong Zionist. The son of an attorney, he joined Zionist organizations in his youth and, at age 20, journeyed to Palestine.

He worked as a farmer for three years and then, hoping to be a Jewish representative in the Turkish Parliament, began to study law at Istanbul University. When World War One broke out, he sided with the Allies, and the Turks expelled him from Palestine.

Israeli Prime Minister David Ben-Gurion (left) with scientist Linus Pauling.

DAVID BEN-GURION 1886-1973 דוד בן-גוריון

ISRAEL إسرائيل

0.25 ישראל

The stamp issued by Israel to honor its first Prime Minister.

In 1918, he helped organize the *Jewish Legion* which fought side-by-side with the British in the campaign to liberate the Holy Land from the Turks.

After the war, Ben Gurion returned to Palestine and assumed increasingly important posts in Zionist organizations. In 1933, he was elected to the executive of the Jewish Agency, representing the interests of the Jewish people in the Holy Land. He became Chairman of the Agency, in effect assuming leadership of the Jews of Palestine.

In May 1939, on the brink of the Second World War, the British issued a White Paper limiting Jewish immigration into Palestine, despite the fact that refugees from Hitler's Germany had few places to go. The White Paper —which violated Britain's pledge to the Jewish people made in the 1917 Balfour Declaration and the terms of the Mandate granted the United Kingdom by the League of Nations—was London's weak response to Arab terrorism.

When World War Two broke out, Ben Gurion declared:

"We shall fight the White Paper as though there was no war, and we shall fight the Nazis as though there was no White Paper."

When the newborn United Nations voted to partition the Holy Land into two states, Ben Gurion responded by proclaiming the independence of the state of Israel on May 14, 1948. The Arab response was to invade the new nation but the Israel Defense Force, despite a lack of weapons and training, defeated seven Arab armies and the war ended with the Jewish defenders occupying more land than was granted them in the partition plan.

David Ben Gurion was Prime Minister of Israel for its first 15 years of modern existence. And he emerged from retirement in 1955.

Golda Meir, who also became Prime Minister of Israel, called Ben Gurion "the greatest Jew in our generation."

He lived in the kibbutz (collective farm) Sde Boker, in a book-filled hut. And in 1973, he was buried beside his wife Paula on a bluff overlooking his beloved Negev desert.

Ben Gurion had a very Jewish sense of humor. When a visiting French socialist met with him, he told B-G "I must make it clear. I am a socialist first, then a Frenchman and, finally, a Jew." "That's fine,' the Prime Minister responded. "Here in Israel we read from right to left."

Novelist Amos Oz said of him:

"Ben-Gurion's iron-will leadership during Israel's early years turned him from 'first among equals' in the Zionist leadership into a modern-day King David."

SIR ROY WELENSKY (1907-1991) was Prime Minister of Rhodesia from 1956 to 1963.

Welensky was born in Salisbury, Rhodesia, of Lithuanian-Jewish parents. He became the only Commonwealth Prime Minister who had been an amateur heavyweight boxing champion in his youth.

He was a trade union official in Northern Rhodesia (now Zambia) and was Founder-Chairman of the Northern Rhodesia Labour Party in 1938.

During World War Two, he directed the utilization of manpower in the area and that experience convinced him that a central African Federation should be formed of the two Rhodesias and Nyasaland.

He was a major figure in the organization of the Federation of Rhodesia and Nyasaland in 1953. His efforts were recognized with a knighthood.

Welensky had hoped that the Central African Federation would achieve Commonwealth status. He became Prime Minister in 1956 and ruled until, with the agreement of the United Kingdom, the three colonies split into separate countries.

Welensky then withdrew from active politics, and ultimately moved to England.

———

ALAN GREENSPAN (1926-   ) has been one of the leading economic advisers to the United States since his first appointment, by President Nixon, in 1974.

He first took office as Chairman of the Board of Governors of the Federal Reserve System in 1987 and has continued as head of the "Fed" under Presidents Reagan, Bush, Clinton, and George W. Bush.

Greenspan, a native of New York City, is one of the most influential people in the world, heading up the body which is the USA's principal monetary policy making instrument.

Every major industrialized nation monitors Greenspan's reports to the US Conference and his announcement of changes in interest rates affect the lives of hundreds of millions of people. The rise and fall of American interest rates, reflecting the strength or weakness of the US economy, affect every modern nation to some extent.

He received all of his degrees from New York University and did advanced study at Columbia.

"The test of democracy is freedom of criticism."

David Ben Gurion, quoted by McDonald in *My Mission in Israel*

Sir Roy Welensky, Prime Minister of Rhodesia, 1956-1963.

Alan Greenspan has served as the leading economic advisor to American Presidents since 1974.

René Cassin was most responsible for the wording of the United Nations Declaration of Human Rights. Here he is seated on the far right with Eleanor Roosevelt and UN radio commentator George Day.

From 1954-1974 and, again, from 1977-1987, Greenspan was Chairman and President of Townsend-Greenspan & Co. Inc., an economic consulting firm. Between 1974 and 1977, he served as Chairman of President Ford's Council on Economic Advisers.

RENÉ CASSIN (1887-1976) was largely responsible for the drafting of the United Nations Declaration of Human Rights. Cassin was a leading world figure in the struggle for recognition of the rights of the individual.

A native of Bayonne, France, he was a brilliant student at the Lycée of Nice and at the University of Aix-en-Province where he took degrees in humanities and the law. In a competitive examination given by the law faculty, he placed first. And in 1914 he received a doctorate in juridicial, economic and political sciences.

He began a legal career—interrupted by World War One in which he was gravely wounded (and decorated with both the Croix de Guerre and Medaille Militaire, for bravery)—and then began to teach law. He served the French government-in-exile during World War Two (apparently he was the first civilian to leave Bordeaux in response to General Charles de Gaulle's broadcast to the French people from London) and, after the conflict, held high positions in both France and in Europe.

From 1965 to 1968, he was President of the European Court of Human Rights at Strasbourg. He served on the United Nations Commission on Human Rights in various senior roles from 1946 to 1957, and was credited with being the most important contributor to the wording of the U.N. Declaration of Human Rights.

In an article written to help mark the International Human Rights Year (1968), Cassin concluded:

"Now that we possess an instrument capable of lifting or easing the burden of oppression and injustice in the world, we must learn to use it." (One cannot help but wonder how René Cassin would react to the activities of the UN Human Rights Commission in the 21st century with a majority of its members among the foremost violators of human rights on the globe.)

CHAPTER EIGHT

JOURNALISTS AND PUBLISHERS

"Of the more than 1,700 daily newspapers published in the United States in the middle 1990s, about fifty were owned by Jewish Americans. That is under 3 per cent, which is the percentage of Jews in the population. About 3.3 per cent of editors and reporters are Jewish, certainly not an important disproportion. On the other hand, newspapers published in New York and Washington, D.C., have a large proportion of Jewish employees, in part because both cities have large Jewish populations."

American Jewish Desk Reference, 1999

Walter Annenberg created *Seventeen* and *TV Guide*.

WALTER ANNENBERG (1908-2002) was head of a huge communications network, including *Seventeen* and *TV Guide* which he created.

Annenberg took over his father's deeply indebted communications network when Moses L. Annenberg died in 1942. The elder Annenberg had started out with a wire service providing the results of horse races to betting offices across the US Ultimately, Moses had a publishing empire including the *Philadelphia Inquirer*, and two horse-racing journals—the *Daily Racing Form* and the *Morning Telegraph*.

Walter Annenberg added *Seventeen* in 1944 and *TV Guide* in 1953, the *Philadelphia Daily News* in 1957 and a variety of radio and television stations.

President Nixon named him US Ambassador to Britain, 1969-1974. (When Queen Elizabeth II politely asked Annenberg if his accommodations were comfortable, he responded: "We're in the Embassy residence, subject, of course, to some of the discomfiture as a result of, uh, elements of refurbishment and rehabilitation.")

Annenberg disposed of his broadcasting and publishing assets between 1969 and 1988, and focused on philanthropy. He donated more than one billion dollars to various charitable causes including the M.L. Annenberg School for Communication at the University of Pennsylvania, a similar facility at the University of Southern California, the Philadelphia Orchestra, the United Negro College Fund, hospitals, art museums, and projects in Israel.

In 1987, in a *Fortune* interview, he stated:

"Adversity either inspires you or destroys you."

He bequeathed his important collection of Impressionist and Post-Impressionist paintings to New York's Metropolitan Museum of Art.

CARL BERNSTEIN (1944-   ) was the Washington Post journalist who, with Bob Woodward, exposed the Watergate Affair.

Their "story of the century" led to the toppling of the President of the United States, Richard Nixon. The Watergate Affair was a break-in of Democratic Party offices in the Watergate Hotel in Washington, and the Nixon administration's efforts to cover up what was done.

The investigative reporting by Bernstein and Woodward won virtually every major American journalism award. Their newspaper, the *Washington Post*, won the 1973 Pulitzer Prize for public service.

The two journalists collaborated on the book, *All the President's Men*, which was made into a successful film in 1976.

Carl Bernstein worked with Bob Woodward to expose the Watergate Affair in their newspaper, the *Washington Post*.

———

ART BUCHWALD's (1925-   ) humorous column is carried by hundreds of newspapers worldwide.

He was born in Mount Vernon, New York, and, when his mother died shortly after giving birth, Buchwald was placed in the Hebrew Orphan Asylum in New York and, later, in five foster homes.

In spite of that difficult start, he became one of America's funniest political satirists. Buchwald himself says those early experiences are "where all the humor comes from—-a defense from the hostility."

He never graduated from high school, but in 1942, aged 17, he enlisted in the US Marine Corps. Assigned to the 4th Marine Air Wing, he spent some three years in the Pacific Theater. He edited the base newspaper at Eniwetok and handled public relations assignments for Special Services.

After his war service, Buchwald attended the University of Southern California—editing the campus humor magazine and writing a column for *The Daily Trojan*.

In 1948, he moved to Paris where he sold a column about Parisian night life to the European editor of the *New York Herald-Tribune*.

That column ultimately was syndicated and read by millions in more than 450 newspapers.

He married Ann McGarry in Paris, explaining "We had the same black market money-changer."

Buchwald claims it is easy to be funny in today's world "Everything is so wild now that all I'm doing is reporting."

Arch Buchwald's brand of humor was carried in hundreds of newspapers.

He told one interviewer: "I never talk to anybody. Facts just get in my way."

In 1959, Buchwald was presented with the French Grand Prix de la Humour.

Seymour Hersh was ranked as one of America's foremost investigative reporters.

SEYMOUR HERSH (1937-   ) is one of the most outstanding investigative American journalists.

Hersh was born in Chicago, and after graduating from the University of Chicago, went to work as a police reporter for the City's News Bureau. His career did not take off until he joined the Associated Press News Agency in 1963 and was assigned to cover the Pentagon.

He built a reputation as a determined, demanding reporter who pushed hard until he had exactly what he wanted.

Hersh left the AP and learned of alleged massacres by American troops in Vietnam. The Defense Department denied the story, but Seymour Hersh uncovered the murders at My Lai and won a Pulitzer prize for it. However, no one would print his story until a lawyer friend promised to defend any publication, free of charge, against libel charges.

He joined the staff of the *New York Times* and won the George Polk Memorial Award for stories on secret US bombings in Cambodia. And in 1974 he was presented with the Sidney Hillman Award for his stories on domestic spying by the Central Intelligence Agency.

Since 1971, he has been a major contributor of in-depth pieces to the *New Yorker*.

Ted Koppel is one of America's most influential journalists.

TED KOPPEL (1940-   ) is one of the most important television journalists in America. He has hosted Nightline on ABC since 1980.

Koppel was born in Lancashire, England, but his family moved to the US when he was 13. (Koppel's father had had a large tire manufacturing company in Germany which he had to abandon in 1938. He was jailed for a time by the Nazis.)

After earning a Master's degree in journalism, he went to work in radio in New York but joined ABC News in 1963. He was a correspondent in Vietnam for two stretches—in 1967 and 1969-1971.

His shelves are heavy with awards. He won Overseas Press Club awards in 1971, 1974, and 1975. In 1979, he was presented with the Dupont-Columbia award for the *ABC World News Tonight* series. He won an Emmy in 1980 for *Nightline*. And in 1982, he was given the George Polk Award for "best television reporting."

Koppel is rated as one of the most incisive interviewers on television yet he goes into interviews almost cold. Unlike most interviewers, he does not have a list of prepared questions developed by research staff.

In an interview with *New York Magazine*, Koppel explained: "It's important to listen and, for me, not to have a bunch of prepared questions." Millions of Americans stay up at night to obtain Koppel's slant on a major news development.

He has been offered senior government positions but, for the moment, is staying with ABC.

Carl Edward Sagan popularized science through television. His popular TV series was *Cosmos*. (NASA photo)

CARL EDWARD SAGAN (1934-1996) was an astronomer and astrophysicist who popularized science through television.

Born in New York, he studied at Chicago University and Berkeley, and became professor of astronomy and space science in 1970.

His research projects ranged from the origin of life on earth to the possibility of extraterrestrial life.

Through his books, and his television program *Cosmos*, he interested many in astronomy and other scientific fields.

His science fiction novel *Contact* pictured contact between our world and life-forms in outer space.

STEPHEN JAY GOULD (1941-2002) was a widely popular lecturer and writer on modern science.

As a child, he was taken to the American Museum of Natural History in New York, and was both "awed and scared" by the skeleton of the towering Tyrannasaurus Rex.

Stephen Jay Gould interested many in science through his best-selling books (Harvard Gazette photo)

Quoting Walter Lippmann

Without criticism and reliable and intelligent reporting, the government cannot govern.

The complexity of modern civilization is a daily lesson in the necessity of not pressing any claim too far, of understanding opposing points of view, of seeking to reconcile them, of conducting matters so that there is some kind of harmony in a plural society.

We are not the policemen of mankind. We are not able to run the world, and we shouldn't pretend that we can.

The opposition is indispensable. A good statesman, like any other sensible being, always learns more from his opposition than from his fervent supporters.

The thinker dies, but his thoughts are beyond the reach of destruction. Men are mortal; but ideas are immortal.

When all think alike then no one is thinking.

Walter Lippmann was one of the most influential journalists of the 20th century.

He became a full professor at Harvard, teaching geology, biology, and the history of science. He, and an associate Niles Eldridge, sought to explain the "missing links" in the fossil record by postulating that evolution may not be gradual, but could come in fits and starts.

The pair's theories triggered a heated debate among academics about this proposed re-think of Darwin's Theory of Evolution.

Gould wrote a weekly column for Natural History from 1974 to 2001. His lectures were popular in part because of his charming sense of humor.

His book titles—*Panda's Thumb*, 1980; *Hen's Teeth and Horse's Toes*, 1983; *The Flamingo's Smile*, 1985; *Eight Little Piggies*, 1993; and *Dinosaur in a Haystack*, 1995—attracted many readers.

———

WALTER LIPPMANN (1889-1974), winner of a special Pulitzer Prize in 1958, was one of the most influential journalists of the twentieth century.

Lippmann's column *Today and Tomorrow* appeared in more than 200 American and foreign newspapers. He was so influential in the determination of both domestic and foreign policy in the US that he was sometimes referred to as the "other State Department."

He was born in New York and his classmates at Harvard included Heywood Broun and T. S. Eliot. He was one of the founders of the liberal *New Republic* magazine in 1914.

With the outbreak of World War One, he was recruited by President Woodrow Wilson to help draft the Fourteen Points the US leader took to the Peace Conference at Versailles in 1919.

He began his journalistic career with the *New York World*, writing brilliant editorials. When the *World* folded, a victim of the Great Depression, Lippmann became a columnist at the *New York Herald-Tribune*, to—in his words—"provide in its ample pages a little corner of mild left-wing philosophy to offset its own conservative columns."

But the writer abandoned the left as the 30s and 40s saw the rise of Hitler and exposure of the cruelties of Joseph Stalin's brand of communism. Despite his brilliance, Lippman lumped the Nazis, the communists, and the mild socialists together, contending "the truly liberal state does not administer the affairs of men. It administers justice among men who conduct their own affairs." In other words, Lippman condemned Big Government and favored laissez-faire capitalism.

He wrote, in 1966:

"We must remember that in time of war what is said on the enemy's side is always propaganda and what is said on our side of the front is truth and righteousness, the cause of humanity and a crusade for peace. Is it necessary for us at the height of our power to stoop to such self-deceiving nonsense?"

Fellow journalist James Reston wrote about Lippman:

"I know that he has given my generation of newspapermen a wider vision of our duty. He has shown us how to put the event of the day in its proper relationship to the history of yesterday and the dream of tomorrow."

A special Pulitzer Prize was awarded to him in 1958 hailing his abilities as a news analyst.

ADOLPH S. OCHS (1858-1935) bought the *New York Times* and made it into one of the world's great newspapers.

Ochs' father reluctantly allowed the 11-year-old boy to go to work because of family financial problems. Adolph Ochs became a printer's devil and compositor on *The Knoxville Chronicle*.

Later he moved to Chattanooga, started his own paper—the *Daily Dispatch* —and in time merged it with the *Chattanooga Times*. The *Times* became one of the most influential newspapers in the post-Civil War South.

During a visit to New York, in 1896, Ochs learned that the *Times* had financial problems. In 1899, he became the owner of the paper and built it into one of the great newspapers of the world.

The Times slogan "All the news that's fit to print" came from Ochs himself.

Among his community activities, Ochs underwrote the research, writing, and printing of the *Dictionary of American Biography*.

Adolph S. Ochs in 1896. (New York Times photo)

Publisher Mortimer Zuckerman. (McGill University Archives)

Baron Paul Reuter founded the news agency bearing his name.

MORTIMER B. ZUCKERMAN (1937-   ) is publisher of *US News & World Report*, but he was a formidable real estate developer before he plunged into journalism.

The Montreal-born Zuckerman bought *The Atlantic*, in 1980, focusing on property that was part of the deal.

However, publishing fascinated him, and in 1984 he acquired *US News & World Report*, and installed himself as editor-in-chief.

He grew up in a strictly religious household. "I couldn't go to the movies until I was 16", he told the *New York Times* in 1983, "so I read." He graduated from McGill University at age 19 with honors in economics and political science. He earned an LL.M. degree from *Harvard* in 1962, and then an M.B.A. from the Wharton School of Finance.

He went into law but detoured into acquisition of prime real estate in downtown Boston. Within five years, he was worth $5,000,000.

In 1971, Zuckerman began construction of the $150 million Park Plaza project, amidst some controversy. By 1986, his Boston Properties had acquired 53 buildings in 15 American cities.

"I've always been fascinated by journalism and public policy," he told the *New York Daily News* in 1986.

In that same year, when the Moscow correspondent for *US News & World Report*, Nicholas Daniloff, was arrested, Zuckerman flew to Russia to intervene. Daniloff had been charged with espionage.

In 1988, *The Atlantic* won three National Magazine Awards. Zuckerman, meanwhile, has broadened his real estate activities but runs an editorial on the back page of *US News & World Report*, expressing his personal views of world events.

BARON PAUL JULIUS REUTER (1816-1899) founded Reuter's News Agency, first using homing pigeons to carry dispatches. His news agency today competes with the major news organizations of the world, such as the Associated Press of the United States.

His working career began with a clerk's job in his uncle's bank. He started out providing information to local newspapers but took advantage of the introduction of the telegraph to expand his operations both in the area he served and in the type of information he carried. Using telegraph lines, he set up a financial news service between Aachen, Germany; and Verviers, Belgium, then used carrier pigeons to set up a link to Brussels. He soon added news to his financial reports. In 1851, he moved to London after a cable was laid between Calais and Dover—linking Britain with the continent.

By 1858, he was providing his informaton services to London newspapers,including *The Times*. He sent his own correspondent to cover the American Civil War. To speed up transmission of information, he laid down his own telegraph line to Ireland. With this link, he was two days ahead of the competition in reporting the assassination of President Lincoln in 1865.

Reuter stated his determination to "come up with solutions for my clients."

By the 1870s, he had bureaus in the Far East. Reuters became a private company in 1916

How the *London Illustrated News* pictured Paul Julius Reuters' innovative pigeon-post service between Aachen and Brussels, in 1850.

EDWARD L. BERNAYS (1891-1995) changed "press agentry" into the far more sophisticated "public relations."

Bernays revolutionized the craft of the publicist—coining the title "public relations counsel."

Bernays was a nephew of Sigmund Freud; he added the "L" to his name, but it didn't stand for anything. He was born in Vienna but his father—a successful grain merchant—moved his family to New York.

Father Bernays hoped his son would become a scientific farmer, and sent him to Cornell University's College of Agriculture. Shortly after graduation, he began working for two small publications—functioning as editor, copy-reader, office boy, promoter, etc—all for $25 a week.

His first involvement in public relations came when an actor sought his help in promoting a play. Bernays set up a "Sociological Fund" with a membership fee of $4.00. But that fee allowed "members" to attend the play gratis. The play was a success.

Eddie Bernays decided that this was what he wanted to do, and he became busy promoting stage and screen stars, including Nijinsky and Caruso.

During World War One, he wrote pamphlets for distribution in Germany and neutral countries, explaining the United States was in the war to promote freedom.

Edward Bernays (right) with US First Lady Eleanor Roosevelt in 1941.

After the war, he convinced businessmen that they would benefit from skilled public relations—and a new occupation was born.

Bernays lectured at a number of universities, including Harvard, Princeton, and Yale on the new "public relations," and encouraged many business figures to hire skilled counselors to guide them.

Indicative of his great imagination was a promotional campaign he developed for Proctor and Gamble. He organized a national sculpture contest for the best figures carved from Ivory Soap, and offered $1,675 in prizes. A committee of well-known artists functioned as judges and the newspapers enthusiastically carried stories on the winners.

To publicize the electric light industry, Bernays arranged for a "Light's Golden Jubilee," and lured the aged inventor of the light bulb, Thomas Alva Edison, to participate and was able to interest President Herbert Hoover in participating in the celebration.

BARBARA WALTERS (1931-   ) is ranked as one of America's top broadcast journalists, co-anchoring 20/20 and hosting the Barbara Walters Specials for ABC.

Walters broke ground as a woman journalist in what, for much of her earlier career, was a man's world.

Walters has the longest on-air service of any woman journalist. She was the first woman evening news anchor—hired in 1976 for ABC's *Evening News*. She was paid a million dollars a year—the highest paid network news personality at that time. (After an interview with the President of Egypt, Anwar Sadat, the Arab leader confided in her that, while she was paid a million dollars a year, he—as President of a large nation—only had a salary of $12,000 annually!)

Barbara Walters was born in Boston. She had a slightly retarded sister, and her father, a nightclub owner, went broke. Because of that, Walters stated, "I always felt I had to work because I felt that I would have to provide for, and take care of my sister."

Since 2000, Walters has worked for ABC—for about $12 million a a year (the highest income of any television news personality) as co-host of *20/20*, produces and hosts *The View*, and turns out two *Barbara Walters Specials* a year.

Possibly, she has interviewed more historic figures than any journalist in history.

Barbara Walters is one of the US' top broadcast journalists. (ABC News)

WILLIAM SHAWN (1907-1992) was the longtime editor of *The New Yorker* magazine and under his direction it became one of the greatest magazines in the world.

William Chon was born in Chicago, attended the University of Michigan but never graduated. He worked briefly as a newspaper reporter in New Mexico before joining *The New Yorker* in 1932.

He began as a reporter for the magazine's "Talk of the Town" section and became editor two years later. He was only 28. He was managing editor from 1939 until 1952, and then became editor-in-chief.

In more than 50 years with the magazine, he put his name on a story only once but, as editor, he was responsible for guiding and encouraging a large coterie of creative people to make the magazine into one of the finest of its kind in the world.

As a boy, Shawn had a close brush with disaster. Richard Loeb and Nathan Leopold planned to kidnap him, but instead chose a schoolmate, Bobby Frank, whom they murdered.

Shawn's predecessor, Harold Ross, meddled in every aspect of the periodical but the new editor was more open; he carefully considered what writers proposed. Nevertheless, he added "I approve everything we publish."

Time magazine called Shawn's editorial style "participatory dictatorship." Whatever grade you gave to his work, under Shawn, *The New Yorker* surged to its greatest reputation ever.

LARRY KING (1933-   ) began his broadcasting career as a disc jockey in Miami but now, on CNN five nights a week, he is known as America's number one talk show host.

The Brooklyn-born King (Lawrence Harvey Zeiger), developed his skill as an interviewer in some of his earliest broadcasting days. Broadcasting from Miami's Pumpernick Restaurant in the 1950s, he chatted with virtually anyone who came to dine.

In 1985, he began his *Larry King Live* on the Cable News Network, one of the channel's most watched segments.

Larry King is known as America's number one talk show host.

From the time he was five, Larry King wanted to be a broadcaster. "I would look at the radio," he says, "sit and listen to it." His father, however, died when he was ten and the family had to go on welfare.

King's first jobs were as a delivery boy and a mail clerk. Tipped he might find a spot on a Miami radio station, he immediately was hired—to sweep floors!

His break came when the station's disc jockey walked out, without notice. Larry King had made no secret of his ambitions and he was given a chance. But his name, Lawrence Harvey Zeiger, was not suitable for a broadcast personality.

The manager chose his new name, pointing to an ad in the Miami Herald for King's Wholesale Liquor store.

—————

HENRY GRUNWALD (1922-   ) had legendary careers in both journalism and diplomacy – serving as Editor-in-Chief of Time Inc. (1979-1987) and as U.S. Ambassador to Austria (1988-1990).

In his later years, he was honored for "helping people overcome the challenges of vision loss." Grunwald suffered from macular degeneration but, in the words of TV broadcaster Mike Wallace: "While his eyesight may be impaired, Henry Grunwald's vision remains impeccable."

David Halberstam writes in *The Powers That Be"* that in one period, when Grunwald was Foreign Editor, "he was not only one of the *Time's* most skilled writers and editors but one of its more skilled politicians as well, and there was no one better at working his way through the minefield of Vietnam."

He became Editor-in-Chief of the newsmagazine in 1978 – 34 years after the 22-year-old immigrant from Vienna had joined the staff as a copy boy.

He had risen quickly, becoming the publication's youngest senior editor, in 1951, when he was only 29.

Legendary *Time* journalist Henry Grunwald with friends at a party in his honor.

WALTER WINCHELL (1897-1972) created the American gossip column and in his radio broadcasts, used colorful language and a staccato style of delivery.

Winchell ran away from home when he was 12 years old. He dropped out of sixth grade and that was the extent of his formal education. He became a dancer in vaudeville, served in the navy in World War One, and then, in 1922, began writing for newspapers.

The gossip column was originated in 1925 when he found himself with no jokes or poems for his usual offering. So he sat down at his typewriter and wrote about gossip he'd picked up. The initial column read like this:

"Helen Eby Brooks, widow of William Rock, has been plunging in Miami real estate ... It's a girl at the Carter de Havens ... Lenore Ulric paid $7 income tax ... Fanny Brice is betting on the horses at Belmont ... S. Jay Kaufman sails on the 16th via the Berengaria to be hitched to a Hungarian ... Report has it that Lillian Lorraine has taken a husband again ...."

Walter Winchell created the American gossip column.

He thus began 40 years of writing gossip for New Yorkers. With his brash style and razor's edge verbiage, he was the king of Broadway. He used his apartment only for sleeping. Every restaurant and nightclub was eager to have him as a guest.

But he spent part of virtually every evening at the Stork Club, picking up tidbits of information from people who dropped by to chat. He was said to have hundreds of informants from politicans to gangsters to celebrities. His syndicated newspaper column was read by more than 35 million people.

He took his gossip column on radio and began every broadcast with "Good evening , Mr. and Mrs. America and all the ships at sea."

He was buddies with prominents on both sides of the law—from the F.B.I.'s J. Edgar Hoover to gangster "lucky" Luciano.

He butchered the English language, dreaming up words. To him "infanticipating" meant being pregnant. "Cupidating" was another original. Even during the depression, Winchell was earning more than $400,000 a year.

Winchell's definition of Hollywood—"a place where they shoot too many movies and not enough actors."

Winchell especially condemned British activity in Palestine, calling it "Brutish." When aviator Charles Lindbergh visited Nazi Germany and spoke favorably about his experience, he renamed the flyer "Berlindbergh."

William Safire has gone from speech-writing for presidents to a position of international prominence as a *New York Times* columnist.

Judaism is transmitted not by the nation or the tribe or the congregation but by the family...Jewish identity is rooted in a distinctive old religion that builds individual character and group loyalty through close family life. That is how the Jewish people have survived through five millennia and is the light the Jews—whatever the number—must continue to offer the world.

William Safire, New York Times, July 17, 1995

He retired in 1969, but by then his column was steadily declining in readership and importance.

One of his few close friends was Broadway writer Damon Runyan. When Runyan died of cancer in 1946, Winchell estabished the Damon Runyan Memorial Fund for Cancer Research.

The *New York Times*, in its obituary—which ran a full page—noted:

"He kept his money in cash in bank vaults. On becoming a millionaire in 1937, he had the Colony Club cater him an elegant meal which he ate alone."

————

WILLIAM SAFIRE (1929-   ) is one of America's most respected journalists, writing a regular column in the *New York Times*. He has played a considerable role, behind the scenes, in American politics.

Safire's father died when he was a child. The family barely got by on what he left them in his will. Bill Safire won a scholarship to attend Syracuse University, but dropped out after his sophomore year and began working as a copy boy for Tex McCrary, a newspaper columnist, and radio and TV broadcaster.

After a few years in radio and TV, he flirted with politics when he organized an "Eisenhower for President" rally, in 1952, at Madison Square Garden.

After a three-year stint in the Army, he began working with McCrary's new public relations firm. One of the people he hired during this period was Barbara Walters.

In 1959 Safire scored a coup when he set up the so-called "kitchen debate" between Vice-President Richard Nixon and Soviet Premier Nikita Krushchev. This occurred at the American Exhibition in Moscow and Safire maneuvered the two leaders into what was featured as a typical American home. Then Safire, using a camera borrowed from an Associated Press photographer, took a widely-distributed picture of the famous encounter.

In the mid-1960s, Safire became a volunteer speechwriter for Nixon who was preparing for the 1968 elections. William H. Honan of *The New York Times Magazine* called Nixon's speechwriter "The Idea Factory."

With Nixon's election, Bill Safire moved into the White House as a member of the Presidential staff.

The *New York Times'* publisher, Arthur "Punch" Sulzberger hired Safire to write a twice-weekly op-ed column to balance the left-wing views of other Times' columnists.

Former US Secretary of State Madeleine Albright commented on his work:

"Whether Safire is being silly or serious, reassuring or provocative, right or wrong, or all of these things at once, he is always read."

In ensuing years, William Safire began writing a popular "On Language" column for the *Times* and wrote novels with mixed success.

He won a Pulitzer Prize in 1978, for zeroing in on budget irregularities in the Carter administration (Carter's Budget Director, Bert Lance, resigned after the column appeared) and was named to the Pulitzer Prize Board in 1995.

ROBERT CAPA (1913-1954) was a courageous war photo-journalist, and his "Death of a Spanish Loyalist," showing a soldier at the moment he is fatally hit dropping to the ground, is ranked as one of the greatest war photos. But Capa (real name Andre Friedman; he took a new name when he couldn't get a visa in 1936 to cover the Spanish Civil War) hated war.

He once said his ambition was to be an "unemployed war photographer."

Capa was born in Budapest. He moved to Paris at age 18 and got a job as a darkroom assistant.

After the Spanish conflict, he took his camera wherever violence flared. He was in China in 1938 for the Japanese invasion, in London to cover the Blitz for Life, in Tunisia with invading US troops, and was the only photographer to splash ashore from a landing craft, at Normandy on June 6, 1944. On May 25, 1954, he was walking up a road in Indo-China, seeking the best angle for a shot for *Life* magazine. He trod on a landmine and died instantly.

In 2003, documentarian Anne Makepeace created *Robert Capa: In Love and War*. One of the commentators in the film says of Capa "Taking pictures was his way of fighting fascism."

Robert Capa was an internationally-renowned war photo-journalist, fatally injured when he stepped on a land-mine in Indo-China.

Wolf Blitzer is one of the best known newsmen in the world. (Harry Walker Agency)

WOLF BLITZER is the anchor journalist for *CNN's Wolf Blitzer Reports* and, as host of the Sunday talk show *Late Edition with Wolf Blitzer*, is seen in more than 210 countries and territories around the world.

Blitzer's first job was with Reuters News Agency, beginning in 1972, as a "very junior reporter" in the agency's Tel Aviv Bureau. He had just been awarded a master's degree in international relations and joined Reuters to train as a journalist.

Later he served as Washington correspondent for *The Jerusalem Post*. He joined CNN in 1990 as the network's military affairs correspondent at the Pentagon.

He describes his coverage of the Gulf War as his "most memorable" story, because he worked for seven months for CNN and became widely known.

Blitzer was awarded the Lowell Thomas Broadcast Journalism Award in 1999 for "outstanding contribution to journalism."

CHAPTER NINE

FROM RAGS TO RICHES

"The Jewish merchant prince thought of wealth as a responsibility, a means of improving public welfare. He spent a large part of his riches on charitable works. ... The merchant princes ..."invented" modern philanthropy. Families ... became patrons of art and education; they donated imposing art collections to museums, funded symphony orchestras, supported the opera and the theater, established trust funds for universities, and endowed chairs in the humanities and sciences."

Max Dimont, *The Jews in America*, 1978

George Soros was a holocaust survivor who became so wealthy he gives away hundreds of millions of dollars every year. Author Andrew Leonard called him the man who bought the world.

GEORGE SOROS (1930-   ) is one of Wall Street's most successful investors and this Holocaust survivor gives away hundreds of millions of dollars every year to prove it.

Born in Budapest, Soros was a teenager when the Nazis seized Hungary.

He posed as the gentile godson of a Hungarian official for a time and later moved from hiding place to hiding place with his family.

After the war, Soros studied at the London School of Economics. After graduating, he worked for an investment firm and then moved to New York.

By 1969, he was manager of the Quantum Fund and had the best earnings record on Wall Street. In 1981 *Institutional Investor* called Soros "the world's greatest money manager."

In 1991, Soros predicted that the British would devalue the pound and made almost one billion dollars for his company in one transaction.

In 1993, *Financial World Magazine* said that George Soros' annual income of $1.1 billion was the highest in the nation. The investment expert has poured hundreds of millions of dollars into Eastern Europe in an effort to make people in those regions more aware of Western ideas and culture.

Business Week called Soros "the single most influential private citizen between the Rhine and the Urals."

SAMUEL BRONFMAN (1890-1971), who went to school in rags, became one of the world's richest liquor distillers.

Sam was the third son (there were also four sisters) of Bessarabian immigrant, Ekiel Bronfman, who settled in Manitoba. The brothers—Abraham (1882-1968), Harry (1886-1963), and Allan (1895-

1980)—all eventually become executives of the powerful Seagram's Liquor Corporation, but Sam was the dominant figure.

And he never forgot the humiliation of being a poor boy, mocked by fellow students because of his torn clothing.

Sam Bronfman vaulted from the hotel business into distribution of liquor, and then became a distiller and a blender of spirits. He actually invented blended whiskeys. And he was a vigorous and imaginative marketing man.

When the Royal Family was scheduled to visit Canada, he created Crown Royal—with a crown-shaped bottle, and offered to put 10 cases, as a gift, on the royal train. The offer was accepted.

Sam Bronfman dominated the Canadian Jewish community for decades, providing leadership and funds. The annual Bronfman gift to the Montreal Combined Jewish Appeal was said to be the largest year-to-year charitable gift in North America.

Leading the Canadian Jewish Congress in the difficult prewar years, he was involved in the rescue of about 7,000 Jews.

While Sam Bronfman swore like a longshoreman, his door was always open to virtually any member of the Jewish community, great or small, and when he visited his distillery in Lasalle, Quebec, he would lunch with his workers.

On his 70th birthday, his four children honored him by donating the Bronfman Biblical and Archaeology wing to Jerusalem's Israel Museum.

He changed his birth date to make it appear that he had been born in Canada. Actually, he was born at sea, en route to North America.

Samuel Bronfman went to school in rags but became one of the world's richest liquor merchants.

HELENA RUBENSTEIN (1872-1965), an immigrant from Poland, founded the cosmetics empire bearing her name.

She was born in Cracow, Poland, but emigrated to Australia where she opened her first salon. She owed her early success largely to one product—Creme Valaze, a cosmetic made from herbs. A Hungarian friend had given her the formula. The cream became very popular in Australia because of its soothing, whitening effect on the skin. More than 100 years later, the cream is still in the Helena Rubenstein cosmetic range.

Helena Rubenstein became a giant in cosmetics.

After a few years, she opened a salon on London's Grafton Street in Mayfair "to attract the carriage trade."

The Helena Rubenstein name and fame thereafter spread to Paris, New York, and to many countries. For the first few years, as she opened a new facility, she would appoint one of her sisters as manager.

She was a very capable promoter and creative in her cosmetics. She pioneered the use of colored face powder and foundation. And she originated the health farm concept of beauty.

———

LEVI STRAUSS (1829-1902) couldn't sell his heavy canvas to California Gold Rush miners for tents so he manufactured sturdy pants, referred to by miners as "Levi's", from the material.

Levi Strauss was a peddler who originated the heavy denim pants called levis.

A Bavarian immigrant, Strauss had arrived in San Francisco (from New York, where he had been a peddler) in 1850, during the Gold Rush. The 21-year-old travelled by clipper ship, around the "Horn", but—during the voyage—sold his entire stock of goods except for a number of bolts of brown canvas. He figured he would be able to find a ready market in California; the miners could make tents and wagon covers from his heavy cloth. But he found people already there selling canvas.

Strauss learned from a miner that ordinary trousers quickly frayed and tore in the miners' work. The idea of "Levi's"—the miners' name for the canvas workpants—caught on. Strauss, himself, called them "waist high overalls." The first "jeans" were made in 1850 (they cost 22 cents a pair) and rivets were added in 1874. The cost of the first riveted jeans was $13.50—-a dozen!

Purchasers of the early jeans would lower themselves into a watering trough so the canvas would shrink to fit them!

Strauss switched from canvas to French denim, and later had the strong cloth dyed a distinctive blue. Denim has been loomed since the Middle Ages in Nimes, France. The word "jeans" comes indirectly from the sturdy trousers worn by Genoese sailors; the French name for Genoa is "Genes."

The word denim came from the French "serge de Nimes," The idea for the rivets came from a tailor in Carson City, Nevada—-Jacob Davis. Davis, a tailor, found the miners were tearing even the heavy canvas because they shoved ore into the pockets. So he went to a harness shop and reinforced the pockets with copper rivets. He journeyed to San Francisco by horse and wagon to show Levi his idea and they took out a joint patent.

Strauss never married. When he died, in 1902, his will directed that the company should go to his nieces and nephews. After all, it was their fathers—his brothers—who had grubstaked him in the first place.

He also was generous to the community, providing funds for 28 scholarships at the University of California.

Nathan Cummings (right) with brother Maxwell, went to work at 14 and became a billionaire – selling everything from brassieres to atomic submarines.

NATHAN CUMMINGS (1896-1985) founded the enormous conglomerate, Consolidated Foods, selling everything from Sara Lee deserts to Electrolux.

He was born in Saint John, New Brunswick, and was hired for his first job at 14—and fired ! "The night I lost that job I swore that someday I would be very, very rich and totally secure."

Living in Montreal for a time, he decided he wanted broader horizons and he went into the coffee importing business.

Today, the company he built sells everything from Sara Lee and Popsicles to Chicken Delight and Electrolux carpet cleaners.

"As a country boy who didn't even finish grammar school," his company racked up billions of dollars in sales annually.

VIDAL SASSOON (1928-   ) was placed in an orphanage after his father ran away with another woman. Sassoon became a world famous figure in hairstyling and hair-care products.

Vidal was five when his father, a carpet salesman, abandoned the family. His mother, unable to provide for her two sons, placed them in a London Jewish orphanage. He remained in the orphanage until he was 13; his mother remarried.

His mother had a dream that her son was styling her hair, and asked London hairdresser, Adolph Cohen, to accept the boy as an apprentice. Sassoon's job was to sweep the floor, shampoo hair and clean combs.

Because of his thick cockney accent, he was considered unlikely to do well. To improve himself, he began attending school. He feels that this experience helped shape his life. "I began to discover a sense of pride, the dignity of achievement."

Sassoon opened his first salon in 1954 at 108 Bond Street. His skilled hairdressing attracted a wide clientele, including actresses and models.

In 1965, he opened his first American salon. As the number of his branches grew, he opened schools for hair stylists in London and New York.

He had been developing his own hair care products for years, but in the late 1960s, began manufacturing them in substantial quantities and offered them for sale in his salons.

By the 1980s, the Sassoon hair care empire was grossing $100,000,000 a year.

CHAPTER TEN

RADIO AND TELEVISION

"American Jews brought the same show business talents of ideas and organization to the new technologies as they developed. In 1926, David Sarnoff created the first radio chain, the National Broadcasting System . . . At the same time, William Paley was putting together the rival Columbia Broadcasting System. In due course, these two introduced black and white television, and then color."

Paul Johnson, A History of the Jews, 1987

David Sarnoff was the person who suggested music and voice could be transmitted over the airwaves to a "radio musical box." (photo courtesy of the David Sarnoff Research Center)

DAVID SARNOFF (1891-1971) first proposed the idea that voice and music could be transmitted over the air waves; he was largely responsible for creating the National Broadcasting Company (NBC).

Sarnoff won fame as the youngster who, on April 14, 1912, picked up the first word of the sinking of the liner "Titanic,"—-"S.S.Titanic ran into iceberg, sinking fast"—- and he remained at his post for seventy-two continuous hours to receive and distribute news of the disaster.

Sarnoff was promoted by Marconi, and in 1915 submitted to the company his idea for a "radio music box." His memorandum read:

"I have in mind a development plan which would make radio useful in the home...The idea is to broadcast music in people's homes .... The receiver could be designed in the form of a simple Radiomusical Box and adapted to different wavelengths, which could be changed by turning a knob or pressing a button."

Radio Corporation of America (RCA) absorbed Marconi, and it was April 29, 1921 before the young man could submit his idea to the new management.

Even then, the directors would risk only $2,000. However, Sarnoff demonstrated his idea boldly, using a borrowed navy transmitter to broadcast the 1921 Dempsey-Carpentier World Championship boxing match.

One newspaper reported: "It created a sensation; about 200,000 amateur wireless operators and others with homemade sets heard it."

Sarnoff was made a vice-president, and in 1922 RCA began manufacturing and selling radios. Sales mushroomed to a staggering $83,000,000 in three years.

He was a visionary in many other ways. The Television Broadcasters Association called him "the father of American television."

Sarnoff recognized the possibilities when he learned of the invention of the iconoscope in 1923 by Dr. Vladimir Zworykin.

In 1928, David Sarnoff erected a special NBC station—B2XBS—to experimentally telecast programs. In 1930, he was named president of RCA.

The first demonstration of television was made by NBC at the New York World's Fair April 30, 1939, with Sarnoff declaring "now at last we add sight to sound."

During the Second World War, Sarnoff became a Brigadier General and was attached to General Eisenhower's staff as communications consultant. He continued to call himself "General" Sarnoff even when peace came.

William S. Paley founded the Columbia Broadcasting System (CBS).

WILLIAM S. PALEY (1901-1990) was a pioneer in making the Columbia Broadcasting System (CBS) a major player, first in radio, and then television.

He began his working career in his father's cigar company but became interested and involved in radio, in Philadephia, in broadcasting's earliest days. In 1928 he bought into a small network, which became CBS.

He attracted major talent to his young network, expanding its reach through 70 affiliates.

Paley recognized the importance of popular programs, and comics he hired included Jack Benny, Burns and Allen, Edgar Bergen, and Red Skelton. He offered listeners a mix of everything from soap operas to game shows, and he built an outstanding news team including Edward R. Murrow, William Shirer, and Eric Sevareid.

When he expanded into television, his outstanding news anchor was Walter Cronkite, and his television shows included *All in the Family, M*A*S*H, I Love Lucy*, and *The Mary Tyler Moore Show*.

The centerpiece of his half-billion dollar estate was an immense art collection which he left to the Metropolitan Museum of Art.

CHAPTER ELEVEN

THE MOVIES

"The motion picture industry was largely a Jewish invention, and it remains predominantly (although not exclusively) a Jewish industry. In a study of most influential writers, producers and executives, the political scientists Stanley Rothman and S. Robert Lichter found that more than three out of five members of the 'movie elite' are Jews. Not surprisingly, since television entertainment is in good measure an outgrowth of film production and is still closely connected with it, Jews make up almost as large a proportion of the 'TV elite.'"

Charles E. Silberman, *A Certain People*, 1985

Samuel Goldwyn was one of the founders of the American moving picture industry.

SAMUEL GOLDWYN (1882-1974) lost both of his parents in the Warsaw Ghetto before he was eleven. He wangled his way across Europe and reached America travelling by steerage. By 34, he was a millionaire; he produced the first feature film in the US, and his people set up shop to make movies in a barn in a place called Hollywood.

In America, the immigrant boy found a job in a glove factory, worked his way up to salesman but, fascinated by "nickelodeons," where five-minute films were shown, he ventured into the movie business.

He and his brother-in-law, Jesse L. Lasky (1880-1958), hired an inexperienced playwright named Cecil B. DeMille to direct their first movie. They sent DeMille to Flagstaff, Arizona, to film some Indians; "if we shoot the picture in Flagstaff, we can get all the Indians we need, free of charge."

However, when the director's train reached Flagstaff, there was a snowstorm, and DeMille continued to the end of the line. He sent a telegram back east:

"Have proceeded to a place called Hollywood. Want authorization to rent barn for $75 a month." Reluctantly the partners agreed, adding "don't make long-term commitment."

That picture, *The Squaw Man*, was a big success and others followed. Ultimately, Goldwyn—who had changed his name from "Goldfish," (he became irritated about people's reaction to his name, so he appeared before Judge Learned Hand to switch to "Goldwyn," whereupon the Judge commented: "A self-made man may prefer a self-made name.") produced such classics as *All Quiet on the Western Front, Arrowsmith, Wuthering Heights, The Little Foxes,* and *The Best Years of Our Lives.*

Goldwyn, whose formal education had ended with the death of his parents, induced some of the greatest writers in America and Europe to come to Hollywood. In 1930, he produced the first talking picture *All Quiet on the Western Front.*

I was always an independent," he stated. "even when I had partners."

On another occasion, he remarked: "I make a picture to please me — if it pleases me there is a good chance that it will please other people. But it has to please me first."

Goldwyn was famous for his so-called "Goldwynisms." Allegedly, he would make remarks like these:

—Kindly include me out.

—Anyone who goes to a psychiatrist should have his head examined.

—A verbal contract is not worth the paper it's written on.

—I'll give you a definite maybe.

—A hospital is no place to be sick.

—I don't think anyone should write their autobiography until after they're dead.

—I don't want any yes-men around me. I want everybody to tell me the truth even if it costs them their jobs.

—If I could drop dead right now, I'd be the happiest man alive.

—Spare no expense to save money on this one.

Many years later, a visitor asked a receptionist to query Goldwyn as to whether he "remembered Hamburg". Goldwyn went into the lobby and there was a Hamburg storekeeper who had helped him get to America.

Goldwyn had used his brother-in-law's name for his first production company in 1910, but in 1916, the company merged with the operation directed by Adolf Zuckor (1873-1976) to become Paramount Pictures.

Zukor had been born in Hungary, and immigrated to the United States at age 15. His first job was sweeping floors. But he saved part of his wages, studied, and become a partner in a furrier's establishment. He formed a brief partnership with another furrier, Marcus Loew, who would also have a great future in the entertainment industry.

In 1903, the partners invested in the first penny arcades and, in time, their investment grew into the Loew Company. Zuckor daringly imported Sarah Bernhardt's feature-length film Queen Elizabeth in 1912. That led to his establishment, with Daniel Frohman, of Famous Players.

There was a major Hollywood celebration in 1973 when Adolf Zuckor marked his hundredth birthday. "If I had known I was going to live this long," he said. "I would have taken better care of myself."

Squaw Man, the first Cecil B. deMille movie produced by Sam Goldwyn and his brother-in-law, Jesse Lasky.

The Hollywood tycoons...were foreigners almost to a man. Some still spoke with foreign accents. Goldwyn used the English language as if it was some Yiddish hybrid ... that one historian of the film industry, Philip French, has described as an "immigrant's adventures with the English language, part mixed metaphor, part malapropism, part illiteracy, that have a power and a pungency of their own."

Chaim Bermant, *The Jews*, 1977

The Warner brothers, Harry, Albert, Sam and Jack, the sons of a Polish cobbler, worked in a variety of trades before combining their resources to open a bicycle shop. In 1904, they acquired a film projector and gave travelling shows with their sister at the piano and Jack, then twelve, as a boy soprano. They prospered sufficiently to join a film exchange and became distributors and exhibitors. In 1912 they moved to California and after a number of false and rather expensive starts, they finally succeeded in launching the Warner Bros. Company.
Chaim Bermant, *The Jews*, 1977

Hollywood's first movie moguls, Louis B. Mayer and Sam Goldwyn, founders of MGM, the Warner brothers, William and Harry Cohn, head of Columbia, were all Jewish immigrants or children of immigrants, fleeing annihilation in Eastern Europe.
Laura Lind, *Reel Life*

THE WARNER BROTHERS (Albert 1884-1967; Harry 1881-1958; Jack 1892-1978; Sam 1887-1927) produced their first movie in 1910 (*Perils of the Plains*). *Warner Brothers* was one of the major film studios in Hollywood history.

They produced the first motion picture with a completely synchronized sound track—*Don Juan*, 1926; the first commercially important film with synchronized music and dialogue—*The Jazz Singer*, 1927; the first full-length all-talking color movie—*Lights of New York*, 1928; the first all-talking color film—*On With The Show*, 1929; the film that initiated the fascination with gangster movies—*Little Caesar*,1930; and some of the greatest film classics of all time including *The Adventures of Robin Hood*, 1938; *The Maltese Falcon*, 1941; *Casablanca*, 1943, *A Streetcar Named Desire*, 1951, and *My Fair Lady*, 1964.

LOUIS B. MAYER (1885—1957), Samuel Goldwyn (1882-1974), and Marcus Loew (1870-1937) teamed up in 1925 to create Metro-Goldwyn-Mayer, which became the largest film production house in the world.

Loew was born to a poor family in New York, but he was the dominant personality in creating MGM.

Furriers Loew and Zukor began their involvement in entertainment running a chain of penny arcades. Then they developed a national chain of movie theaters. They had the outlets and therefore decided to produce films themselves.

Louis B. Mayer founded his first film production company in 1916 and by 1924 it had evolved into Metro-Goldwyn-Mayer (MGM).

Louis B. Mayer, another major partner, bought a rundown Massachusetts burlesque theater and converted it into a cinema.

In 1915 he helped form Metro Pictures Corporation, then left New England for California which was becoming the heartland of movie production. In 1919 Loew purchased Metro Pictures Corporation; five years later, he absorbed Goldwyn Pictures and, when Loew died in 1927, completed development of the legendary MGM.

WILLIAM FOX (1879-1952) worked as a paperboy and in the fur industry before buying a nickleodeon in Brooklyn.

By 1913, he was a powerful figure in exhibiting and distributing films and, in 1915, he formed the Fox Film Corporation. He was an innovator—introducing organ accompaniment to silent films and presented the first commercially successful sound film in 1927. His firm ultimately became 20th Century Fox, but he himself was bankrupted by the Great Depression.

HARRY COHN (1891-1958), with his brother JACK (1889-1956) founded Columbia Pictures (originally called C.B.C. Film Sales Company) in 1920.

They shared management duties. Harry was in charge of production, while Jack produced some of the earliest newsreels and cartoons. Jack's son, Robert (1920-1996) formed Screen Gems—the television subsidiary of Columbia Pictures, 1949.

"Movies were the product of a marriage between California and Ashkenazi Jews. This followed an earlier union between Jewish productive and creative genius in New York. In 1890 there was not a single amusement arcade in New York.
By 1900 there were over 1,000, and fifty of them already called Nickelodeons. Eight years later there were 400 of them in New York alone and they were spreading all over the Northern cities. They cost five cents and appealed to the poorest of the urban poor. The hundreds of movies made for them were silent. That was an advantage. Few of the patrons spoke English."

Paul Johnson *A History of the American People* 1997

Spielberg triumphant after winning two Oscars.

STEVEN SPIELBERG (1946-   ) is ranked as one of Hollywood's greatest producers, and to date, has provided the public with a dozen of the highest-grossing productions in the industry's history.

Spielberg began making films as a little boy, taking moving pictures as he crashed his toy Lionel trains. During his 19th summer, he donned his Bar Mitzvah suit every day, borrowed his father's briefcase and managed to outwit the guards at Universal Studios—pretending he had business on the lot.

He enrolled at California State University, but when Universal took notice of one of his student productions, he quit school. His first assignments for Universal were episodes for television.

Spielberg's first major film was *Jaws*, and he followed that success with *E.T.* He will be producing startling new productions for a long time to come. Spielberg says: "I don't have enough time in a lifetime to tell all the stories I want to tell."

CHAPTER TWELVE

THE PLAYWRIGHTS

"George S. Kaufman ranks without peer as the wit of the American twentieth century. George's comment, George's cool-off, George's swiftness to pick up the answer was breath-taking...He was taciturn. He didn't say much, but what he did say was stringent, always to the point, cutting acid, true or true enough. Which was his great trick. His trick of wit and his trick of criticism wasn't that he found what was true, but he would find what was true enough"

Garson Kanin

George S. Kaufman, with Moss Hart, featured in a display at the James A. Michener Museum.

Duveen

The Story of the Most Spectacular Art Dealer of All Time

S. N. BEHRMAN

With an Introduction by Glenn Lowry

S.N. Behrman wrote the best-selling biography of Lord Duveen as well as many successful plays.

GEORGE S. KAUFMAN (1889-1961) wrote more than 40 plays—all but one of them in collaboration with another author. Moss Hart (1904-1961) and he won the Pulitzer Prize for *You Can't Take it with You*, and they co-authored *The Man who Came to Dinner*. Kaufman worked with Morrie Ryskind and Ira Gershwin on the Pulitzer Prize winning *Of Thee I Sing*.

Kaufman, known as the "gloomy dean of American humor," also wrote musical comedies, was a producer and director, and appeared on radio on the *Information Please* program and on television, on *This is Show Business*.

For years he was a drama critic at the *New York Times* and continued to work for the paper long after he was a success on Broadway.

Kaufman collaborated with Morrie Ryskind and Irving Berlin in writing the comedy *Coconuts* for the Marx Brothers. Since the madcap brothers rarely paid much attention to the written script, Kaufman's comment on the experience was: "*Coconuts* introduced me to the Marx Brothers. *Coconuts* was a comedy, the Marx Brothers are comics, meeting them was a tragedy."

Nevertheless, Groucho Marx—in an interview with Howard Teichmann, for his book *George S. Kaufman, an Intimate Portrait*—acknowledged "Kaufman molded me. Kaufman gave me the walk and the talk."

George Kaufman was active in the theatre for 40 years and during that four decades worked with 16 collaborators on 45 plays. Twenty-six were hits. And he won two Pulitzer Prizes.

Humorist James Thurber called Kaufman "the man who was comedy."

S.N. (SAMUEL NATHAN) BEHRMAN (1893-1973) wrote *No Time For Comedy* and other succesful plays.

Behrman was born in Worcester, Massachusetts, to immigrant parents.

He became one of America's most successful playwrights. His more popular plays included *The Second Man*, in 1927; *End of Summer*, in 1936, *Jacobowsky and the Colonel*, 1943, and *But For Whom Charley*, in 1964. The latter play was presented as part of the opening season of the Lincoln Center Theater in New York.

He also wrote a best-selling biography of Lord Duveen, an art dealer who revolutionized the art world by persuading American millionaires to collect great art, and then donate their collections to institutions.

———

EUGENE IONESCO's (1912-1994) most famous play was *Rhinoceros*.

Ionesco was born in Slatina, Romania, but grew up in France.

He did not write his first play until he was 41. The idea of that first play, *The Bald Soprano*, grew out of Ionesco's intense efforts to teach himself English.

In all, he wrote 20 plays. And he won a basketful of awards after the quality of his work was recognized.

In 1970, he was elected to the Academie Francaise. He is regarded as a pioneer of the theatre of the absurd.

Eugene Ionesco is best-remembered for his play *Rhinoceros*.

———

ARTHUR MILLER (1915-   ) won several Pulitzer Prizes and is regarded as one of the three greatest American playwrights of the 20th century.

He was born in Harlem, New York, and started writing plays while still in university.

He was 32, however, before he first drew accolades, and this was for his 1947 play *All My Sons*, which focussed on wartime profiteering. A year later, he wrote one of America's greatest plays—*Death of a Salesman*, challenging Americans' fascination with success. This play received the New York Drama Critics Circle Award, the Pulitzer Prize and the Antoinette Perry Award—all in 1949. More than half a century later, the play is still being performed.

In 1953, Miller wrote *The Crucible*, ostensibly about seventeenth century witch-hunting in Massachusetts, but clearly aimed at the Congressional anti-communist tribunals. He himself fell victim to the witch-hunt in 1956 when he was summoned before the notorious House Committee on un-American Activities and cited for contempt.

His plays have been described as "powerful slices of post-war American life."

Arthur Miller is ranked as one of the three greatest American playwrights of the 20th century.

Neil Simon was one of the most important playwrights on the American scene in the second half of the 20th century.

NEIL SIMON's (1927-   ) runaway successes include *The Odd Couple, Barefoot in the Park* and *The Sunshine Boys.*

Born in the Bronx, he began to write while serving in the Army.

He wrote stories for the Army camp newspaper. Discharged from the Army, he became a mailroom clerk. He and his brother Danny began writing comedy reviews. They moved on to radio, and then television—in good company. They wrote for *The Phil Silvers Show* and Sid Caesar's *Your Show of Shows* with Woody Allen, Mel Brooks and Larry Gelbart.

He was nominated for Emmy Awards several times for his TV writing.

Finally, he tried his hand at writing plays for Broadway, and became one of America's most successful commercial playwrights. His first hit was *Come Blow Your Horn*, and this was followed by *Barefoot in the Park, the Odd Couple, Sweet Charity* and *The Star Spangled Girl*—all during the 1966-1967 season!

For the 1970-1971 season, he offered *Plaza Suite, Last of the Red Hot Lovers* and *Promises, Promises.*

After the death of his wife, he wrote two failures but moved to California and went on to write *California Suite, Chapter Two, Brighton Beach Memoirs, Biloxi Blues* and *Broadway Bound.*

And in 1991, he wrote the Pulitzer Prize-winning *Lost in Yonkers.*

Lillian Hellman, in addition to important plays, wrote three books of memoirs.

LILLIAN HELLMAN (1905-1984) was a playwright who adapted many of her plays for the screen.

The greatest influence on her life and career was detective-story writer Dashiell Hammett, an alcoholic. She met him, in Hollywood, in the early 1930s. They lived together for about 30 years, until his death in 1961. And it was under his stern direction that she began to be successful.

Her first Broadway success was in 1934 with the controversial *The Children's Hour*, boldly touching on lesbianism.

Other major plays she penned included: *The Little Foxes* (1939); *Watch on the Rhine* (1941); *Another Part of the Forest* (1946).

She wrote three books of memoirs; *Pentimento*, in 1974, was developed into the film *Julia* three years later. Her earlier memoir, *An Unfinished Woman*, won the National Book Award. And she won the New York Drama Critics Circle Award for *Watch on the Rhine* and *Toys in the Attic.*

CHAPTER THIRTEEN

ACTORS AND ACTRESSES

"Many highly talented performers who got their professional start on the Yiddish stage or in the Yiddish-speaking environment, made the transition to Broadway and Hollywood, as well as to radio and later television. Early examples were Paul Muni, Al Jolson, Eddie Kantor (sic), Sophie Tucker, Molly Picon and Fanny Brice. Those were followed by screen greats like Edward G. Robinson, Danny Kaye, Lauren Bacall, Shelley Winters, Esther Williams, Johnny Weissmuller, Kirk Douglas, the Marx Brothers, Jerry Lewis, Zero Mostel, Walter Matthau, and Mel Brooks in the US, and Claire Bloom and Peter Sellers in England."

The Shengold Jewish Encyclopedia, 2001

LORNE GREENE (1915-1987) began his career as a newscaster on the Canadian Broadcasting Corporation, but was best known as the kindly patriarch on the television series *Bonanza*.

Greene was born in Ottawa. He went from Queen's University, in Kingston, Ontario to the radio broadcast booth where his deep expressive voice and delivery won him an immense national audience across Canada.

He began to act with the Neighborhood Playhouse in New York but journeyed to Hollywood—not to act, but to market a stopwatch he had developed.

His career bounded forward when he won the part of Ben Cartwright on the weekly TV show *Bonanza*. The show was a tremendous success and remained in production for a remarkable 13 seasons. At its peak, the show was watched by an estimated 400,000,000 people in 83 countries.

Lorne Greene felt *Bonanza* was well received because "our show is about love. It's about people who love and respect each other."

Lorne Greene is best known as Ben Cartwright on Bonanza.

Ruth Gordon's career on stage, in the movies, and on television spanned 70 years! Here she stars as Maude in *Harold and Maude*.

RUTH GORDON (1896-1985) performed on both the Broadway and London stages and her career spanned some 70 years.

Ruth Gordon Jones was 19 when she made her Broadway stage debut—appearing as one of the lost boys in *Peter Pan*. She caught the attention of critic Alexander Woolcott who noted, approvingly, "Ruth Gordon was ever so gay as Nibs."

Thornton Wilder wrote the part of Dolly Gallagher Levi in *The Matchmaker* especially for her.

She received an Academy Award for her performance in *Rosemary's Baby* in 1968, and an Emmy in 1979 for an appearance in *Taxi*.

Michael Douglas is a popular actor and producer.

MICHAEL DOUGLAS (1944-   ) is a powerhouse in Hollywood in the dual role of actor and producer. He is the eldest son of the legendary actor Kirk Douglas (1916-).

Michael Douglas was born in New Brunswick, New Jersey, and turned to acting reluctantly. Kirk, after seeing his son in a production of *As You Like It*, commented "Michael was terrible."

However, he was outstanding in *Romancing The Stone*, (1984); *Jewel of the Nile*, (1985); and *Fatal Attraction*, (1987). With Hollywood stardom established, he became a producer.

Kirk Douglas was called the "dimpled-chin he-man of the American screen." He was featured frequently as an anti-hero in such movies as *Champion* in 1949, *Ace in the Hole* in 1951, and *The Bad and the Beautiful*, 1952.

He played more sensitive roles in such films as *Paths of Glory*, in 1957 and *Lust for Life*, 1955, in which he played the part of artist Vincent Van Gogh.

Any Jewish actor or actress hoping to be built up as a star had to be processed and turned into an all-American boy or girl before they could be exposed to the public. Marian Levee had to become Paulette Goddard; Bernard Schwartz had to become Tony Curtis; Judith Tuvim, Judy Holliday; Danny Kaminsky, Danny Kaye; Joseph Levitch, Jerry Lewis; Shirley Schrift, Shelley Winters.

Chaim Bermant, *The Jews*, 1977

Michael's father, Kirk Douglas, in his heyday.

Goldie Hawn as Private Benjamin.

GOLDIE HAWN (1945-   ) laughed her way to stardom playing the dizzy blonde on Rowan and Martin's *Laugh-in*.

She began her career as a go-go dancer in nightclubs. Her giggling in a first movie drew the attention of the producers of *Laugh-in* and a legend was born. "I've been a giggler since I was three years old," she told an interviewer. In fact, to get attention, she doffed all her clothes as a child.

She won an Academy Award for her first major film *Cactus Flower* (1969) and made a big hit with her performances in *Private Benjamin* and *The First Wives Club*.

—————

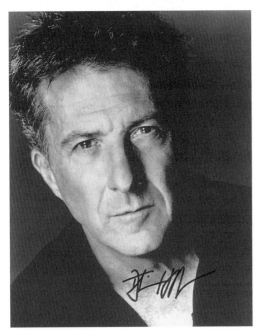

Dustin Hoffman is known as the actors' actor.

DUSTIN HOFFMAN (1937-   ), whose father was a prop man at Columbia Studios, is known as the Actor's Actor because of his versatility.

Hoffman has been nominated seven times for Academy Awards and has won two—in 1979 for *Kramer vs. Kramer* and in 1988 for *Rain Man*.

At first, he wanted to be a pianist. But a professor at Santa Monica City College suggested his talents lay elsewhere.

He signed up for the Actors Studio in New York and shared an apartment with fellow student Gene Hackman. Finding work is often difficult for an actor, and Hoffman worked at a variety of jobs—ranging from weaving Hawaiian leis to working as an attendant in a hospital psychiatric ward.

His big break came when director Mike Nichols spotted him acting off-Broadway.

His first movie was *The Graduate*, in which he convincingly played the part of a university undergraduate in his early 20s; he was 31. He was nominated for an Academy Award and attained instant star status.

Since then he has played a rich variety of character roles. His perfectionism is legendary in the business. Arthur Penn, who directed him in *Little Big Man* stated: "everything involves his total attention."

Actor Sir Laurence Olivier commented on Hoffman's perfectionism: "Dustin is very talented—but why doesn't he just act?"

PAUL MUNI's (1895-1967) real name was Mehilem Weisenfruend and he was virtually born into Yiddish theatre.

He was born in Lemberg, Austria, and his parents were both Yiddish entertainers.

The family moved to America in 1901 and Muni's first stage appearance came seven years later when—aged 13—he was called upon to replace an old actor in the play *Two Corpses at Breakfast*. He did well and began playing elderly men in Yiddish plays.

Muni switched to the cinema in 1926 when he was hired to replace Edward G. Robinson in *We Americans*. He used his new name for the first time, in 1929, appearing in *The Valiant*. That performance won him an Oscar nomination.

He became a full-fledged star acting in *Scarface* in 1932.

Muni won an Academy Award for *The Story of Louis Pasteur*.

In all, Paul Muni appeared in 23 movies and in 12 Broadway plays.

Paul Muni was the son of Yiddish entertainers.

GENE WILDER (1935-   ), known as a madcap actor, is also a scriptwriter, director, and producer.

Jerome Silberman was born in Milwaukee, Wisconsin. His mother became an invalid when Wilder was only six, and he started performing to cheer her up.

He made his first stage appearance in 1947, age 13, at the Milwaukee Playhouse. He acted in student plays at the University of Iowa and earned small amounts appearing in summer stock.

Intent on an acting career, he attended the Old Vic Theatre School in Bristol, England.

After a stint in the army, he became a member of the Actors Studio and beginning in 1961 worked with Lee Strasberg. That same year, he made his Broadway debut—acting as the confused valet in Graham Greene's comedy *The Complaisant Lover*. His performance won him the Clarence Derwent Award.

Wilder moved from Broadway to Hollywood in 1967 and began to work with the multitalented Mel Brooks. He appeared as the bewildered accountant in Brooks' first movie *The Producers* working opposite Zero Mostel.

Gene Wilder is actor, script-writer, director, and producer.

Peter Lorre often played the villain in movies.

Since then the actor has appeared in many movies including two other Brooks' productions: *Blazing Saddles* and *Young Frankenstein*.

Gene Wilder remains a popular movie and television actor, but he has steadily widened his reach—writing, directing, and producing.

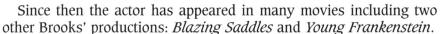

PETER LORRE (1904-1964) played the villain in many of his pictures. A star in the *Maltese Falcon* and *Casablanca*, he studied psychiatry under both Sigmund Freud and Alfred Adler.

Although he appeared in a number of films, he starred in only one: *M* in 1931. That was his first film. In that production, he played a demented child-murderer. In the *Maltese Falcon* he played a crazed hitman. His final appearance on screen was in *The Patsy*, in 1964, winding up a 33-year career.

His best-known films were *The Maltese Falcon*, *Casablanca*, and *Mr. Moto*.

Ed Asner played the tough desk editor on TV.

ED ASNER (1929-   ), the hardboiled editor on television's *The Mary Tyler Moore Show* and *Lou Grant* was the son of a scrap iron dealer.

Asner was born in Kansas City, Missouri, and was raised as an Orthodox Jew. To pay for his university education, he drove a taxicab, sold books door-to-door, and picked up part-time jobs where he could.

He began to act while attending the University of Chicago, and was drafted into the army for a four year stint.

The Playwright Theater Club of Chicago invited him back to the Windy City in 1955 and from there he turned to Broadway.

However, Asner did not become well-known until he moved to Hollywood and was cast as the short-tempered news editor, Lou Grant, in *The Mary Tyler Moore Show*. He won three Emmys. And when, after eight seasons (1970-1977), the show came to the end of its long run, Asner was given his own *Lou Grant Show*.

He used his own show to make numerous statements about what he felt was wrong in the society of the day. In 1979, he told an interviewer:

"With the exception of *Lou Grant, Family,* and *Little House on the Prairie*, no fully-developed human beings exist (at this time) on television."

RICHARD DREYFUSS (1947-   ) started his acting career in Hebrew school plays and is an Oscar winner.

Born in Flatbush, Brooklyn, he began to act after his family (almost flat broke) drove to California. Dreyfuss appeared professionally at the Gallery Theatre in Los Angeles. As a conscientious objector, he dropped out of college for two years and worked as a file clerk.

His career was slow in taking off. He appeared in minor roles in television and movies, and even on Broadway.

His big break came when he took the part of Bill Walker in George Bernard Shaw's *Major Barbara*. He was offered the part of Curt Henderson in *American Graffiti* in 1973.

His later movies included *The Apprenticeship of Duddy Kravitz* in 1974, and *Jaws* in 1975.

He won a Golden Globe and an Academy Award, as best actor, in *The Goodbye Girl*—both in 1978. In that year, he starred in Steven Spielberg's science-fiction hit *Close Encounters of the Third Kind*.

Richard Dreyfuss' long acting career began in Hebrew school.

WALTER MATTHAU (1920-2000) won an Oscar nomination for his performance in *The Sunshine Boys*; he got his start acting in Yiddish plays.

Walter was born in New York. His real name was Walter Matuschanskayasky. His father abandoned the family when Walter was three, and his mother—with two little boys to support—became a sewing machine operator in a sweatshop.

Matthau lived in poverty and the family often had to move because they couldn't afford to pay the rent.

Nevertheless, Walter became fascinated by the plays of Shakespeare, and at age seven decided he would become an actor and a writer. When he was eleven, Matthau was hired to sell soft drinks at a Yiddish theatre and he began to get small parts in the plays. (The job paid 50 cents a performance.) After high school, where he did some acting, Matthau worked at odd jobs to survive. He scrubbed

Walter Matthau started his acting career in the Yiddish theater.

floors, trained boxers and was a file clerk for a time. He enlisted in the US Army Air Force during World War Two, serving from 1942 until 1945.

He was a radio operator and gunner, and by war's end had earned six battle stars.

On the G.I. Bill of Rights, he enrolled in the New School's Dramatic Workshop. Fellow students at the time included Rod Steiger and Tony Curtis.

Walter Matthau had a tough time getting parts. He was tall and lanky, hunched over and hardly handsome. But he began to be noticed, and his big break came when playwright Neil Simon approached him at a cocktail party and said: "You're going to be in my next play!" "Who are you?" responded Matthau.

The play was *The Odd Couple*, and Walter played sportswriter Oscar Madison—and won a Tony Award.

Matthau referred to himself, on one occasion, as "a Ukrainian Cary Grant." Neil Simon described him as "the greatest instinctive actor I've ever seen."

HENRY WINKLER's (1945-   ) greatest success was playing "Fonzie," in the television series *Happy Days*.

Winkler's father was in the lumber business in New York (the family had fled Germany before World War Two), and he wanted Henry to follow in his footsteps. But young Winkler had other ideas. He majored in drama at Emerson College in Boston, and then earned a master's degree at *Yale University's School of Drama*.

For three years, he found parts only in TV commercials. He plugged frozen pizzas and toothpaste, but accepted that the experience was part of the learning process.

He and another newcomer, Sylvester Stallone, appeared in the movie *The Lords of Flatbush*.

Nervously he faced an audition for the part of a brash biker on a new sitcom *Happy Days*. The next day—on his 28th birthday—he was hired to play Arthur Fonzarelli—the "Fonze". The producers had planned Fonzarelli as a minor role, but with his outstanding characterization of a drop-out biker (he never learned to ride a motorcycle) relating to lead Ron Howard, *Happy Days* became the most watched show on TV. And Winkler was nominated three years in a row for an Emmy as lead actor.

Henry Winkler's career peaked when he played Fonzie on TV's Happy Days.

Since those heady days, he has worked as a director and producer as well as an actor.

In 1996, the French government awarded him its highest honor, Chevalier de l'Ordre des Arts et Lettres, for his work on behalf of children.

———

TONY RANDALL (1920-   ) has been an outstanding performer for more than four decades on radio, in movies, on television and on stage.

The role that won him the greatest acclaim was as the clean-crazy "Felix" in *The Odd Couple*.

He was born in Tulsa, Oklahoma, and at 19 was learning drama under the expert guidance of Sanford Meisner.

He started his acting career with radio performances but got his big break, after serving in World War Two, playing Harvey Weskit on the *Mr. Peepers* TV show (1953-1955). In between *The Odd Couple* and *Mr. Peepers* he performed in the movies, in television, and on stage.

He is a man of firm opinions—and expresses them. "I love classical music with the same passion with which I despise rock 'n' roll."

Tony Randall's most celebrated role was as Felix in *the Odd Couple*.

———

LAUREN BACALL (1924-   ) won Tony Awards for her performances in the Broadway musicals *Applause* in 1970 and *Woman of the Year* in 1981, and she has had a long and outstanding film career.

Her real name is Betty Perske, and she is a cousin to former Israeli Prime Minister Shimon Peres, whose original name is also Perske.

While studying at the American Academy of Dramatic Arts, in New York, she had a crush on fellow student Kirk Douglas.

Her first starring role was at age 20, when she appeared in *To Have And Have Not*, opposite Humphrey Bogart. (She married him the next year and remained devoted to him until his death in 1957.) She was offered that role because she, working as a model, was on the cover of *Harper's Bazaar*. Director Howard Hawks, shown the magazine by his wife, recognized that this was the girl he wanted for *To Have And Have Not*.

Hawks, after telling Bogart he was "the most insolent man in Hollywood" warned the actor he was going to perform with a woman who was "even more insolent." Director Hawks sent Bacall to a voice coach to produce the throaty tones by which she became known.

Lauren Bacall won two Tonys on Broadway and was a movie star.

(I am) just a nice Jewish girl from New York. Going back through my life now, the Jewish family feeling stands proud and strong, and at least I can say I am glad I sprang from that. I would not trade those roots—that identity.

Lauren Bacall in her memoirs, 1979

Bacall appeared opposite Bogart in four outstanding films—*To Have and Have Not* (1944); *The Big Sleep* (1946); *Dark Passage* (1947); and *Key Largo* (1948).

When Bogart died, Lauren Bacall placed a small gold whistle in the urn containing his ashes. On it she had engraved: "If you want anything, just whistle." She spoke this line in *To Have and Have Not*, the first movie she had made with Bogart.

She was nominated for an Academy Award in 1996 for her role as a bitter mother in *The Mirror Has Two Faces*.

In 1999, she appeared with her fellow student of half a century before, Kirk Douglas, in the movie *Diamonds*.

SHELLEY WINTERS (1922-   ) is a highly versatile actress who has won an Academy Award and was nominated for many others.

Shirley Schrift was born in East St. Louis, Illinois, daughter of a fashion designer father and an opera singer mother.

The family moved to New York, and Winters worked as a model to help pay for acting lessons at the New Theater School. She performed in the chorus line at a nightclub, and acted in summer stock.

She was impressive during a performance in the operetta *Rosalinda* in 1942 and was given a contract by Columbia Pictures. She appeared in minor roles in seven films but Columbia did not renew the contract.

Director George Cukor was impressed by her acting ability in a minor film *The Gangster*, and cast her in the part of a frumpish waitress in *A Double Life*. She was nominated for an Oscar.

She received another Oscar nomination for her role as a murder victim in *A Place in the Sun*. She won an Oscar as best supporting actress playing a Dutch housewife in *The Diary of Anne Frank*. She won another Oscar, as supporting actress, in *A Patch of Blue*, in 1965.

Winters has actively supported Israel and has said :

"I think the whole world must be concerned with Israel—this country is the hope of the future. It combines the wisdom of the old and the energy of the young. If Israel goes, the whole free world goes."

Shelley Winters was nominated for several Academy Awards but won only one.

TONY CURTIS (1925-   ) has been one of Hollywood's most enduring stars appearing in such successful films as *The Boston Strangler* and *Some Like it Hot*.

He was born, Bernard Schwartz, in the East Bronx. He managed to win a minor role in a film in 1949. He then played a variety of parts in everything from *Houdini* to *The Defiant Ones*, in which he played a fugitive from a chain gang.

Possibly the film that was closest to home for him was *City Across the River* in which he played a gang member. Recalling problems with bullies in his own youth, he commented: "Where I come from, being good looking was a passport out of a garbage can."

Tony Curtis has played roles in movies for more than half a century.

NATHAN LANE (1956-   ) only became a star after 20 years of performing.

1996 was the magic year for the actor, born Joseph Lane. In that year, he played a leading role in *The Birdcage* and won a Tony for his performance in the revival of the musical *A Funny Thing Happened on the Way to the Forum*. Even greater days lay ahead when he appeared in Broadway in the revival of the smash hit *The Producers*.

EDWARD G. ROBINSON (1893-1973) was Hollywood's most famous movie gangster.

Early in his career, in 1930, he portrayed *Little Caesar*, and that performance launched him on a long run of playing villains.

Charles Higham, in *Celebrity Circus*, described the seventy-eight year old Robinson, only a short time before his death, in these words: "The voice is still Little Caesar's: harsh, stabbing, authoritative. The eyes still have a fierce intensity, the wide frog mouth as tight with determination as ever behind the grizzled Hemingway beard."

His film career lasted some 40 years and he played a realistic death scene in his final film *Soylent Green*—a scene which became all too real a few months later.

The greatest tragedy of his life, in his eyes, came when he was compelled to sell his magnificent collection of art to pay a divorce settlement.

Nathan Lane performed in relative obscurity for 20 years.

Edward G. Robinson was Hollywood's favorite gangster.

Robert Clary was LeBeau in *Hogan's Hereos*.

He had been a major collector of French Impressionist paintings.

"I had put my money," he noted, "my whole life's blood into paintings."

Dealers purchased the paintings for Niarchos, a Greek shipping magnate.

Robinson adds: "He acted very miserably in the whole matter. He wouldn't let me buy back what I wanted when I finally got the money."

ROBERT CLARY (1926-   ) is best known for his role as Corporal Louis LeBeau on *Hogan's Heroes*, which ran on television for seven seasons—1965-1971. He is a Holocaust survivor.

Clary, whose real name is Robert Widerman, was taken—at age 16 with a dozen other members of his family from Paris to concentration camps. He was the only one who survived, and he managed to do so because he could entertain Germans in the camp.

During the day, Clary was a slave laborer in a shoe factory. But, as he worked, he would sing. "Singing was my escape from the suffering."

In 1949, he made it to the United States and appeared on Broadway. Then came his big break: *Hogan's Heroes*, set in a Nazi prisoner of war camp.

At age 76, he considers himself "semi-retired," but he still records a new compact disc of his songs every year. And he is a great-grandfather.

WERNER KLEMPERER (1920-2000) played Colonel Klink in *Hogan's Heroes*, a pompous, bumbling prisoner of war commandant. He was the son of the music director for the Los Angeles Philharmonic, Otto Klemperer.

Werner was born in Germany, but the family fled, to America, in the mid-30s following Hitler's rise to power. After graduation from high school, Werner Klemperer studied at the Pasadena Playhouse. He made his professional debut acting in the play "The Trojan Horse."

He served in the American Army in World War Two; he was a military policeman in the 33rd Infantry.

He played many German roles, in the movies and on television, but his longest run was six years on *Hogan's Heroes*, where each year he was nominated for an Emmy as best supporting actor—and won twice.

Did he feel comfortable playing a Nazi officer? The *Washington Post* quoted Klemperer as saying, about the part:

"He was a little greedy, a little pompous, a little vain and a little insecure. All those things are very much part of our personalities in many ways, so that's what made him fun."

William Shatner forged to stardom as Captain Kirk in Star Trek, but his other roles included T.J. Hooker.

WILLIAM SHATNER (1931-   ) played 100 different roles in his career, but remains fixed in much of the public's mind as Captain James T. (for Tiberius) Kirk, commander of the spaceship USS. Enterprise.

The Montreal-born Shatner studied commerce at McGill University, but left to try his luck as an actor in New York.

He did well in numerous television roles and, at first, his role on *Star Trek*, from 1966 to 1969, appeared to be only a blip on the screen of his career. The series was regarded as a failure, but Shatner kept returning to the Enterprise—for a year as a voice on an animated series and then on a number of *Star Trek* movies. In all, six movies were made.

In addition to the science fiction series, Shatner has starred in a number of other TV series including *Barbary Coast, T.J. Hooker*, and *Rescue 911*.

He has turned to writing, including several successful novels: his TEK series.

Leonard Nimoy's most important role was as Spock in *Star Trek*.

LEONARD NIMOY's (1931-   ) greatest role was "Mr. Spock," part-human and part-Vulcan, on *Star Trek*. The show ran for only three years on television (1966-1969), but is still a popular rerun.

In developing the character, there was a need for a salute, and Nimoy, recalling the use of the division of the four fingers of both hands, in synagogue, to create the Hebrew letter "shin" (representing Shad-dai, the name of God) introduced that as the space crew's salute. "I can call that salute my Vulcan shalom, my greeting of peace, my yearning for the blessing of peace—the age-old quest of the Jewish people, my people."

Nimoy had been only a minor player until Mr. Spock came along. After that he was a superstar. In addition to the TV series, he played the part in six *Star Trek* movies and directed the fourth production.

He then widened his role to include involvement as a director and writer.

CHAPTER FOURTEEN

AUTHORS

"Nobel Laureate Saul Bellow, Bernard Malamud, and Philip Roth scorned the materialism and sterile ethnicity of their elders but also found American society wanting. The critical acclaim these writers received reflected the discontent shared by intellectuals in general. The themes of alienation and the anti-hero were depicted through Jewish characters and circumstances, but they struck a universal chord."
Harvard Encylopedia of American Ethnic Groups, 1970

Isaac Asimov wrote nearly 500 books – most of them science fiction.

ISAAC ASIMOV (1920-1992) was the most popular writer on science in America. He authored nearly 500 books.

Asimov was born in Petrovichi, Russia, and the family moved to the United States in 1923; he was three years old. He taught himself to read both English and Yiddish, and graduated from Brooklyn Boys High School at age 15.

He studied chemistry at Columbia University and graduated at 19. After service in the armed forces in World War Two, he completed his education (Ph.D., Columbia, 1943). He then taught until 1958 when he took up writing full-time.

He is best remembered for his imaginative science fiction, based on a wide knowledge of science and an ability to fascinate the reader.

After early, successful sales of stories to magazines, he began writing books. One of the best known is *I, Robot*, in which he presented "three laws of robotics—-robots must not harm humans, must obey the law and, unless it was in conflict with laws one and two, protect their own existence."

His *Foundation* trilogy earned him the first of five Hugos.

When he had achieved great success, Asimov proudly showed off one of his books to his father. "How did you learn all this?" he asked his son. "From you, poppa," came the reply. "But I know nothing of these matters" "You didn't have to, Poppa. You valued learning, and you taught me to value it. All the rest came without trouble."

It is change, continuing change, inevitable change, that is the dominant factor in society today. No sensible decision can be made any longer without taking into account not only the world as it is, but the world as it will be."
Isaac Asimov, article in
The Encyclopedia of Science Fiction,
1978

———

SAUL BELLOW (1915-   ), son of Russian immigrant parents, won the 1976 Nobel Prize for his novels. His name was Solomon Bellows, but he dropped the "s" from Bellows and switched from Solomon to Saul.

Bellow was born in the Montreal suburb of Lachine but spent much of his childhood living in the Jewish district of the City, "The Main."

He acquired four languages as he grew up: English, Yiddish, French, and Hebrew.

The family moved to Chicago and Bellow studied anthropology and sociology at the University of Chicago and Northwestern.

He served in the US merchant marine during World War Two, and then wrote his first novel *The Dangling Man* (1944).

His most famous novels are *The Adventures of Augie March* (1953) and *Herzog* (1964).

Bellow received the National Book Award three times, won the International Literary Prize in 1965, France's "Croix de Chevalier des Arts et Lettres" in 1968, and he received the Nobel Prize in Literature in 1976 "for the human understanding and subtle analysis of contemporary culture that are combined in his work."

The author is amused when he is referred to as an American Jewish novelist. "The concept of my being an American Jewish novelist is accurate only insofar as it is true that I am an American and a Jew and a writer."

On the world today, Bellow comments: "Our society like decadent Rome, has turned into an amusement society, with writers chief among the court jesters."

Saul Bellow won a Nobel Prize for his fiction.

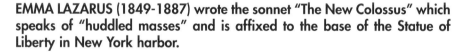

EMMA LAZARUS (1849-1887) wrote the sonnet "The New Colossus" which speaks of "huddled masses" and is affixed to the base of the Statue of Liberty in New York harbor.

Lazarus was the daughter of a wealthy sugar refiner. Her essays and poems had drawn favorable attention from Walt Whitman and Ralph Waldo Emerson. She also translated medieval Spanish-Jewish and German poems. But she is remembered most for these immortal lines:

"Not like the brazen giant of Greek fame, With conquering limbs astride from land to land; A mighty woman with a torch, whose flame Is imprisoned lightning, and her name Mother of Exiles. From her beacon-hand Glows world-wide welcome; her mild eyes command The air-bridged harbor that twin cities frame.

'Keep ancient lands, your storied pomp,' cries she with silent lips. 'Give me your tired, your poor, Your huddled masses yearning to breathe free, The wretched refuse of your teeming shore, Send these, the homeless tempest-tot, to me; I lift my lamp beside the golden door!'"

Lazarus' historic sonnet was lost for years and recovered from the pages of a book in a shop (University of Virginia Library).

In 1883, the campaign to pay for the pedestal for the Statue of Liberty was not going well. Constance Cary Harrison approached a number of prominent artists and writers to donate examples of their work to be auctioned off.

Walt Whitman, Mark Twain and Bret Harte all had made contributions. But Emma Lazarus said she "could not possibly write verses to order." Harrison responded: "Think of the Goddess of Liberty standing on her pedestal yonder in the bay and holding the torch out to those refugees you are so fond of visiting at Ward's Island."

Two days later, Lazarus turned in her poem; it was auctioned off for $1,500—and then forgotten.

President Grover Cleveland dedicated the Statue on October 28, 1886, with the sculptor, Frederic-Auguste, among the honored guests. Emma Lazarus had not been invited and died the following year. She was only 38 years old.

In 1903, New York artist Georgiana Schuyler found the poem portfolio in a bookshop. She was so moved by the words that she asked for and received permission to have the lines engraved on a bronze plaque and affixed to the base of the statue.

In 1883, that same year, Lazarus had written "Exodus," recalling her ancestors' expulsion from Spain in 1492:

"The Spanish noon is a blaze of azure fire, and the dusty pilgrims crawl like an endless serpent along treeless plains and bleached highroads, through rock-split ravines and castellated, cathedral-shadowed towns.

"The hoary patriarch, wrinkled as an almond shell, bows painfully upon his staff. The beautiful young mother, ivory pale, wellnigh swoons beneath her burden; in her large enfolding arms nestles her sleeping babe, round her knees flock her little ones with bruised and bleeding feet. 'Mother, shall we soon be there?'

"The halt, the blind, are amid the train. Sturdy pack-horses laboriously drag the tented wagons wherein lie the sick athirst with fever.

"The panting mules are urged forward by spur and goad; stuffed are the heavy saddle-bags with the wreckage of ruined homes.

"Hark to the tinkling silver bells that adorn the tenderly carried silken scrolls.

"Noble and abject, learned and simple, illustrious and obscure, plod side by side, all brothers now, all merged in one routed army of misfortune.

"Woe to the straggler who falls by the wayside! No friend shall close his eyes.

"They leave behind the grape, the olive, and the fig; the vines they planted, the corn they sowed, the garden-cities of Andalusia and Aragon, Estramadura and La Mancha, of Granada and Castile; the altar, the hearth, and the grave of their fathers.

"The townsmen spits at their garments, the shepherd quits his flock, the peasant his plow, to pelt with curses and stones; the villagers sets on their trail his yelping cur.

"Oh, the weary march ! oh, the uptorn roots of home ! oh, the blankness of the receding goal !

"Listen to their lamentations. *They that ate dainty food are desolate in the streets; they that were reared in scarlet embrace dunghills. They flee away and wander about. Men say among the nations, They shall no more sojourn there; our end is near, our days are full, our doom is come. (Lam. 4. 5, 15, 18)*

"Whither shall they turn? for the West hath cast them out, and the East refuseth to receive."

——

EDNA FERBER (1885-1968) won the 1925 Pulitzer Prize for *So Big*.

Ferber was born in Kalamazoo, Michigan, and was one of the most popular women writers of the 20th century. Most of her plays were written in collaboration with George S. Kaufman.

They often worked together in Ferber's suite in the Algonquin Hotel, where—on one occasion— a hotel clerk, concerned about possible impropriety called about midnight to ask, "I beg your pardon, Miss Ferber, but is there a gentleman in your room?"

"I don't know," Ferber responded, "wait a minute and I'll ask him."

Edna Ferber wanted to be an actress but her father began to go blind and her mother had to work in the family store.

Edna went to work for local newspapers. When she couldn't find a publisher for her first novel *Dawn O'Hara*, she threw the manuscript into the garbage can.

Her mother quietly retrieved it and sent it to a publisher. It was published in 1911 and sold more than 10,000 copies. Edna started writing and selling short stories, and then returned to novels.

Her third novel *So Big*, published in 1924, sold more than 300,000 copies and twice was made into moving pictures.

Edna Ferber as a young woman. (State Historical Society of Wisconsin Visual Archives, Negative No. WHI (x3) 11476

Joseph Heller's Catch-22 is regarded as one of the major novels of the 20th century.

She wrote *Show Boat* in 1926 (which Jerome Kern and Oscar Hammerstein turned into a well-received Broadway show), *Cimmaron* in 1930, *Saratoga Trunk* in 1941, and *Giant* in 1952. All were produced as movies.

Her best known plays—both written with Kaufman—were *Dinner at Eight*, 1932, and *Stage Door*, 1936.

JOSEPH HELLER's (1923-1999) *Catch-22* was one of the major novels of the 20th century.

More than 10,000,000 English copies of the book were sold in the United States and many more were sold in other languages.

Catch-22, which has entered the language to describe an impossibly frustrating situation, tells the story of a flyer who wanted to be grounded because he was insane, only to be told that he had to be sane to want to be taken out of combat.

Heller served in the US Army Air Corps from 1942, and flew 60 combat missions as a bombardier. But his actual experiences apparently had nothing to do with his fictional situation.

At first, Heller was going to call his novel Catch-18, but discovered that Leon Uris had a book about to appear on the bookshelves entitled *Mila 18*.

Franz Kafka's best known works were published after his death.

FRANZ KAFKA (1883-1924) was one of the most important writers of the 20th century.

Kafka was a tortured spirit. During the day, he worked as a clerk for The Workers' Accident Insurance Institute of Prague, and at night he struggled to write, despite harassment by an intrusive family.

He penned five incomplete novels and considered himself such a failure that he asked a friend to burn his manuscripts. The friend, Max Brod, refused.

His best-known novels were published, in Germany, between 1925 and 1927, shortly after the author's death from tuberculosis.

The Nazis banned his books, but translations appeared quickly in several countries.

His best known novels are *The Trial, The Castle*, and *Amerika*.

BERNARD MALAMUD (1914-1986) won the 1967 Pulitzer Prize for The Fixer.

Malamud was both a writer and an educator, and, unlike many of his contempories, continued to teach after he had achieved success with his short stories and novels.

He taught at Oregon State University (1949-1961) and at Bennington State College (1961-1986).

The Fixer won him a National Book Award in addition to the Nobel Prize. He also won a National Book Award for his short story collection *The Magic Barrel* in 1958, and a Gold Medal in Fiction by the American Academy and the Institute of Arts and Letters, 1983.

Bernard Malamud won the Pulitzer Prize for *The Fixer*.

DOROTHY (ROTHSCHILD) PARKER (1893-1967) was one of the most influential women writers of the 20th century. She was a poet, a playwright, critic, and short story writer.

The United States, in its first 200 years, is said to have produced six great humorists; Dorothy Parker was the only woman amongst them.

She became widely known through her writing for the *New Yorker* Magazine, four books of poetry (*Enough Rope*, 1926; *Sunset Gun* 1928; *Death and Taxes*, 1931; *Not Deep as a Well*, 1936) and a small number of finely-crafted short stories. She won the O. Henry Prize for her short story "Big Blonde".

She claimed that the only thing she learned in school was "if you spit on a pencil eraser, you can erase ink."

In school, she wandered about whispering "a girl's best friend is her mutter."

In the early days of the *New Yorker*, when money was tight, publisher Harold Ross was startled to find her in a bar. " Why aren't you at work?," he asked. "Someone was using the pencil," she replied.

Dorothy Parker was a wit and one of the most prominent women writers of the 20th century. Here she is in her younger days.

For the American public, she became widely known for her wit as a member of the Algonquin Round Table, a daily luncheon at the Hotel of that name where writers, playwrights, poets, and artists congregated (usually less than a dozen) to be seen and heard.

Other Jewish regulars at the Round Table group included playwright George S. Kaufman, New Yorker publisher Harold Ross, author Edna Ferber, columnist Franklin Pierce Adams, and actress Ruth Gordon.

Newspaper columnists had a field day quoting the remarks of Round Table participants, but no one had a more telling impact than Parker.

One of her most famous remarks: "Men don't make passes, at girls who wear glasses." Parker was near-sighted but rarely donned her horn-rimmed spectacles in public.

When she had enough funds, she ordered her soaps and perfumes from Cyclax of London—always the tuberose scent, which undertakers use on corpses. For a time, she subscribed to an undertakers' magazine and posted some of its articles on the wall by her desk.

On her death in 1967 (aged 73), longtime *New Yorker* editor William Shawn, told the *New York Times*:

"The humorist's personal and literary style had an influence on the character of the twenties—at least that nonserious, unsolemn, sophisticated literary circle she was an important part of in New York City."

Parker's maiden name was Rothschild, but she kept the name of her first husband. Her final marriages were to Alan Campbell (she married him twice), and they worked as a writing team in Hollywood.

Her last published poem *War Song* was published in 1944, and was her personal favorite:

"Soldier, in a curious land All across a swaying sea, Take her smile and lift her hand—Have no guilt of me.

Soldier, when were soldiers true?
If she's kind and sweet and gay,
Use the wish I send to you—-
Lie not alone until day.
Only, for the nights that were,
Soldier, and the dawns that came,
When in sleep you turn to her
Call her by my name."

She had suggested the wording on her gravestone should read: 'excuse my dust'."

JEROME WEIDMAN's (1913-1998) first novel was the best selling *I Can Get It For You Wholesale.*

He grew up in an immigrant Jewish neighborhood on the Lower East Side of Manhattan and sold short stories to magazines before his first novel became a best-seller in 1937.

After penning 22 novels, he worked with George Abbott on the Pulitzer Prize-winning book for the musical *Fiorello!* in 1959, and the book for the musical *Tenderloin* in 1960.

His other ventures on Broadway included the musical adaptation of his *I Can Get It For You Wholesale* in 1962 and, in 1969, a play, *The Mother Lover.*

S. J. PERELMAN (1904-1979) was one of America's greatest humorists.

He was born in Brooklyn, but as a child the family moved to Providence, Rhode Island, where his father worked spasmodically, but not successfully, as a machinist, a dry goods storekeeper and a farmer.

While attending Brown University (he never graduated; he was short one credit, but Brown hastened to give him an honorary degree when he became a best-selling author), he tried his hand at cartooning, but he put more humor into the captions than the drawings.

After writing for humor magazines, he began writing satirical pieces for the *New Yorker* and he was a regular contributor to what has been called "the best magazine in the world" for more than 30 years.

His first book, *Ginsbergh's Revenge*, was published without his name on the title page. He was so excited that, when correcting the galleys, he never noticed his name was not there.

He had a tremendous command of the English language. A display of his original manuscript *Swiss Family Perelman*, in the New York Public Library, showed text from a portable typewriter virtually free of pencilled changes.

His screenplay for *Around the World in 80 Days* won him an Oscar.

New Yorker editor William Shawn commented on Perelman: "He was one of the world's funniest writers."

Sample: "A farm is an irregular patch of nettles bounded by short-term notes, containing a fool and his wife who didn't know enough to stay in the city." or "I've got Bright's disease and he's got mine."

S.J. Perelman was one of America's greatest humorists.

Isaac Bashevis Singer wrote his stories, originally, in Yiddish.

Ayn Rand has become a cult figure for her right-wing philosophy.

Perelman's description of himself:

"Under a forehead roughly comparable to that of Javanese and Piltdown Man are visible a pair of tiny pig eyes, lit up alternatively by greed and concupiscence."

Otherwise, he wrote: "before they made S.J. Perelman, they broke the mold."

ISAAC BASHEVIS SINGER (1904-1991) won the 1978 Nobel Prize for Literature.

Born in Poland, this Yiddish story-teller arrived in New York City in 1935. He devoted his entire life to telling stories of life as it was in the Jewish shtetls of Eastern Europe before World War Two, and particularly before Adolf Hitler and the Nazis, destroyed it.

His *A Crown of Feathers* won the Nobel Prize for literature in 1978. The Nobel citation read "for his impassioned narrative art which, with roots in a Polish-Jewish cultural tradition, brings universal human conditions to life."

In accepting his Prize, he said of Yiddish, it is a "language of exile without a land, without frontiers, not supported by any government, a language which possesses no words for weapons, ammunition, military exercises, war tactics."

Many of his stories were translated into English and widely read, and some were adapted for the stage or the movies—most notably *Yentl* in 1983.

He was someone who didn't mince words. When, during an interview, Singer was asked if he became a vegetarian for religious reasons, or for health. "Neither, responded the author. "It was out of consideration for the chicken."

AYN RAND (1905-1982) received worldwide acclaim with publication of *The Fountainhead,* in 1943, and 14 years later *Atlas Shrugged* secured her fame.

Born Alice Rosenbaum in St. Petersburg, she changed her name — -taking "Ayn," the name of a Finnish writer she admired, and Rand because she was typing on a Remington-Rand typewriter.

Her hatred of the left came from seeing Russian soldiers, during the Revolution, bursting into her father's chemist shop—seizing it in the name of the people. She later stated:

"That's the principle of communism. They were saying that the illiterate and the poor had to be the rulers of the earth, because they were illiterate and poor."

With her books, expounding bitter opposition to government interference into people's lives, she became a cult figure. Even though most reviewers didn't like her books, the public did and Ayn Rand Clubs were organized in the 50s and 60s.

"I'm opposed to mysticism, religion and other departures from reason," she stated.

The funeral home, on her death, was decorated with a six-foot high dollar sign; she had often worn a gold brooch in the shape of a dollar.

Some other outstanding authors:

Stefan Zweig saw his books burned by the Nazis.

STEFAN ZWEIG (1881-1942) was oppressed by the Nazis and saw his books burned.

He fled first to Britain, and then to Brazil, where, overwhelmed by what he had experienced, he committed suicide.

BEN HECHT (1894-1964) is best remembered as co-author of *The Front Page*, but he also was an outstanding screenwriter, a playwright, and novelist.

He was born on New York's Lower East Side, to Russian immigrant parents. His first language was Yiddish.

Hecht attended the University of Wisconsin for three days and then dropped out. The world became his university.

He worked as a journalist. His first novel *Eric Dorn*, was based on his experiences in Berlin, 1918-1920. He collaborated with Charles MacArthur on *The Front Page*, a great success as a play. And it was twice made into films.

Ben Hecht was an award-winning writer of screenplays.

He was one of Hollywood's greatest screenwriters—the first script writer to earn $1,000 a day. His scripts for *Underworld*, 1927, and *Scarface*. 1932, established him as a master of the gangster film.

Underworld won him an Oscar. He worked on 150 films and penned eight novels.

NORMAN MAILER (1923-   ) won the Pulitzer Prize for non-fiction.

Born in Long Branch, New Jersey, Mailer grew up in Brooklyn. He enrolled in Harvard University in 1939—aged 16—and published his first story two years later.

He graduated from Harvard, in 1943, with a degree in aeronautical engineering.

Mailer was drafted into the US Army in 1944 and served in the Philippines until 1946. He enrolled in the Sorbonne in Paris immediately after writing *The Naked and the Dead*, in 1948. It is regarded as one of the finest World War Two novels.

He won the Pulitzer Prize and the National Book Award for *Armies of the Night*, describing the Washington peace rallies of 1968, in which he participated. He was sent to jail in 1967 for taking part in anti-Vietnam War demonstrations.

In addition to his books, Mailer has written, directed, and acted in a number of motion pictures.

BORIS PASTERNAK (1890-1960), author of *Dr. Zhivago*, twice refused the Nobel Prize for Literature.

Pasternak was the son of a painter and a pianist. He grew up in Moscow and became a major Russian poet (Some speak of him as the leading Russian poet and even the leading world poet) as well as a novelist. But to get his *Dr. Zhivago* published, he had to have it smuggled out of the Soviet Union.

In 1958, he was awarded the Nobel Prize for Literature, but was pressured into refusing it. His book remained banned in the USSR, but in the West it became a best-seller and a classic, and was made into a film.

Boris Pasternak was offered the Nobel Prize for his *Dr. Zhivago*, but had to turn it down.

163

CHAIM POTOK (1929-2002) wrote *The Chosen*.

He was born in New York City—son of Polish Jewish immigrants.

He left his parents' orthodoxy, affiliating himself with Conservative Judaism; he became a rabbi and, in 1964, editor of *Conservative Judaism*.

He began writing novels in 1967 and his first book was *The Chosen*, focusing on the Hasidic community.

The Promise, published two years later, was a sequel to *The Chosen*.

Chaim Potok wrote *The Chosen*.

HAROLD ROBBINS (1916-1997) was one of the best-selling authors of all time.

He published more than 20 books, with sales of more than 50,000,000 copies! His work was translated into 32 languages.

Harold Robbins (originally Rubin) was born in New York City, son a successful pharmacist. The author has been vague about his past, and stories of his having lived in an orphanage and losing millions (made in deals with sugar) are taken by most with a grain of salt.

Robbins moved to Hollywood, working as a shipping clerk for Universal Studios. But he rose to become an executive in the company.

His book *The Dream Merchants* is about Hollywood, intertwining fiction and fact. Another best-seller was *The Carpetbaggers*, in which the formidable Howard Hughes was easily recognized.

His *A Stone For Danny Fisher* was produced as a musical under the title *King Creole*.

Harold Robbins was one of the best-selling authors of all time.

IRVING STONE's (1903-   ) *Lust for Life* and *The Agony and the Ecstasy* were both made into films.

Irving Stone's *Lust for Life* and *The Agony and the Ecstasy* were made into movies.

Leon Uris was one of America's best-selling authors.

Alvin Toffler, who wrote *Future Shock*. (McGill University Archives)

LEON URIS (1924-2003) was one of America's best-selling authors with such books as *Exodus* and *Topaz*.

Uris was born in Baltimore, Maryland, and dropped out of high school in 1942 to enlist in the United States Marine Corps. During World War Two, he participated in the brutal battles on the islands of Guadalcanal and Tarawa. He was shipped back to the US after he became sick with malaria.

Uris was not a good student. He failed English three times.

Nevertheless, his best-selling *Exodus*, published in 1958, was translated into fifty languages and was made into a film. It was the biggest best-seller in the United States since *Gone With the Wind*. He wrote *Exodus* after covering the 1956 war, in the Middle East, as a newspaper correspondent.

In 1961, after a long journey to Eastern Europe, he wrote *Mila 18*, an historical novel set in the Warsaw Ghetto in 1943, when Jews fought their German oppressors with little more than their bare hands.

Topaz, published in 1967, was rooted in dislosures made to him by an exiled French diplomat who differed with Charles de Gaulle on foreign policy. And *Trinity* (1976) stemmed from material absorbed by Uris during a long stay in Dublin.

In all, the author wrote 19 novels and screenplays.

To me," Uris told the *New York Herald Tribune* in 1959, "a writer is one of the most important soldiers in the fight for the survival of the human race. He must stay at his post in the thick of fire to serve the cause of mankind."

———

ALVIN TOFFLER's (1928-   ) *Future Shock* caused a considerable stir.

In all, Toffler, with his wife and collaborator Heidi Toffler, has written more than a dozen books—all of them best-sellers. The first of these titles was launched in 1970 with the blockbuster *Future Shock*.

FRANZ WERFEL (1890-1945) wrote *The Song of Bernadette.*

Born in Czechoslovakia, Werfel was a poet, a playwright, and a novelist.

Although a pacifist, he served with the Austrian Army on the Russian Front, but he was charged with treason because of his opposition to all wars.

His best-known books include *The Forty Days of Musa Dagh*, written in 1933, to chronicle the clash between the Turks and Armenians, and *The Song of Bernadette* in 1941. Werfel was fleeing the Nazis when he found sanctuary and solace in Lourdes. This is where Bernadette, who was beatified, had visions of the Virgin. Werfel promised to "sing the song" of the saint if he managed to escape to the United States.

He died in California, but he never converted.

NATHANIEL WEST (1904-1940) made his mark in a brief lifespan of 37 years with *Day of the Locust.*

Born in New York City (original name Nathan Weinstein), he attended Brown University where he met and befriended humorist S.J. Perelman. Perelman married West's sister.

Lacking ambition, West wrote one novel and then drifted back to the US from a stay in Paris, and managed a number of small hotels.

His book *Miss Lonelyhearts*, written in 1933 was a critical success but did not sell well. That same year, he moved to Hollywood where he worked as a scriptwriter for small studios.

During this period, he wrote *The Last Tycoon*, ranked as one of the best novels written about Hollywood.

However, while things were looking up for West, he never lived to enjoy the fruits of his labor. He went through a stop sign in El Centro, California, and was fatally injured in a collision.

Mordecai Richler dropped out of university, journeyed to Europe and was increasingly successful in writing about the Montreal he left behind.

Elie Wiesel won the Nobel Prize in 1986 for his promotion of human rights. (Montreal Jewish Public Library Archives)

MORDECAI RICHLER (1931-2001) was a Canadian curmudgeon, snatching the brass ring with his novel *The Apprenticeship of Duddy Kravitz*, and drawing on his experiences growing up in Jewish Montreal in the 40s and 50s.

He dropped out of university, age 19, to try his hand at writing about his roots—but at a distance ... in England and then Spain.

Robert Gottlieb, writing in *Time* magazine (the Canadian edition) after Richler's death, stated "he was both cherished as a literary treasure and resented as a national gadfly."

He was deliberately provocative—offending particularly Quebec separatists (his essays on the topic in the *New Yorker* magazine sold out the publication in Montreal) and his fellow-Jews. The guest speaker at a well-attended meeting of the Montreal Jewish Federation—with two enormous head-tables—he mocked the vanity of those who felt they had to be in privileged seating.

The movie version of *The Apprenticeship of Duddy Kravitz* was filmed in the precise area where Richler had grown up and included scenes shot in Wilensky's cafe—unchanged in the 21st century from the 1930s when the author would down a "special" and leaf through a comic book (2 cents if intact; one penny if the cover had been torn off.)

In all, he wrote ten novels and several children's books. Anthony Wilson-Smith, in *Maclean's* magazine, wrote of the author:

"By the time he died ... he had achieved success on the two fronts that, by any measure, matter most: he was an internationally acclaimed literary figure with 10 novels, three children's books and a vast collection of essays, journalistic reports and polemics behind him—and he had a happy home life with his wife of four decades, Florence, and his three sons and two daughters."

———

ELIE WIESEL (1928-   ) won the Nobel Prize in 1968 for his promotion of human rights.

He was born in Romania, but in 1944—when he was 16—the Nazis deported their entire community to the Auschwitz concentration camp. Both of his parents died in the camp. Wiesel survived and, after the war, studied at the University of Paris and became a journalist.

He began writing books in 1958; his first publication was *Night*, describing his experiences in the concentration camp.

In 1963, he became a citizen of the United States and taught at Boston University.

He served as Chair of the President's Commission on the Holocaust, 1980-1986. In 1985 he received the Congressional Gold Medal. And two years later, he established the Elie Wiesel Foundation for Humanity.

———

Budd Schulberg's *What Makes Sammy Run* established him as a major author.

BUDD SCHULBERG (1914-   ) wrote *What Makes Sammy Run?*, the story of a Hollywood hustler.

Schulberg was inducted into the International Boxing Hall of Fame in 2003.

His father started taking him to boxing matches when he was ten years old and the youngster became fascinated with the ring. He used this knowledge ultimately to write the screenplay for *On The Waterfront*. It won him an Oscar.

CHAPTER FIFTEEN

PHILOSOPHERS AND HISTORIANS

"A people's memory is history; and as a man without a memory, so a people without a history cannot grow wiser, better."

Peretz, *Vegn Geshichte*, 1890

Martin Buber influenced both Christian and Jewish theologians with his commentaries.

MARTIN BUBER (1878-1965) wrote some of the most important religious and philosophical books of all time.

Both Christian and Jewish theologians have been influenced by his commentaries on the relationship between God and man.

Buber was born in Vienna, but when his parents separated he went to live with his grandparents. Displeased at what he felt was the alienation between man and God, he joined the Hasidic movement.

In 1930, he was appointed Professor of religion at Frankfurt University, but the Nazis, on assuming power, drove him out of the country. In 1938, he journeyed to Palestine where he taught at the Hebrew University in Jerusalem. He sought to establish ties between Arabs and Jews.

After many years in Jerusalem, Buber was asked "How well do you speak Hebrew?" "Good enough to lecture in," responded the philosopher, "but not sufficiently good to be obscure."

Buber became the first president of the Israeli Academy of Sciences and Arts. In an interview in *Encounter* magazine, Buber stated:

"The real struggle is not between East and West, or capitalism and communism, but between education and propaganda."

HERBERT MARCUSE (1898-1979) was the philosopher of the student revolt of the 60s.

Born in Berlin, he was educated in German universities and became a Marxist.

He was a member of the "Frankfurt School" of Marxists who emigrated to America when the Nazis seized power in Germany.

While teaching at Brandeis University (1953-1965), he wrote *Eros and Civilization* in 1955. This was followed, in 1964, by his *One-Dimensional Man*, making him a major figure to student protest movements in the United States and Europe.

He was critical of the student revolt in his *Counter-revolution and Revolt*, in 1972, but—by that time—Marcuse was already yesterday's man.

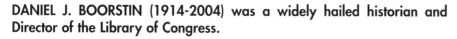

DANIEL J. BOORSTIN (1914-2004) was a widely hailed historian and Director of the Library of Congress.

Herbert Marcuse was an influential Marxist philosopher.

Daniel J. Boorstein is a celebrated historian and author, and onetime Director of the Library of Congress. His best-selling "popular" books included *The Creators* and *The Discoverers*.

He was born in Atlanta, Georgia, but grew up in Oklahoma.

He graduated from Harvard with honors, and attended Oxford as a Rhodes Scholar. His Ph.D. is from Yale.

He taught at the University of Chicago—and then overseas at the University of Rome, the University of Geneva, Cambridge, and at the Sorbonne.

In 1975, he became the 12th Librarian of Congress—a position he held for 12 years.

He is a popular and award-winning author. His trilogy of books on American history—*The Colonial Experience* (Bancroft Prize); *The Democratic Experience* (Pulitzer Prize); and the *National Experience* (Francis Parkman Prize) established him as an outstandingly important chronicler of American history.

His other works include *The Creators* and *The Discoverers*.

Never have people been more the masters of their environment. Yet never has a people felt more deceived and disappointed. For never has a people expected so much more than the world could offer.

Daniel Boorstin, *Image*, 1961

Sir Martin Gilbert is the official biographer of Winston Churchill.

SIR MARTIN GILBERT (1936-   ) is one of the great modern historians and is the official biographer of Winston Churchill.

Gilbert, who has written many histories, including a three-volume history of the 20th century, completed the longest biography in publishing history in 1988. It was the life of Sir Winston Churchill.

The task had originally been undertaken by Churchill's son, Randolph, who completed—with Gilbert—two volumes of a planned eight. The two worked together on the story covering the great British leader's life from 1874 to 1914. Gilbert wrote the next six volumes—7,285 pages—alone. He also organized 6,500 pages of documents in additional volumes.

Martin John Gilbert was born in London. His grandparents had emigrated from Eastern Europe at the turn of the century. He graduated from Oxford with first-class honors and in 1962 he was made a fellow of Oxford's Merton College.

Gilbert has written extensively on Jewish subjects, including the Holocaust.

His publications include numerous historical and ethnographic atlases.

———

BERNARD LEWIS (1916-   ) is the world's leading writer on Islamic history.

Lewis is Professor Emeritus of Near Eastern Studies at Princeton University.

Professor Lewis believes that the clash between Christianity and Islam is rooted in the fact that—unlike Judaism from which both evolved—both claim to provide the only pathway to paradise.

However, he feels that there are enough similarities that "may in time lead to a dialogue."

Lewis has surged to the fore in the early part of the 21st century with enthusiastically-received books, analyzing what has been happening in the Middle East and its consequences for the Western World. While he has spent most of his life studying and teaching about Islam and the history of the Middle East, he did study law for a time "but decided I didn't like it, and returned to study, and later teach, Middle Eastern History. It was a choice I never regretted."

Bernard Lewis is a world-class authority on the history of Islam. (Princeton University)

BARBARA TUCHMAN (1912-1989) received Pulitzer Prizes for *The Guns of August* and *Stilwell and the American Experience in China*.

Tuchman was born in New York City, and was a member of a very distinguished family. Her father, Maurice Wertheim, was a banker, publisher, and philanthropist. Her maternal grandfather was Henry Morgenthau Sr., who served as US Ambassador to Turkey and her uncle, Henry Morgenthau Jr., was Secretary of the US Treasury.

Experiences convinced Barbara Tuchman to become an historian. The first came when she was only two and half. While travelling in the Mediterranean with her family, a British warship, the *Gloucester*, engaged two German naval craft—*Breslau* and *Goeben*. She was too young to remember the encounter, the first naval battle of World War One, but she wrote an entire chapter on the battle in *The Guns of August*.

She was hired by the Nation magazine, became a writer and editor, and was sent to cover the Spanish Civil War for the publication.

Her first truly great book, *The Guns of August*, was not published until she was 50. Four years later, she wrote *The Proud Tower* covering the years and the events leading up to World War One.

Her book on the 14th century, *A Distant Mirror*, was published in 1975. Four years later, she became the first woman president of the American Academy of Arts and Letters.

Ranked as one of America's greatest historians, she once explained "I am a seeker of small facts, not the big explanations; a narrator, not a philosopher."

Barbara Tuchman was a Pulitzer-award winning historian.

WALTER LAQUER (1921-   ) is a prolific author and Director of the Institute of Contemporary History.

Born in Breslau, Germany, the Laquer famly fled Hitler's Germany in 1938, journeying to Palestine where Walter studied at the Hebrew University. He worked briefly on a farm and then, moving to London, he became the founder and editor of *Survey* from 1955 to 1967. Ultimately he settled in Washington as Director of Georgetown University's Center for Strategic and International Studies.

Laquer has been a productive author, writing about the Holocaust, (which he narrowly escaped), Zionism, the Middle East, the confrontation between East and West, and terrorism.

Berlin, with umbrella at the ready, in a university setting.

There exists a great chasm between those, on one side, who relate everything to a single central vision...and, on the other side, those who pursue many ends, often unrelated and even contradictory... The first kind of intellectual and artistic personality belongs to the hedgehogs, the second to the foxes.
Isaiah Berlin, *Hedgehog and Fox*, 1953

Yigael Yadin was a warrior and an award-winning archaelogist.

While churning out a multitude of books, he also found time to teach—at Brandeis, Tel Aviv University, and Georgetown.

SIR ISAIAH BERLIN (1909-1997) was an outstanding authority on the history of ideas.

He was born in Riga, then part of Latvia (now Russia) but was educated in England. His probing mind has shown how modern society has evolved.

He was President of the British Academy from 1974 to 1978, was knighted in 1957, and presented with the Order of Merit in 1979. He was educated at Corpus Christi College, where he spent his entire academic career.

Berlin was involved in conventional philosophical research until, during the Second World War period, he decided to devote the rest of his life to studying the history of ideas.

YIGAEL YADIN (1917-1984) was an immensely important archaeologist, delving deeply into Israel's past with his digs.

Yadin was born in Jerusalem, and at age 16 became active in the defense of the as-yet-unborn Jewish State. It was 1933 and the Arabs were revolting against the British Mandate authority and Jews living in the Holy Land.

He rose to prominence in the Haganah, the Jewish self-defense force. After Israeli dependence was declared, he became the new nation's second Chief of the *Israeli Defence Forces* (IDF). He left the army in 1952 and followed in the footsteps of his father, archaeologist Eliezer Sukenik, studying at the Hebrew University of Jerusalem.

His excavations included Masada, where Jews made their last stand against the Romans in the first century of the first millenium, and Meggido, the so-called Chariot City of the north where many layers of habitation have been uncovered.

He decoded and interpreted several of the Dead Sea Scrolls and, for that, was awarded the Israel Prize in Jewish Studies in 1956.

He broke away from archaeology to enter politics, serving as deputy prime minister during the period from 1977 to 1981.

CHAPTER SIXTEEN

PSYCHOLOGISTS AND PSYCHOANALYSTS

"War was not the sole agent in the demolition of the established European order. Sigmund Freud pioneered scientific psychoanalysis and offered evidence that men are driven principally by unconscious instincts rather than rational calculation. Meanwhile, Albert Einstein demonstrated that space and time are not absolute and universal, as earlier scientific theories had supposed, but in fact varied according to the position of the observer. Both ideas, although apparently technical and specific, undermined popular confidence in a fixed, rational and predictable world."

The Times (of London) Illustrated History of the World, 1986

Sigmund Freud was one of the greatest figures of the 20ᵗʰ century.

SIGMUND FREUD (1856-1939) founded psychoanalysis. He also developed modern theories of psychiatry. Friedrich Heer describes Freud's efforts as "one of the landmarks of the twentieth century."

He once said "the mind is an iceberg—it floats with only one-seventh of its bulk above water."

Freud set out to break through to the other six-sevenths through psychoanalysis. He treated many clients, some of whom became psychoanalysts themselves. During the sessions, Freud would puff away endlessly on cigars—smoking fifteen to twenty a day.

Harassed by anti-Semites in his native Austria when Hitler invaded the country, Freud was made to pay a fine of 250,000 Austrian schillings.

He was forced to leave his native Austria, aged 81. Freud continued to work in London, often in partnership with his daughter Anna.

The psychoanalyst raised questions about religion, but remained Jewish himself and raised his six children as Jews. He wrote his fiancée in 1882, "something of the core, of the essence of this meaningful and life-affirming Judaism will not be absent from our home."

Lawrence Wilson, in *100 Great Events That Changed the World*, wrote:

"Since Freud, we know not only what we do, but approximately why we do it. The consequences have been immense. There is hardly a sphere of modern life which has not been influenced by Freudian thought."

Yale historian Peter Gay noted:

"For good or ill, Sigmund Freud, more than any other explorer of the psyche, has shaped the mind of the 20th century."

Conflicts of interest between man and man are resolved, in principle, by recourse to violence. It is the same in the animal kingdom, from which man can not claim exclusion; nevertheless men are also prone to conflicts of opinion, touching on occasion, the loftiest peaks of abstract thought, which seem to call for settlement by quite another method.
Sigmund Freud in letter to
Albert Einstein, 1932

Alfred Adler identified the inferiority complex.

ALFRED ADLER (1870-1937) was one of the great figures in early modern psychology.

He identified the inferiority complex. Adler was a pupil of Sigmund Freud in his earliest teaching period, but broke away in 1911. He was founder of the school of individual psychology.

He fundamentally disagreed with Freud on the master's emphasis on sex.

Adler felt that man's "main problem" was a struggle to compensate for feelings of inferiority.

To be a human being means to possess a feeling of inferiority which constantly presses towards its own conquest. The paths to victory are as different in a thousand ways as the chosen goals of perfection.

The greater the feeling of inferiority that has been experienced, the more powerful is the urge to conquest and the more violent the emotional agitation.

Alfred Adler, 1933

ANNA FREUD (1895-1982) was a major figure in the development of child psychology.

She was born in Vienna, youngest child of Sigmund Freud. Anna was the only one of his six children to follow in his footsteps.

However Anna Freud had no formal training. She was her father's secretary and obviously, in that position, was privy to extraordinary conversations and analyses.

She became a leading figure in the fields of psychoanalysis, ego psychology, research methodology, and child analysis.

Anna was exposed, at an early age, to experts in all of these fields. At 14, she would sit "on a little library ladder in the corner," at meetings of the Vienna Psychoanalytic Society.

She taught school, rather than plunging into her father's field.

She never married; her world revolved around her famous parent.

The Psychoanalytic Society accepted her as a member in 1922, and in 1923 she started a private practice in Vienna. By 1925, at only 30 years old, she was named chairman of the Society. Through a private school, seminars, lectures, and books, she became a leading figure in the field of child analysis.

She and her father fled to London after the Nazis took over Austria.

Anna Freud with her father in 1913.

Creative minds always have been known to survive any kind of bad training.

Anna Freud

Max Wertheimer founded Gestalt Psychology.

Melanie Klein created play therapy to help children.

The British capital, largely through her efforts, became the center for reestablishment of psychoanalysis in Europe. And she managed to help a number of psychoanalysts to escape from Germany and Austria.

MAX WERTHEIMER (1880-1943) was the founder of Gestalt psychology.

He studied law for several years, but ultimately graduated with a degree in philosophy. He taught at several German universities. But in 1910 he developed an interest in perception after viewing a stroboscope in a toy store.

He studied the scientific principles behind the toy and, with colleagues, developed theories of perception and perceptual grouping, but left the country in 1934 after the Nazis gained control.

In 1906 he had a famous controversy with C.G. Jung about "word association technique." And in the critical four years beginning in 1910, he developed the fundamental ideas of Gestalt theory.

He was professor of psychology at the University of Frankfurt from 1929 until 1933, when the Nazis began to govern Germany. Wertheimer emigrated to the United States by way of Czechoslovakia. He joined the faculty of the New School for Social Research in New York City—the so-called "University in Exile."

MELANIE KLEIN (1882-1960) created "play therapy," introducing ideas which changed the way children were treated by psychologists.

Born in Austria, Klein became interested in psychoanalysis after reading Sigmund Freud's book *On Dreams*. She herself underwent psychoanalysis with one of Freud's followers, Sandor Ferenczi. Ferenczi was impressed by the young woman and encouraged her to undertake analysis of children.

She originated play therapy, whereby very young children could express their feelings.

Klein increasingly differed with Freud in her thinking.

CHAPTER SEVENTEEN

THE ACTIVISTS

"Israel's sages burned with anger over the abuses of the world. The prophets were fanatics in the cause of social justice."
Ernest Renan (1823-1892) French philologist and historian from *History of the People of Israel,* 1887

A woodcut portrait of Karl Marx.

KARL MARX (1818-1883) did not live into the 20th century but his ideas led to the creation of communism, and the world was split in two by the theories he developed.

The twentieth century was many decades old before communism was discredited and the symbol of the movement, the Union of Soviet Socialist Republics, collapsed. However, the deliberate misinterpretation of his theories, adopted by leaders of the communist movement was far from Marx's thinking.

Author Jacques Barzun wrote: "It was surely out of a passionate hatred of injustice that Marx spoke of exploitation."

Marx came from a family of rabbis. Both of his grandfathers had been men of the cloth. In fact, David McLellan, in his *Karl Marx: His Life and Thought* declares "it would be difficult to find anyone who had a more Jewish ancestry than Karl Marx."

Yet his father converted to Christianity, because a Jewish lawyer could not practice in the higher courts. As for Karl Marx, he turned his back on all religions, feeling that organized religion collaborated in the exploitation of the working class. As for his Jewishness, Edmund Wilson commented in *To The Finland Station*:

"Nobody but a Jew could have fought so uncompromisingly and obstinately for the victory of the dispossessed classes."

Karl Marx left, as his legacy, 40 volumes of his writings—launching the concept of communism ... a concept that, for a time, claimed the allegiance of a large proportion of humankind.

He basically summarized his attitude towards society with these famous statements:

"The workers have nothing to lose but their chains. They have a world to gain. Workers of the world, unite." (From his *The Communist Manifesto*.)

"From each according to his abilities, to each according to his needs."

"Religion...is the opium of the people."

"The dictatorship of the proletariat."

As for his impact on the 20th century—even though he never lived to see it, Theodore Zeldin, in *An Intimate History of Humanity* wrote:

"Marx's journey into the sufferings of the working class, and his invitation to revolution, tore the world apart for a hundred years, though it soon became obvious that revolutions are incapable of keeping their promises, however honestly made."

Karl Marx died on March 14, 1883—in his 66th year—and was buried three days later in London's Highgate Cemetary. Less than a dozen people attended the funeral.

"Just as Darwin discovered the law of evolution in organic nature, so Marx discovered the law of evolution in human history."
Friedrich Engels, Funeral oration,
March 17, 1993

BETTY NAOMI FRIEDAN (1921-   ) wrote the best-selling *The Feminine Mystique* (1963) and thereby helped launch the women's liberation movement.

She became the spokesperson for the movement, demanding equal rights for the "weaker sex" across the board.

She was born Betty Naomi Goldstein in Peoria, Illinois ... attended Smith College, receiving a B.A. degree in psychology in 1942. She married Carl Friedan in 1947, a marriage that lasted 22 years.

By 1969, Friedan—divorced—was heading up the National Organization for Women (NOW)—serving as president from 1966 to 1970. She took her campaign on behalf of women's liberation another leap with her book *The Second Stage* in 1981 and an article in the *New York Times Magazine* which Friedan summed up in these words:

"How do we transcend the polarization between women and women, and between women and men, to achieve the new human wholeness that is the promise of feminism and get on with solving the concrete, practical, everyday problems of living, working and loving as equal persons?

"I think that implicit in the women's movement is the idea that women will share in the economic burden, and men will share more equally in the home and the family."

Betty Friedan helped map the campaign for the liberation of women.

Gloria Steinem, one of the major figures in the heightened equality for women.

GLORIA STEINEM (1934-   ), one of the founders of the American feminist movement saw her journalistic career take off after she infiltrated a hutch of Playboy bunnies and wrote an exposé.

Steinem was born in Toledo, Ohio, (her older sister, Susanne, had demanded that her parents provide her with a sister to be named "Gloria" after one of her dolls) graduated from Smith College, magna cum laude (She earned a scholarship; her divorced mother was too financially strapped to help her) and went from doing research and writing articles to co-found *New York* magazine (1968) and, in 1972, she was editor and co-founder of *Ms* magazine.

Joelle Attinger of *Time* magazine called Ms. Steinem "the leading icon of American feminism."

She has had a number of widely-publicized romances, but turned down all marriage proposals.

————

ABBIE HOFFMAN (1936-1989) was a self-styled revolutionary and cofounder of the Youth International Party, or "Yippies".

Abbott Hoffman was born in Worcester, Mass., and was a troublemaker even as a child.

He studied psychology at Brandeis University where he soaked up the radical ideas espoused by Herbert Marcuse. Graduating from the University of California in Berkeley, in 1960, he worked for a time as a salesman for a pharmaceutical company.

But, by 1967, he was intensively involved in the radical movement of that turbulent decade.

He moved to the East Village, in Manhattan, and worked with Jerry Rubin to organize the Youth International Party or "Yippies."

Seeking media exposure, Hoffman organized a variety of stunts. He disrupted activities at the New York Stock Exchange by sprinkling dollar bills over the trading floor. He organized a protest against the Vietnam war by circling the Pentagon with protestors planning, it was claimed, to levitate the building 300 feet off the ground.

He was among those arrested in Chicago in 1968 for allegedly "crossing state lines with intent to riot." The conviction was later overturned.

We must not overlook the important role that extremists play. They are the gadflies that keep society from being too complacent, or too self-satisfied; they are, if sound, the spearhead of progress."

Abraham Flexner

He continued to actively protest everything from apartheid in South Africa to US activities in Central America.

He died of an apparent self-administered drug overdose on April 12, 1989, in New Hope, Pennsylvania.

———

EMMA GOLDMAN (1869-1940) was known as "Red Emma" and was an American anarchist.

Goldman was born in Lithuania, but moved to St. Petersburg, Russia in 1882 where she found work in a glove factory. She also absorbed the radical thinking of much of pre-revolution Russia.

She emigrated to the United States three years later, and worked in the garment industry where working conditions horrified her. When four anarchists were executed for the Haymarket bomb throwing in Chicago in 1886, she helped lead the protests.

In 1893, she was imprisoned for incitement to riot in New York City. She worked with Alexander Berkman to found and edit an anarchist monthly *Mother Earth*, begun in 1906 and continued for 11 years.

Goldman became an international celebrity because of her passionate speeches.

In 1917, she was sentenced to two years in prison for opposing the registration of recruits for service in World War One. Two years later, she was deported to the Soviet Union. But she found the Soviet Union no better for her than America. In 1923, she wrote a book *My Disillusionment in Russia*, and the following year she managed to reenter the US

She was a vigorous supporter of the anarchists in the Spanish Civil War.

"All wars are wars among thieves," Emma Goldman, said in 1917, "who are too cowardly to fight and therefore induce the young manhood of the whole world to do the fighting for them"

"With trenchant power they (the Prophets) hammered into the hearts of their people and through their writings, into the hearts of all mankind, the truth that the essence of sin among men is oppression of the lowly, and that righteousness consists in worthy treatment of the poor and the oppressed."
Hermann Gunkel (1862-1932) What Remains of the OT 1914

Emma Goldman on a streetcar.

"The ultimate end of all revolutionary social change is to establish the sanctity of human life, the dignity of man, the right of every human being to liberty and well-being."
Emma Goldman, 1924

CHAPTER EIGHTEEN

THE WORLD OF ART

"The Jews are a people of artists, of intrinsic dreamers. That's what makes them achieve the impossible, and that is why they have survived."
Gabrielle D'Annunzio (1864-1938) Italian poet and soldier

SIR JACOB EPSTEIN (1880-1945) was born in New York, studied in Paris but made his mark as a sculptor largely in the United Kingdom.

The son of Polish Jewish parents, he sketched the colorful immigrants in his Lower East Side neighbourhood. He studied art in the evening and worked in a foundry during the day.

He was commissioned to illustrate a book and used the fee to pay his way to Paris. There he studied at the École des Beaux Arts and the Académie Julien.

He moved to London in 1905 and began an often controversial career as a sculptor. Much of his work was condemned as obscene and it was as a portrait sculptor that he earned a living.

This drawing of Epstein was by Augustus John.

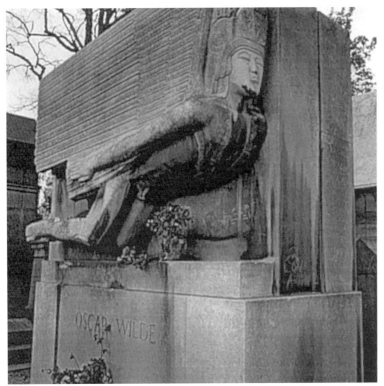

Sir Jacob Epstein was one of Britain's most distinguished sculptors. This was his sculptured tribute to Oscar Wilde.

He (Sir Jacob Epstein) was helped during his early years in London by a fund set up by the older Anglo-Jewish families to assist struggling young Jewish artists. When he was invited during his prosperous years—and he became a fairly wealthy man—to contribute to the fund he retorted that he had done enough for the fund by accepting its money."
Chaim Bermant, The Jews, 1977

MARC CHAGALL (1887-1985) was born in Russia but rose to prominence in Paris; he became one of the most popular painters of the 20th century.

He was also one of the longest living modern artists, and was still active in his 90s.

In addition to dreamlike paintings and lithographs, he designed the sets and costumes for a Metropolitan Opera production of Mozart's *The Magic Flute*.

Chagall's work reflects the influence of Hasidic legends blended with European modernism. He grew up in a shtetl near Vitebsk, Russia—a traditional east European village where animals wandered the streets. The chickens, goats, and cows the artist remembered from his childhood frequently turned up in his work. Examples of his work are in most major museums around the world.

Michael Gibson, writing in the International Herald Tribune (March 23, 2003) says of the artist: "While Chagall was obviously an exceptionally gifted young man, he clearly appeared on the scene at a crucial point, just when the oppressed Jews of Russia were beginning to express their full poetic, humorous and spiritual essence as never before."

Chagall's definition of art was interesting;

"Art is the unceasing effort to compete with the beauty of flowers—and never succeeding."

Marc Chagall, one of the most celebrated artists of the 20th century.

LORD DUVEEN OF MILLBANK (1869-1939) revolutionized the world of art by convincing wealthy Americans to collect art and then donate it to museums.

As a boy, he worked in his father's store—selling delft, furniture, and objets d'art. He learned from the experts, and began investing in art, paying, in 1901, the highest price ever paid for a picture at a British auction—14,000 pounds.

He began buying entire collections, including the Rodolph Kann collection, in Paris, for five million dollars and then he acquired a second Paris collection for three million.

With a huge stock, he sailed to the United States and spent the next half century transforming the American taste in art. Ultimately, he had elegant galleries in New York, London and Paris.

He was knighted in 1919, became a baronet in 1927 and then was elevated to the peerage. He took his title from the Millbank district of London where the Tate Gallery is located.

Despite critical illness, one of the final acts of his life was to convince Andrew Mellon to endow the National Gallery of Art in Washington.

S.N. Behrman, in his *Duveen* encapsulates Duveen's career in these words: "Early in life, Duveen . . .noticed that Europe had plenty of art and America had plenty of money, and his entire astonishing career was the product of that simple observation."

The artist must penetrate into the world, feel the fate of human beings, of peoples, with real love. There is no art for art's sake; one must be interested in the entire realm of life.

Marc Chagall, 1951

Lord Duveen of Millbank was the world's greatest art dealer in his time – and perhaps for all time. Walter Tittle executed this portrait print in the 1920s.

Bernard Berenson became the top authority, world-wide, on Renaissance art.

Art is not based on actuality, but on the wishes, dreams and aspirations of a people.

Bernard Berenson, 1941

BERNARD BERENSON (1865-1959), son of poor Lithuanian immigrants, became one of America's greatest art historians and connoisseurs.

He impressed art collector Isabella Stewart Gardner with his interest in Renaissance artists and she became his patron, and later accepted his guidance in purchasing major paintings.

With Mrs. Gardner's support, he set out to become a connoisseur and after years of study, settled into a villa, I Tatti, near Florence, Italy.

Here, wealthy collectors called on him to advise them on acquisitions. He became artistic adviser to Lord Joseph Duveen, the greatest art dealer in the first decades of the 20th century.

Eric Linklater, in his book *The Art of Adventure*, described Berenson in these words: ... a little tiny man, more of a genial fox than roaring lion, spruce and grey, so formally and neatly dressed that he looked like a miniature banker in Wall Street, though his voice was gentler." His books on artists of the period are regarded as the ultimate authority.

During World War II, friends hid him from the Fascists. He bequeathed his villa, his immense art library and his collection of paintings to Harvard University.

LUCIAN FREUD (1922-   ) is regarded as Britain's greatest living painter; he is the grandson of Sigmund Freud, founder of psychoanalysis.

Lucian Freud was born in Berlin; his father was the youngest of Sigmund Freud's six children. The family moved to London in 1933 when Hitler came to power.

He studied art at the Central School of Arts and Crafts and at the East Anglian School of Painting and Drawing.

Freud served briefly in the Royal Navy, but was discharged on medical grounds.

He first came to prominence in 1951—winning a prize from the Arts Council of Britain for a painting of the neighborhood in which he lived for many years.

Freud paints powerful portraits, taking three to six months to finish each picture. He has turned down requests to paint certain people, including the late Princess Diana. Freud's dealer told the *Guardian* "he couldn't paint Diana .... He said he couldn't get past that sheen of glamour. The image was so strong that I couldn't get at the real person."

He spent a year and a half painting Queen Elizabeth II in 2001, but the critics were furious about the portrait. "Freud should be locked in the Tower for this," declared Robert Simon, editor of the *British Art Journal*.

Gloria Goodale, commenting on Freud's work in the *Christian Science Monitor*, (March 16, 2003) said: ; "Observing the forensic intensity of detail, especially in the mature works, one is tempted to suggest that this grandson of Sigmund Freud, the father of modern psychoanalysis, has inherited at least the proclivity for peering deep beneath the skin of his subjects."

The *Times of London* (Jan. 12, 2003) estimated that Freud was earning at least 12,000,000 pounds a year. He broke into the American market in 1993. William Acquavella, who has represented the British artist for more than a decade, says he paints 12-15 pictures a year. His large paintings go for as much as $4,500,000 each.

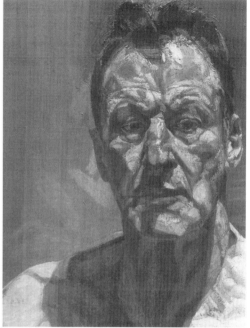

Lucian Freud is regarded as Britain's greatest living artist. Herewith a self-portrait.

ANTHONY CARO (1924-   ) is regarded as the most influential living British sculptor.

For a time, he worked as an assistant to Henry Moore. Caro's experience with Moore was his first encounter with modernism.

He moved on from figurative modeling, or carving, to creating imaginative assemblages. He welded or bolted chunks of metal together.

In his own words "All I want to do is to give vitality to the form. I do not intend to break with the past, but to stay vital, sculpture needs to be re-invented again and again."

All of the arts, poetry, music, ritual, the visible arts, the theatre, must singly and together create the most comprehensive art of all, a humanized society, and its masterpiece, free man.
Bernard Berenson Quoted in Atlantic Monthly November, 1957

Albert Hirschfield was an outstanding New York caricaturist.

ALBERT HIRSCHFIELD (1903-2003) was the great New York caricaturist; on his death, the *Times* gave him a front-page obituary and a full page tribute to his work.

The Martin Beck Theatre was to be renamed to honor Hirschfield on his 100th birthday, June 21, 2003. "It's a great honor," he gasped when told. "But I won't speak. Just take a bow." However, the caricaturist passed away in his sleep on January 20th—the day before the great event.

His career spanned much of the century. And Broadway was his beat. He rarely missed a play or musical. And he captured the essence of literally hundreds of subjects in his striking caricatures.

Many stars could be recognized from the few skilled lines he used to represent them. He drew perched on an old barber chair. And he hid his daughter's name "Nina" in each of his drawings, from her birth in 1945.

He grew up in St. Louis where he has a plaque honoring the City's greatest. But in life and even in death, he belongs to New York. The New York City Landmarks Conservancy, in 1996, actually named him as one of six "New York City Landmarks."

Mel Gussow, in *The Broadway Artist* speculated that "he has probably been to more shows than anyone else in the history of the theater." His wife states that, even in his final days in bed, he was waving his hand—drawing invisible caricatures in the air.

Herbert L. Block was better known as Herblock, drafting powerful political cartoons.

HERBERT L. BLOCK (1909-2001) was one of the most powerful political commentators of his time, signing his work "Herblock."

He became a staffer with the *Chicago Daily News* in 1929 but only four years later, his cartoons were syndicated nationally.

His first Pulitzer Prize was awarded him in 1942 and a year later he joined the US Army—drawing cartoons for Army information and education.

The war over, he was hired by the *Washington Post* where he used his biting artistic and language talents to target such people as

President Richard Nixon and Senator Joseph R. McCarthy. He coined the word "McCarthyism" in 1950.

He shared the 1957 Pulitzer Prize with the *Washington Post* for the paper's coverage of Watergate—leading to the resignation of Nixon. That same year, he was invited to deliver the annual Joseph Pulitzer Memorial Lecture, during which he declared that the responsibility of the press is to "use its freedom to protect the rights and liberty of all individuals."

He was made a fellow of the American Academy of Arts and Sciences.

CAMILLE PISSARRO (1830-1903) was one of the great French Impressionist painters.

He was born in St. Thomas in the West Indies, son of a prosperous merchant. The Pissarro family was of French and Jewish origin.

He was educated in France and then returned to St. Thomas, a Danish colony, but was not interested in working in his father's business.

He settled in France when he was 25 and began painting and sketching in small towns and villages near Paris. He became friendly with artists who later became members of the Impressionist group. His early friends were Paul Cézanne and Claude Monet. His landscapes were praised by the important critic Emile Zola.

Pissarro spent time in England during the Franco-Prussian war (1870-1871) and he was a key figure in organizing the first Impressionist exhibition (1874). He was the only member of this important group to participate in all eight Impressionist exhibitions.

In the 1880s, he began to paint in company with a younger generation of artists, including Georges Seurat, Paul Signac and his own son, Lucien. He steadily modified his style, moving from "Neo-impressionism" to his new world of cityscapes.

He was an active painter almost until his death in 1903 at age 73.

Camille Pissarro with fellow artists. He is seated.

Arthur Syk's biting 1942 artwork showing Hermann Goering, Benito Mussolini and Emperor Hirohito.

ARTHUR SZYK (1894-1951) used his artistic skill to pillory the Nazis and he became known as "Franklin Roosevelt's soldier with a pen."

He was born in Lodz, Poland, but left home at 15 to study art in Paris. During the First World War, he served in the Russian Army, but—after the revolution in St. Petersburg—pulled out of the war against Germany. He fought in the Polish Army against the communist Red Army.

He resumed his art studies in Paris in 1921, and developed an intricate and decorative style.

In 1931, he was commissioned by the League of Nations to do the artwork on its charter.

With the rise of Hitler, Szyk moved first to England and then, with the German invasion of Poland, he went to the United States. He used his skills as a caricaturist to pillory the Nazis. Both the *New York Post* and the *New York Times* used his work.

In late 1941, an *Esquire* magazine survey showed that Szyk's political cartoons were more popular with young soldiers than photos of movie actresses and pin-up girls.

The artist attacked all forms of prejudice and was one of the first to criticize prejudice against blacks.

Germany's postage stamp tribute to Max Lieberman. It's a self-portrait.

MAX LIEBERMAN (1847-1935) was sent to university to study philosophy but rebelled; this German-Jew became a prominent artist.

While Lieberman studied in Germany, he appeared to find inspiration in the early phase of his career during repeated trips to Holland and France. And the acceptance by Parisians of his work convinced him to stay in Paris, where he was impressed by the painting of Courbet, Millet, Corot, and Daubigny.

Lieberman later settled in Munich where he joined the Berlin Secession Movement, defying the art establishment, and ultimately became its president.

He became a member of the Berlin Academy and later served as its president. His favorite subjects were the common people, but he was in demand as a portraitist.

When the Nazis came to power, in 1933, he was stripped of all his honors and classified as a "degenerate." Nevertheless, he remains one of Germany's most respected painters.

AMEDEO MODIGLIANI (1884-1920) became interested in art at age 14 and rose to be one of Italy's greatest painters and sculptors.

Born in Leghorn, ill health forced him out of regular schooling, and he started to visit the studio of Guglielmo Micheli, who became his teacher. After recovering from an illness, he was taken by his mother on an exciting journey to Naples, Amalfi, Rome, and Florence.

After studying in Venice, he moved to Paris, rented a studio in Montmartre and lived in a tenement at rue Delta 7. He exhibited paintings, drawings, and sculpture—working in wood (he used railway ties left behind in the construction of the Paris metro.)

Later he used limestone from construction sites or he picked up stones at night and took them to his studio. He was extremely poor, selling little at first. And his mother's limited financial assistance dried up.

He stopped sculpting with the start of World War I. There was no more construction, and therefore no more odds and ends for him to use.

Influenced by the Polish poet Leopold Zboroswki, he began painting nudes which were among his finest work. But the police closed his only one-man show because it was illegal to show pubic hair.

In 1919, in London, author Arnold Bennett became the first collector to recognize Modigliani as one of the most important artists of the 20th century. (70 years later, in 1989, a Modigliani portrait was sold by Sotheby's, at auction, for $8 million.)

Amedeo Modigliani, an improverished, ailing Italian painter and sculptor in Paris, has been hailed as one of the greatest painters and sculptors of the 20th century. This is one of his portraits.

ALFRED STIEGLITZ (1864-1946) is known as the Father of Modern Photography.

He was born in Hoboken, New Jersey. His father, a prosperous wool merchant, took him to Germany where he studied engineering. In Berlin, he bought a camera and, excited by the images he captured, he sent 12 prints to a London competition for amateur photographers. He won first prize—the first of more than 150 medals he would win in worldwide competition. But, of course, the first recognition was the most important.

He studied photo-chemistry and ultimately published several very high quality magazines on photography. He recognized photography as a new art form. And he won fame for his imaginative work.

Alfred Stieglitz is known as the father of modern photography. This is a photographic self-portrait.

Chancellor Conrad Harrington of McGill University (l.) confers an Hon. LL.D. on architect Moshe Safdie.

In 1924, the British Royal Photographic Society awarded him the Progress Medal, its highest honor.

Paul Rosenfeld, in *America and Stieglitz* (1989) wrote:

"His handling of the photographer's tool of natural light reveals depth and form, not a mere static record, but conscious perception—a work of art."

MOSHE SAFDIE (1938-   ), a native of Haifa, Israel, became an internationally respected architect only six years after graduating from McGill University.

His breakthrough to fame came with his award-winning design of Habitat '67, in Montreal. It won him the Massey Medal of the Royal Architectural Institute of Canada.

His construction technique used concrete cubes to construct a building as if he were playing with children's blocks. The technique has been adopted and adapted for many other buildings.

Safdie has taught at Harvard, Yale, McGill, and Israel's Ben Gurion University.

Henry Dreyfuss with the model 500 telephone he designed for Bell Telephone in 1946. (Cooper-Hewitt National Design Museum)

HENRY DREYFUSS (1904-1972) was one of the world's most important industrial designers.

He began his career in the theatre—apprenticed to the brilliant Norman Bel Geddes. He went from designing for the stage to designing for mass production. His hundreds of designs included the round Honeywell thermostat, the Polaroid "swinger" camera, several modern telephone designs including the Trimline and Princess, an improved Deere tractor, the interior of the Boeing 707 airliner and streamlined passenger trains.

An exhibition of his designs at the Cooper-Hewitt Design Museum of the Smithsonian Institution notes that "Dreyfuss had a profound impact on the daily lives of millions of Americans."

JOSEF ISRAELS (1824-1911) is touted as one of the discoverers of the Dutch landscape.

He was born in Groningen, son of a money-changer. He first studied at the Amsterdam Academy and later at the Académie des Beaux-Arts in Paris.

He returned to Amsterdam in 1847 and was sufficiently skilled to make a living as an artist. He painted portraits and historical subjects. For health reasons, he began living in a fishing village, Zandvoort, where he began painting the fishermen and the locals.

Finally, in 1871, he moved to The Hague and joined a group known as the Haagse School.

While his landscapes were hailed as the work of one of Holland's best 19th century artists, he often turned to Jewish subjects.

Self-portrait of artist Josef Israels. (Hecht Museum, Haifa University)

CHAPTER NINETEEN

CONDUCTORS AND COMPOSERS

"Oscar Hammerstein I (1847-1919) arrived there (New York) in 1863, working (like countless other Jews) in a cigar factory. Twenty years later his son Oscar Hammerstein II went on to play a major part, as librettist, in making the America 'musical play' a new form of integrated drama. From Rose Marie (1924) and the Desert Song (1926), he joined Jerome Kern, another New Yorker, to create the quintessential American musical, 'Show Boat' (1927) and then from the early forties he joined with Richard Rodgers to raise the genre, perhaps the most characteristic of all American art forms, to a new peak, with Oklahoma (1943), Carousel (1945), South Pacific (1949), The King and I (1951) and The Sound of Music (1959)"

Paul Johnson, A History of the Jews, 1987

Aaron Copland was known as the Dean of American composers.

AARON COPLAND (1900-1990) was known as the "Dean of American Composers"; his most popular work was "Appalachian Spring."

The family's name was Kaplan, but an immigration officer marked it down as "Copland."

Copland became fascinated with classical music, at 13, when he attended his first recital. And he began to study music—first in the United States and then in Europe. He met and was influenced by such giants as Stravinsky, Hindemith, Prokoviev, Schoenberg and the "French Six." Copland wrote ballets, symphonies, chamber music, operas, and choral works.

Although some of his early work proved too modern for American audiences, he found his voice in a blending of American folk themes, jazz rhythms, and Hebrew music.

"I think of my music as Jewish," he told an interviewer, "because it's dramatic, it's intense, it has a certain passionate lyricism in it."

Copland received a Guggenheim Fellowship, a Pulitzer Prize (in 1945 for *Appalachian Spring*), the Presidential Medal of Freedom, and membership in the American Academy of Arts and Letters.

In 1981, Queens College of the City University of New York named its School of Music for him.

Aaron Copland (centre) in 1950 with pianist Artur Rubenstein (2nd from left).

GUSTAV MAHLER (1860-1911) is best known for his song-symphony Das Lied von der Erde. He began composing at age four!

As a child, he became fascinated by the playing of military bands, in a barracks in his village, and by workers' folk songs. He learned to play the music on both the accordion and piano.

The deep emotions expressed in his music may be traced, at least in part, to the anti-Semitism he experienced in his native Bohemia and to his father's violence towards his mother.

Many composers, including Benjamin Britten, Schoenberg, and Shostakovich acknowledge the influence of Mahler's compositions on their work.

Gustav Mahler began composing at age four.

Arnold Schonberg influenced the shape and form of 20th century classical music.

ARNOLD SCHOENBERG (1874-1951) was an important composer of 20th century music.

Born in Vienna, he was largely self-educated. He served in the Austrian Army in 1916.

He taught composition on both sides of the Atlantic—in Berlin and Vienna, then from 1933 in Boston, Hollywood and Los Angeles. His major compositions include the opera *Moses and Aron* (1932); *Five Orchestral Pieces*, (1909); *Pierre Lunaire*, 1912; *Concerto for Violin and Orchestra*, (1935); and *Four string quartets* (1905-1936).

SIGMUND ROMBERG (1887-1951) first achieved success with *The Student Prince* and his most popular compositions include *The Desert Song* and *New Moon*.

This Hungarian-born American composer wrote about 50 operettas and musical comedies.

His most successful shows were *Blossom Time* (1921), *The Student Prince*, *The Desert Song* (1926), and *The New Moon* (1928).

Sigmund Romberg was famed for his light operas.

Leonard Bernstein.

"Any work of art is great because it creates a special world of its own."

Leonard Bernstein

LEONARD BERNSTEIN (1918-1990) was the first native American to serve as conductor of a major symphony orchestra in the US

Louis Bernstein was born into a family of Russian-Jewish immigrants in Lawrence, Massachusetts. He changed his name to Leonard to avoid confusion with another Louis Bernstein in the family.

He studied piano in Boston and entered Harvard at 17. Later, he studied conducting in Philadelphia with maestro Fritz Reiner. And in 1940 and 1941, at Tanglewood, he studied under Serge Koussevitsky.

His talent was quickly recognized and he became assistant conductor of of the New York Philharmonic in 1943. In November he was called upon to substitute for the regular conductor and won the praises of audience and critics alike. He was proclaimed the greatest musician of the age. For the next decade and a half, he was welcomed to the podiums of some of the greatest orchestras in the world.

He was also a composer of note—providing the world of music with three symphonies, and the musical theatre with *West Side Story*, *Candide*, and *On the Town*.

A multitude of Jews were outstanding conductors, including:

SERGE KOUSSEVITSKY (1874-1951), conductor of the Boston Symphony Orchestra, established the concert series at Tanglewood.

ARTHUR FIEDLER (1894-1979) was the legendary, longtime conductor of the Boston Pops.

BRUNO WALTER (1876-1962) conducted the New York Philharmonic.

FRITZ REINER (1888-1963) led the Cleveland Symphony Orchestra.

SIR GEORG SOLTI (1912-1997) conducted both the Chicago and Paris Symphony Orchestras.

WALTER SUSSKIND (1913-1980) was the revered conductor of the Cincinnati Symphony.

Arthur Fiedler was the legendary, longtime conductor of the Boston Pops.

EUGENE ORMANDY (1899-1985) was music director of the Philadelphia Orchestra for a remarkable 44 years! He made his debut in Philadelphia in 1931, then co-directed the orchestra with Leopold Stokowski in the late 30s, taking over the baton alone in 1938.

WALTER J. DAMROSCH (1862-1950) conducted the Metropolitan Opera.

OTTO KLEMPERER (1885-1973), one of the outstanding conductors of the 20th century, was removed by Hitler from his post as conductor of the Berlin State Opera.

ANDRE KOSTELANETZ (1901-1980) first came to prominence as a conductor on the radio. Later he appeared as a guest conductor with a number of leading orchestras.

ERICH LEINSDORF (1912-1993) conducted the Metropolitan Opera, the Cleveland Orchestra, the Rochester Philharmonic, and the Boston Symphony; his career sparred more than half a century.

JAMES LEVINE (1943-   ) performed on the piano at age 10 with the Cincinnati Symphony Orchestra. In 1972, he was appointed principal conductor and music director of the Metropolitan Opera.

Levine, with his appointment to the Met at age 29, was dubbed the "kid who conquered the mighty Met." and one critic said of him that he is "possibly the most significant operatic conductor/ administrator since Toscanini."

ANDRE PREVIN (1929-   ) is a brilliant pianist, conductor and composer; as a child, he played piano, four-hands, with his father.

Andre Previn is among the US's best-known conductors and musicians.

CHAPTER TWENTY

THE CLASSICAL MUSICIANS

"It is among violinists that Jews are particularly numerous: Jascha Heifetz, Mischa Elman, Nathan Milstein, David Oistrakh, Leonid Kogan, Isaac Stern, Yitzhak Perlman, Gil Shaham, Maxim Vengerov—to name only a few...For most of the 20th century, Jews seemed to dominate the ranks of top violinists."
George Jochnowitz, Emeritus Professor, Midstream, Feb/Mar., 2003

Mischa Elman enjoyed sales of more than two million recordings of his violin playing.

MISCHA ELMAN (1873-1967) began studying the violin at six; more than two million of his records were sold during his lifetime.

He was born in Talnoye, Ukraine, and his grandfather was a distinguished violinist. He made his debut in St. Petersburg at age 13. He made a successful tour of Britain in 1905 and in 1911 he settled in the United States.

Donald Brooks wrote of him:

"The outstanding feature of his playing is not the technical mastery of his instrument, nor yet the satisfying breadth of tone, but that spiritual Hebraic quality that artists of Jewish ancestry seem to be able to put into music of a somber mood."

With the exception of Francescatti, Szigeti and Thibaud, it is difficult to think of a violinist of the first rank who is not Jewish, usually of Russian origin, frequently from Odessa. Yehudi Menuhin, whose very name has become almost an evocation of all that is noble in the violin, was, indeed, born in America, but his parents were from Russia. Jascha Heifetz is from Lithuania; Mischa Elman is from the Ukraine, as is Isaac Stern; Efrem Zimbalist is from Rostov; Ida Haendel is from Poland; Nathan Milstein and David Oistrakh are from Odessa, as are a host of lesser players.

Chaim Bermant, The Jews, 1977

JASCHA HEIFETZ (1900-1987) was the greatest violin virtuoso of his time; he gave his first concert at age five. By then, he had been practicing for two years.

His father, first violinist with the Vilna Orchestra, had bought the youngster a five-dollar instrument when he was three. At age nine, young Heifetz was enrolled in the Russian Imperial Conservatory in St. Petersburg. His father enroled with him because that was the only way, as a student, that a Jew could live in the capital city.

The young violinist made his debut, at age 12, with the Berlin Philharmonic Orchestra, and a sixty year career was launched.

The family emigrated to the United States in 1917; young Heifetz was 16. And his debut at Carnegie Hall was an historic event.

Carl Flesch wrote "There probably has never been a violinist who has approached the summit of perfection more closely."

Heifetz travelled all over the world to perform and, during World War Two, he joined the United Services Organization (USO) and performed in the war zones for servicemen.

Harold Schonberg of the *New York Times* wrote that perhaps Heifetz was "the greatest violin virtuoso of his time."

Jascha Heifetz is regarded as the greatest violin virtuoso of his time.

—————

VLADIMIR HOROWITZ (1903-1989), during his performing career, was judged to be the world's greatest living pianist.

He was born in Kiev, Russia, and his love for music came from his mother, who was an amateur pianist. Vladimir began taking lessons at the Kiev Conservatory, where his teacher was Felix Blumenthal, a student of Anton Rubenstein.

He had hoped to become a composer but in the wake of the Russian Revolution, he began performing to help support his family.

His early performances were so exciting that he was sent on a tour of Russia in 1923-1924. In 1925, he left the Soviet Union on a study permit and did not return.

For two years he toured Europe to rave notices, and then in 1928 he made his American debut at Carnegie Hall. Critics called his playing "sensational" (he played the Tchaikovsky concerto in B-flat minor), and received a standing ovation.

Twenty-five years later, he repeated that performance at Carnegie Hall, and critics remarked on the great depth and sophistication of his playing.

He won 15 Grammy awards.

Vladimir Horowitz in his day was recognized as the world's greatest living pianist.

Knighted by the British, Sir Yehudi Menuhin added conducting to his skills.

SIR YEHUDI MENUHIN (1916-1999), taken to concerts because his parents could not afford a baby-sitter, became one of the world's finest violinists.

Menuhin was born in New York. He was given a toy violin when he was three. Shortly thereafter, his parents invested in a real instrument. By the time he was five, when it was apparent that Yehudi was very talented, he began studying with Sigmund Anker, whose specialty was working with small children.

Menuhin's first public solo appearance was in 1923. The next year, a San Francisco attorney, Sidney Ehrman, began sponsoring Menuhin's studies and touring program.

The New York Times critic, Olin Downes, wrote of a performance in New York: "A boy of 11 proved conclusively his right to be ranked, irrespective of his years, with the outstanding interpreters of this music."

Menuhin became known as "America's Best Ambassador," because he helped arrange cultural exchanges with other countries.

He settled in England, and in 1959 he became the head of the Bath Festival which ten years later was moved to Windsor and renamed the Menuhin Festival Orchestra.

Mstislav Rostropovich has won worldwide acclaim for his cello playing.

MSTISLAV ROSTROPOVICH (1927-   ) studied the cello with his father as a youngster, and the piano with his mother. He has won worldwide acclaim for his cello performances.

He was born in Baku, but the family moved to Moscow when he was four. He made his debut at age eight. And, having chosen the cello over the piano, he studied with eminent musicians and composers—including Shostakovitch and Prokofiev.

He won the International Competition for Cellists in Prague in 1950. And the following year, he performed for the first time in the West, appearing in Florence. As he performed concert after concert, his reputation grew.

He made his American debut at Carnegie Hall, in New York in 1956 and won extraordinary critical acclaim.

He married the soprano Galina Vishnevskaya, and on occasion accompanies her on the piano.

However, he was too independent-minded for Soviet authorities, who harassed both husband and wife, periodically canceling performances. In 1974, travel restrictions were lifted for the couple, and their two children.

He made a brilliant debut as guest conductor of the National Symphony Orchestra in Washington, in 1975, and two years later he was appointed its music director.

In 1990, the Soviet Union—which had stripped the musician of citizenship, restored it and invited him to bring the National Symphony Orchestra to Russia. Rostropovich is recognized as one of the greatest cellists of the century and his many honors and awards include the French Legion d'honneur (1982) and an honorary knighthood from Queen Elizabeth II (1987).

ARTUR RUBINSTEIN (1887-1982) was fascinated with the piano at age seven; he became one of the finest interpreters of Chopin's music.

He was born in Lodz, Poland, but his performance on the piano was so brilliant that he was sent to Berlin to study.

He then became an impressive pianist, contracted to play all over Europe—but lazy! "When I was young," he admits, "I was lazy. There were many things in life more important than practicing. Good food, good cigars, great wines, women."

But in the early thirties, he settled down, studied intensively and became one of the greatest interpreters of the music of Chopin—focusing on the Polish composer's work because of criticism of his interpretation of Chopin's work. Oscar Thompson, in his *International Cyclopedia of Music and Musicians*, declares: "As a Chopin player, Rubenstein is supreme, possessing the superb technique, poetic temperament, sensitivity, and imagination to bring this music to life as few have been able to".

PINCHAS ZUKERMAN (1948-   ) became an outstanding violinist and conductor.

He was a native of Tel Aviv, son of two concentration camp survivors. His father, Yehuda, had been a violinist in the Warsaw

Artur Rubenstein became one of the finest interpreters of Chopin's music.

Pinchas Zukerman is both an outstanding violinist and a conductor.

Itzhak Perlman is considered one of the world's finest violinists today.

Philharmonic, and he gave Pinchas a child-size violin when he was seven. He would play duets with his father.

The lad studied at the Israel Conservatory and the Academy of Music in Tel Aviv. When Isaac Stern, on a visit to Israel, heard Zukerman play, he arranged for the young man to study at the Juilliard School of Music in Manhattan.

He gave his first concert in New York, at Town Hall, in 1963.

Impresario Sol Hurok arranged a tour for him of the United States and Canada.

ITZHAK PERLMAN (1945-   ) began playing his violin for audiences when he was 10; today he is considered one of the world's finest violinists.

At 19, he won the coveted Leventrit Prize.

He is a native of Tel Aviv, Israel; his father, Chaim, was a barber. Perlman first tried his hand on a toy violin, but when his parents saw he was serious, they bought him a second-hand instrument for $6.00.

He gave his first solo recital at 10.

Perlman has become one of the world's greatest violinists, despite the fact that polio left him permanently disabled from age four.

Perlman was brought to the United States to appear on the televised *Ed Sullivan Caravan of Stars*, and the family stayed in the US

One of his teachers at the Juilliard School, Dorothy Delay, declared: "What set Itzhak apart from the beginning was his sheer talent and enormous imagination."

He made his Carnegie Hall debut in 1963, and attracted the attention of Isaac Stern, Yehudi Menuhin, and Zino Francscatti.

In 1980, a critic for *Newsweek* wrote:

"The music seems not so much played as felt, spilled out in great rushes of warm, lyrical sound."

ISAAC STERN (1920-2001) was one of the top virtuosos of his generation and helped save New York's Carnegie Hall. He was the first American-trained world-class violinist.

He was born in Russia but brought by his parents to San Francisco as an infant. His violin studies began when he was eight and he soon left school to study music full-time.

After studying for three years with Naoum Blinder, concertmaster of the San Francisco Symphony, he made his debut with that orchestra conducted by Pierre Monteux.

He then toured the country for six years before playing at Carnegie Hall in 1943, where he received an enthusiastic response.

He had had a difficult time making it in the world of classical music and, with that in mind, he encouraged and supported a number of young, promising musicians.

During World War Two, he visited and played for troops in Iceland, Greenland, and the South Pacific. He refused to perform in Germany.

When the storied Carnegie Hall was slated for demolition in 1960, Isaac Stern led the campaign to save it. He became President of the Carnegie Hall Corporation. The main concert stage in the Hall is called the Isaac Stern Auditorium.

In 1991, while the Gulf War was raging, an air-raid siren sounded while Stern was performing in Israel. Stern continued to play while the audience donned gas masks. The violinist said later he did not wear a mask because it would have interfered with his playing.

The onetime managing director of the Los Angeles Philharmonic, Ernest Fleischmann, told the *Los Angeles Times*:

"Isaac was in many ways a fairly unique combination—a natural, instinctive musician, intellectual musician and absolute master of his instrument. You normally get great virtuosos or natural musicians, but not the intellectual capacity—you don't get that combination. He was very rare."

Isaac Stern was the first American-trained world-class violonist. His records sell worldwide.

CHAPTER TWENTY-ONE

THE OPERA SINGERS

"Sing, O heaven, be joyful, O earth, and break forth into singing, O mountains!"
Bible, Isaiah, 49.13

Robert Merrill was an outstanding operatic baritone.

ROBERT MERRILL (1919-   ), an outstanding operatic baritone, first performed in synagogues at weddings and Bar-Mitzvahs.

Initially, he studied with his mother, Lillian Miller Merrill, a former concert singer; then under Samuel Margolis in New York.

After making his debut in 1944, Merrill won a Metropolitan "Auditions of the Air," in 1945. He sang Posa in *Don Carlos* on the opening night of the Rudolph Bing regime at the Metropolitan in 1950. But he was dismissed from the company the following year for failing to show up at engagements on a tour. He was reinstated the following season.

Back at the Met for the 1953-1954 season, Merrill—performing as Valentine in *Faust* lay mortally wounded on stage while Mildred Miller, as Siebel, bent over him only to have the singer mutter in her ear "Oi vey. It hoits."

Toscanini chose him to perform in his broadcasts and recordings of *La Traviata* and *Un Ballo in Maschera*.

JAN PEERCE (1904-1984), at the peak of his 26-year career at the Metropolitan Opera, often returned to the synagogue to lead services.

This great American tenor began his musical career as a violinist, played with dance bands, and on occasion sang a little. His singing drew attention, and he was engaged to perform at the Radio City Music Hall, where he was featured from 1933 to1939.

He made his opera debut in
Baltimore in 1939. He was the
leading tenor at the Met from
1941 to 1966—15 years!

Arturo Toscanini selected him
to sing *Boheme, Fidelio, Traviata,*
and *Ballo in Maschera* in his
broadcasts.

His real name was Jacob Pincus
Perlemuth.

**Jan Peerce's career spanned 26 years
at the Metropolitan Opera. His
cantorial records are still popular.**

Roberta Peters was a lead soprano at the
Met for 30 years!

**ROBERTA PETERS (1930-   ) was a lead soprano for a remarkable 30
years at the Metropolitan; she was spotted as a talented singer by tenor
Jan Peerce when she was 13.**

She studied with William Hermann, and the Met signed her up at
19 even though she had no experience. Her official debut was set for
early 1951, as the Queen of the Night, but she was hustled onstage to
replace Nadine Conner.

On her 25th anniversary with the Met, it was calculated that she
had given 303 performances of twenty roles in 19 operas.

She was one of the leading coloraturas of the 1950s.

Beverly Sills was one of America's most
popular sopranos.

**BEVERLY SILLS (1929-   ) began singing on radio and television at age
three, and at 18 made her operatic debut with the Philadelphia Civic
Orchestra.**

Her original name was Belle Miriam Silverman, and she was born
in Brooklyn. Her mother, in a discussion with her husband, declared
"The two boys (their sons) will go to college and be smart. This one
(Beverly) will be an opera singer."

This American soprano studied in New York with Estelle Liebling,
and debuted in Philadelphia in 1947.

She was reputed to be the most popular American soprano since Grace Moore. She had a repertory of more than 60 roles, and retired, at 50, to support the opera in other ways. She served as director of the New York City Opera for ten years (1979-1989).

In 1994 Sills became chairman of New York City's Lincoln Center.

Her most important recognitions were the Presidential Medal of Freedom, 1980, and a Kennedy Center Honor, 1985.

Tucker in full operatic regalia.

RICHARD TUCKER (1913-1975), an orthodox Jew, was called "the best Italian tenor in the world."

This American tenor (original name Reuben Ticker) studied in New York with Althouse, Martino, Borghetti, and Wilhousky.

He made his debut in New York in 1943, and two years later joined the Met. He was the Met's leading tenor until his death, 30 years later.

He sang more than 600 performances of some 30 roles in the Italian and French repertory. His ambition was, as the son of a Romanian Jew, to sing the role of Eleazor in *La Juive*, which he did in 1973.

On one occasion, Tucker was put out by the selection of Franco Corelli to perform at the Met in *Tosca*. However, he was pleased when the younger man came to him for advice on how to sing an aria. "To sing it properly," Tucker explained to the Italian tenor. "You have to be Jewish."

CHAPTER TWENTY-TWO

TIN PAN ALLEY

"You know how amazing it is that, except for a handful like Cole Porter, almost everybody in musical comedy on Broadway have been Jews...I think it has something to do with growing up in a Jewish home where there is melodic singable music.... I grew up in a home where there was always Yiddish and Hebrew songs....Cole Porter said when he wanted to be super melodic he'd put a Jewish melody in his song. An example is 'I Love Paris.'"

Jerry Herman

Irving Berlin wrote more than 1,500 tunes.

IRVING BERLIN, (1888-1989) who spoke no English until he was 12, was one of America's greatest composers of popular songs from his "Oh How I Hate to Get Up in the Morning" to "God Bless America."

Born in Russia, Berlin—whose real name was Isidor Baline (he accepted "Berlin" when a printer made a typesetting mistake)—was four years old when he arrived in the United States. His father, a cantor, died when he was eight and the youngster had to do what he could to help maintain the family. He sang on the streets of New York, for pennies; in his teens, he plugged songs for music publishers and, later, he became a singing waiter in a Bowery cafe.

Berlin first came to notice when the *World's* Herbert Bayard Swope wrote a story about the waiter who refused to take a tip from Prince Louis of Battenburg. While working in the cafe, Berlin wrote his first big hit *Alexander's Ragtime Band.*

He wrote about 1,500 songs in his lifetime, many of them timeless classics. Among those tunes was *God Bless America*, which for some is a second national anthem. Furthermore, he wrote 19 musicals and scores for eighteen movies.

He is a Jewish songwriter who composed two of the greatest tunes associated with Christian holidays—-*White Christmas and Easter Parade.* Also intriguing was that, unlike most of his colleagues, he wrote the words as well as the music. And he published his own compositions !

Jerome Kern said of him:

"Irving Berlin has no place in American music; he is American music."

Berlin married twice. When his first wife died of typhoid, he composed his first ballad *When I lost You.* And when his second wife's father disinherited her because she had married a Jew, Berlin wrote *Always* as a wedding present.

217

In 1955, President Dwight D. Eisenhower presented Irving Berlin with a gold medal recognizing his immense services to the country, and particularly for his patriotic songs.

Some of his most popular tunes, were *Oh How I Hate to Get Up in the Morning, This is the Army, I Left My Heart at the Stage Door Canteen, There's no Business Like Show Business, All by Myself* and *What'll I Do?*

All this from a man who, as a child, hid with his family in the woods fearing attacks by Russian Cossacks.

MEL TORME (1925-1999) was a singer, songwriter, arranger, pianist, drummer, actor and author; he was called the "velvet fog."

His full name was Melvin Howard Torme. He made his professional debut as a singer in Chicago, aged four. By age six, he was performing in vaudeville. His first published song was *Lament for Love*, which Harry James' big band made a jukebox hit in 1941. Torme was only 16!

He co-wrote his best known tune, *The Christmas Song* ("Chestnuts roasting on an open fire...."), which was recorded by Nat King Cole in 1946. He performed in nightclubs, on stage, television, and in the movies.

In 1983 and 1984 he won Grammy Awards for best male jazz vocalist for albums recorded with George Shearing. And, in 1999, he received a Grammy Award for Lifetime Achievement.

SAMMY CAHN (1913-1993) often wrote lyrics for Jimmy van Heusen and received Academy Awards for *Call me Irresponsible*, *High Hopes* and *Three Coins in the Fountain*.

In all, he won a remarkable four Oscars for his work.

Cahn (real name - Samuel Cohen) was born on New York's Lower East Side in the same area as Ira and George Gershwin, and Irving Berlin. Typically his parents wanted him to be a doctor or a lawyer but Cahn began to play the violin and found work in burlesque houses. He

Some of Irving Berlin's greatest hits

Alexander's Ragtime Band - All Alone - Always - Anything You Can Do I Can Do Better - Change Partners - Cheek to Cheek - Easter Parade - Isn't This A Lovely Day - I've Got My Love To Keep Me Warm - Let's Face The Music and Dance - Oh How I Hate to Get Up In the Morning - Over There - A Pretty Girl is Like a Melody - Puttin' On The Ritz - The Song is Ended - There's No Business Like Show Business - This is the Army - Top Hat - What'll I do? - White Christmas

Mel Torme was a multi-talented performer.

Lyricist Sammy Cahn's received four Academy Awards for his compositions.

delighted in improvising parodies of popular songs as performers, on stage, were stripping.

But he knew he would never make it as a muscian. "I played the violin so badly," he told a Chicago Tribune interviewer, "I was almost forced into making up songs."

Teaming up with Saul Chaplin, their first big hit was an adaptation of the Yiddish tune *Bei Mir Bist du Schoen*, which they sold to the (then unknown) Andrews Sisters.

Moving to Hollywood, he teamed up with Jules Styne, and together they wrote such hit songs as *Let it Snow, Let it Snow, Let it Snow*, and *I'll Walk Alone*.

Singer Frank Sinatra depended on Cahn, and various collaborators, to come up with some of his best songs. These included *All The Way, Three Coins in the Fountain, High Hopes, Call me Irresponsible, My Kind of Town, Come Fly With Me,* and *Only The Lonely*.

Shortly before his death, in 1993, Cahn told an interviewer from *Gentlemen's Quarterly*:

"Would I like to be a successful architect? Nothing's wrong with that, but who walks down the street humming a building?"

George Gershwin's first great hit was *Swanee* sung by Al Jolson.

GEORGE GERSHWIN, (1898-1937) whose compositions included *Porgy and Bess, An American in Paris,* and *Rhapsody in Blue,* first sat down at a piano at age twelve. His first great hit was *Swanee* sung by Al Jolson.

He began writing songs, with his lyricist brother Ira, at age 18. For Tin Pan Alley, he wrote such hit songs as *Lady be Good, Strike up the Band,* and *Funny Face*.

By age 19, he was an accomplished performer and accompanied actress Louise Dresser on tour. His song *Swanee* was picked up by Al Jolson who sang it at the Winter Garden. It became a national sensation. In one year, *Swanee* sold more than 3,000,000 records and copies of sheet music. At 21, George Gershwin was a star composer.

Popular tunes poured out of the composer's fertile mind.

Orchestra leader Paul Whiteman recognized the latent talent in Gershwin for more serious work and persuaded him to write what became *Rhapsody in Blue.*

Gershwin recalls that he began to work out *Rhapsody* in his head during a train ride from New York to Boston. "I heard it as a musical kaleidoscope of America, of our vast melting pot, of our national pep, of our blues, our metropolitan madness." George Gershwin was 25 years old at the time.

Rhapsody was premiered by Whiteman on Feb. 12, 1924, and earned tremendous recognition for both the orchestra leader and the composer.

In 1936, the brothers journeyed to Hollywood and began to compose songs for the movie song-and-dance team of Fred Astaire and Ginger Rogers. However, a year later, he began to have blackouts and, ultimately—too late—doctors found he had a brain tumor. Two of his greatest songs, *Our Love is Here to Stay* and *Love Walked In*, were released after his death.

Gershwin bridged the worlds of classical and popular music. His greatest classical works included the opera *Porgy and Bess* and *An American in Paris.*

His brother, Ira, a celebrated lyricist, is quoted in *The Gershwin Years* (by Edward Jablonski and Lawrence D. Stewart) as saying of George:

"From Gershwin emanated a new American music—not written with the ruthlessness of one who strives to demolish established rules, but based on a new native gusto and wit and awareness."

His was a modernity that reflected the civilization we live in as excitingly as the headline in today's newspaper."

Ira continued to write lyrics for other composers.

A Selection of songs by George and Ira Gershwin

But Not For Me - Embraceable You - Fascinating Rhythm - A Foggy Day - I Got Rhythm - It Ain't Necessarily So - Oh, Lady Be Good - Let's Call The Whole Thing Off - Love Walked In - Nice Work If You Can Get It - Our Love Is Here To Stay - The Man I Love - Somebody Loves Me - Someone To Watch Over Me - Strike Up The Band - Summertime - They All Laughed

---

OSCAR HAMMERSTEIN II (1895-1960) and RICHARD RODGERS were partners on many Broadway shows. Their compositions included *Oklahoma, Show Boat, South Pacific, The King and I, Annie Get Your Gun,* and *Carousel.*

Oscar Hammerstein II had solid family credentials for a career in show business. His father, William, was director for years of Hammerstein's Victoria, the most popular vaudeville house of the day.

Oscar Hammerstein II and Richard Rodgers were partners in some of Broadway's greatest shows.

His grandfather, Oscar Hammerstein, was a famous opera impresario.

Oscar II began writing song lyrics while studying law at Columbia. His earliest musical comedies were written with Richard Rodgers (1902-1979), a Columbia undergraduate. Lorenz Hart (1895-1943) helped write the lyrics.

Hammerstein collaborated on eight musicals with Jerome Kern (1885-1945) climaxed by their masterpiece *Show Boat*.

Oscar II then began to work exclusively with Rodgers and the famous team was born. That partnership shook up the whole world of the Broadway musical, beginning with *Oklahoma* in 1943. This was followed by such triumphs as *Carousel, South Pacific, The King and I, Flower Drum Song,* and *The Sound of Music*.

They wrote *State Fair* specifically for the movies.

Altogether, they picked up 34 Tony Awards, 15 Academy Awards, two Pulitzer Prizes and Two Grammy Awards. They also worked as producers, and their biggest triumph outside of their own productions, was Irving Berlin's *Annie Get Your Gun*.

Meanwhile, Lorenz Milton Hart worked with Rodgers on *Pal Joey* and *The Boys from Syracuse*.

Hart, at 23, was introduced to the 16 year old Rodgers. Rodgers played his music and Hart read some of his lyrics. They formed a partnership that day that resulted in the composition of some of the greatest musicals of the first half of the 20th century.

Their hits included *Babes in Arms, The Boys from Syracuse* and *I Married an Angel*. But they were very different people. Hart was short, a homosexual, and an alcoholic. Rodgers was disciplined and unemotional. When they broke up, Hart fled to Mexico, while Rodgers launched a whole new chapter in his career when he teamed up with Oscar Hammerstein II.

Hart attended the premiere of *"Oklahoma,"* but died six months later.

JEROME KERN's (1885-1945) compositions, among the hundreds he wrote, included *Smoke Gets in Your Eyes*, and *Ol' Man River*.

He was born in New York City, and while his parents encouraged his interest in music, his father thought composing likely would not provide his son with a good living. So Mr. Kern pressed his son, at age 16, to join him in the business. That adventure came to a distressing end when Jerome, sent to order two pianos for the store, got so drunk over lunch that he upped the order to 200 .

Turfed from the business, he studied at the New York College of Music, plugged songs and wrote a few, and then studied composition in Germany and England.

His first big hit was the operetta *The Red Petticoat*, in 1912. He began composing Broadway shows.

After 1931, he wrote the scores for many films. The most outstanding was *Show Boat*. He won an Academy Award for his song *The Way You Look Tonight*.

Kern returned to Broadway for his collaboration with Hammerstein on the revival of *Show Boat*. But the composer never lived to see the revival staged. He died of a heart attack, with Hammerstein at his bedside.

He had composed nearly 700 songs for 117 shows and films in a 40-year career. His greatest hits included *All The Things You Are, Smoke Gets in your Eyes, The Way You Look Tonight*, and *The Last Time I Saw Paris*.

Hammerstein, in his tribute to Jerome Kern, declared:

"He devoted all his lifetime to giving the world something it needs and knows it needs—-beauty."

Kern was one of Broadway's greatest composers of popular melodies.

ALAN JAY LERNER (1918-1986) , who usually worked with FREDERICK LOEWE (1904-1988), wrote *Paint Your Wagon, Brigadoon, Gigi, My Fair Lady, Camelot*, and *An American in Paris*.

In addition, he worked with composer Burton Lane on the Broadway musical *On A Clear Day You Can See Forever*.

Lerner and Loewe met by chance at New York's Lambs Club in 1942. They had different backgrounds. Lerner was the son of a successful business man, and was educated in England and then Harvard. He studied at the Juilliard School of Music. Loewe was the son of an eminent operetta tenor, learned to play the piano at age four, and at 15 wrote *Katrina*. It sold 3,000,000 copies in Europe.

Some of Richard Rodgers' Songs

Bewitched, Bothered and Bewildered - I'm Gonna Wash - that Man Right Out of My Hair - It Might As Well Be Spring - Mimi - Mountain Greenery - My Favorite Things - My Funny Valentine - People Will Say We're in Love - Some Enchanted Evening - The Lady is a Tramp - The Most Beautiful Girl in The World - There's A Small Hotel - There's Nothing Like a Dame - This Can't be Love - Thou Swell - Oh, What a Beautiful Morning - With A Song In My Heart

Frank Loesser.

Lerner and Loewe's first great collaboration was *Brigadoon* in 1947. Another giant success was *My Fair Lady* in 1956, presented for a record 2,717 performances on Broadway alone. *Camelot* followed, but then Loewe suffered a heart attack in 1958 and retired.

FRANK LOESSER (1910-1969) wrote *Guys and Dolls* and *How to Succeed in Business Without Really Trying.*

During World War Two, he wrote the popular song *Praise the Lord and Pass The Ammunition*.

He was born in New York.

After writing scores for the movies, he turned his talents towards Broadway. He made a hit with the song *Once In Love With Amy* but caused a sensation with the show *Guys and Dolls* in 1950. It won him Tonys for Best Musical and Best Score.

He repeated his success with *How To Succeed in Business Without Really Trying*.

In addition to the Tonys, it won a Pulitzer Prize.

Stephen Sondheim was an outstanding composer if not THE outstanding composer after the remarkable 40s and 50s.

STEPHEN SONDHEIM (1930-   ) is both a composer and lyricist—writing the lyrics for Leonard Bernstein's *West Side Story* and composing, among other shows, *A Little Night Music* and *Sweeney Todd.*

Sondheim launched his career auspiciously, writing four librettos under the guidance of Oscar Hammerstein at age 21.

In 1957, he worked with Leonard Bernstein on *West Side Story*. And two years later he collaborated with Jules Stein on *Gypsy*.

His first solo flight—writing both the words and the music—was *A Funny Thing Happened on the Way to the Forum*.

He walked away with a number of distinguished awards in the years that followed, including *A Little Night Music, Merrily We Roll Along, Sunday in the Park with George*, and *Passion*.

KURT WEILL (1900-1950) composed light opera and broadway shows, including *One Touch of Venus, Knickerbocker Holiday* and *The Threepenny Opera.*

He was born in Dessau, Germany—the son of a cantor. He showed talent—composing songs and presenting amateur concerts and theatrical presentations to family and friends.

By 1925 he had won a reputation as an important composer. He collaborated with Brecht on such shows as *The Threepenny Opera* in 1928. But his music was condemned by the Nazis and in 1933, Weill fled Germany.

In America, his first collaboration was *Knickerbocker Holiday* followed by *Lady in the Dark*, written by Moss Hart with Ira Gershwin penning the lyrics (his first effort since his brother's death in 1937).

One Touch of Venus, with book by S.J. Perelman and lyrics by Ogden Nash, was an even greater success. He worked with Ira Gershwin on an original film musical, *Where do we go From Here*, in 1945.

Virgil Thomson wrote in Weill's obituary that he was "the most original single workman in the whole musical theater, internationally considered, during the last quarter century."

Kurt Weill was the son of a cantor; he became one of the leading composers of his generation.

ABE BURROWS' (1910-1985) hits included *Can-Can, Silk Stockings*, and the Pulitzer prize winning *How to Succeed in Business Without Really Trying.*

Burrows (his real name was Abram Solman Borowitz) studied at City College of New York and New York University. His first job was as a script writer for the radio show *Duffy's Tavern*. He later joined the writing staff of *The Rudy Vallee Show*.

He received both a Tony Award and a New York Drama Critics Award for the libretto he wrote for *Guys and Dolls*.

He also directed *Happy Hunting, Silk Stockings, First Impressions, Can-Can, Say, Darling* and *How to Succeed in Business Without Really Trying*. The latter won him three awards—a Pulitzer, a Tony, and the New York Critics Award.

Abe Burrows made his mark in Manhattan's music world.

Betty Comden and Adolph Green have won the highest awards of their craft but are best known for *Singin' in the Rain.*

ADOLPH GREEN (1915-2002) was one of America's greatest lyricists, writing the words for *Singin' in the Rain* while he worked, for many years with **BETTY COMDEN (1919-   )** and **JULES STYNE (1905-1994)**, on such hits as *Wonderful Town* and *Bells are Ringing.*

Styne wrote the lyrics for such hits as *Gentlemen Prefer Blondes, Gypsy*, and *Peter Pan.*

Director Harold Prince called Green "the quintessential New Yorker: buoyant, optimistic and resilient."

Green and Comden collaborated for decades, working with such composers as Leonard Bernstein, Jules Styne, and Cy Coleman.

"The great thing about their lyrics," suggested director George Wolfe, "was their wonderful combination of elegance and joy."

They won five Tony Awards for their Broadway productions. And their most celebrated screenplay was the one they wrote for *Singin' in the Rain.*

Dale Wasserman collected more than 40 top awards – but only attended one award ceremony.

DALE WASSERMAN (1917-   ) won both a Tony Award and the New York Drama Critics Circle Award for *Man of La Mancha.*

In all, Wasserman, who called himself "a showbiz hobo," started his theatrical career at age 19 and has won about 45 awards. He rarely turned up to accept an award. However, he made one exception: he donned cap and gown to receive an Honorary Doctorate from the University of Wisconsin "because a scant quarter-mile from where I was being doctored, I had hopped my first freight at the age of 12."

He was born in Rhinelander, Wisconsin, and endured one year of high school in Los Angeles.

His *Man of La Mancha* ran for five years on Broadway, and *One Flew Over the Cuckoo's Nest* had, among other long runs, six years in San Francisco.

BURT F. BACHARACH (1929-   ) is one of America's most popular composers of popular songs; his hits include *Raindrops Keep Fallin' On My Head, Alfie, Twenty Four Hours from Tulsa* and *Walk on By*.

He has been writing hit songs for four decades. His career as a performer began in the United States Army! He served in Korea as a concert pianist.

After doffing his uniform, he became an accompanist for a number of prominent entertainers including Vic Damone, Joel Gray, and Polly Bergen.

He only became prominent, however, when he worked as conductor-arranger for the legendary Marlene Dietrich, on a world concert tour. At the same time, he was composing songs for both Broadway and the movies.

In 1969, he won two Academy Awards—for the soundtrack for *Butch Cassidy and the Sundance Kid*, and for the song *Raindrops keep Fallin' on My Head*.

Burt Bacharach.

JERRY HERMAN (1933-   ) was a composer, lyricist, director, performer, and musician.

Some of his greatest hits were *Hello, Dolly!* (he wrote the music and the lyrics, and supervised production); *La Cage Aux Folles* (wrote both words and music); *Mame* (music, lyrics and production supervision), *Dear World*, (music and lyrics)

He was born in New Jersey, son of two teachers. His mother played the piano and sang on radio for a time.

Ruth Herman arranged a meeting for her enthusiastic youngster with one of the giants of Broadway, composer-lyricist Frank Loesser.

Herman recalls that Loesser "made me play everything I'd ever written." The established composer later phoned the Hermans and told them "I believe your son can make it in this business."

His Broadway assignment, and a big hit, was *Milk and Honey*, in 1963, followed by *Hello, Dolly!* and *Mame*, both in 1970

Jerry Herman has written some of the greatest Broadway shows including *Hello Dolly, Mame* and *La Cage Aux Folles*.

CHAPTER TWENTY-THREE

OTHER ENTERTAINERS

"Jews were heavily involved in entertainment as entrepreneurs and artists, beginning in the 1920s. Florenz Zeigfeld, Lee Strasberg, and the Schubert brothers were prominent directors and producers . . . The list of Jewish entertainers includes Fannie Brice, Eddie Cantor, Al Jolson, Groucho, Harpo and Zeppo Marx, Milton Berle, Danny Kaye and Zero Mostel."

Harvard Encyclopedia of American Ethnic Groups, 1980

Theodore Bikel is a multi-lingual folksinger and actor.

THEODORE BIKEL (1924-   ) starred as both a folksinger and an actor; he is fluent in five languages.

His family fled Austria when the Nazis seized the country in 1938. They moved to Palestine, and Bikel studied acting at the Hebrew National Theatre, Habimah, in Tel Aviv. In 1946, he left Palestine to study at the Royal Academy of Dramatic Arts in London.

Sir Laurence Olivier saw him perform in an Academy play and cast him as "Mitch" in the London production of *A Streetcar named Desire*. This, in turn, led to his appearance as a German soldier in the classic Humphrey Bogart-Katharine Hepburn film, *The African Queen*.

Journeying to the United States in 1954, he began appearing on television and in movies. He was nominated for an Academy Award for his performance as the Sheriff in *The Defiant Ones*.

In addition to his acting, Bikel was a popular folksinger.

VICTOR BORGE (1909-2000) made his debut in 1926 as a pianist in his native Denmark but, after fleeing to the US in 1940, enjoyed a highly successful career, coupling humor with his piano playing.

His original name was Borge Rosenbaum.

Borge was born in Copenhagen; his father was first violinist with the Danish Royal Opera Orchestra. As a small child, he began to learn how to play the violin but, at five, switched to the piano. He found it more comfortable. He studied classical music and played with the Copenhagen Philharmonic. But he was disturbed by the insistence on perfection in playing so he began to inject humor into his performances.

To earn extra money, he began playing at funerals, and in the evenings in nightclubs.

He became a star in his native Denmark, but had to flee when the Germans invaded. He was performing in Sweden when word came of the Nazi attack, coupled with a report he was on the list of intellectuals and artists to be arrested. He made his way to Finland where he rendezvoused with his wife, and managed to clamber aboard a crammed vessel, departing for the US, just as the gangplank was being raised.

He arrived in the United States flat broke and unable to speak English. He learned the language by watching movies, and reading comic strips.

In *Higher and Higher* (1943), with Frank Sinatra, a bystander comments to Borge "Lovely thing you're playing. What is it?" Victor pauses, rises from the bench and—after some careful consideration—replies "The piano."

Denmark knighted him and he was also honored by Sweden, Norway, and Finland.

Cyd Charisse (1921-   ) was famed for her dancing in such films as *Singin' in the Rain* and *Brigadoon* (both with Gene Kelly), and *Silk Stockings* (with Fred Astaire).

She was born in Amarillo, Texas, and her original name was Tula Ellice Finklea.

She began taking ballet lessons at age eight, and at 12 moved on to advanced dancing classes in Hollywood with Nico Charisse. Colonel de Basil of the famed *Ballet Russe* signed the dancer, at 14, and took her on his company's tour of the United States and Europe.

Cyd married Charisse when she returned to Los Angeles where she began dancing, and acting, in movies. Her performances as an actor were not noteworthy, but the moment this long-legged beauty began to dance, the audience paid rapt attention.

Fred Astaire, one of her dancing partners, said "when you've danced with her you stay danced with."

One of her most sparkling performances was as a gangster's moll dancing with Gene Kelly in *Singin' in the Rain*. She also partnered with Kelly, as a Scottish highland lass, in *Brigadoon*.

Metro-Goldwyn-Mayer publicist Howard Dietz once described the circuitous route the dancer took as her name evolved:

Victor Borge had to flee his native Denmark after taunting the Nazis during pre-invasion performances.

I want to thank my parents for making this possible—and I want to thank my children for making this necessary.
Quip with which Victor Borge ended his concerts

Cyd Charisse danced, in the movies, with both Gene Kelly and Fred Astaire.

Harry Houdini in Chains, 1899. (Library of Congress)

"She was born Tula Ellice Finklea. Her baby brother nicknamed her Sid. She joined the Ballet Russe and became Felicia Sidarova. This was subsequently changed to Maria Estamano. She married and became Mrs. Nico Charisse. At the start of her screen career she took the name Lily Norwood. MGM changed that to Sid Charisse and she was finally billed Cyd Charisse."

HARRY HOUDINI (1874-1926), son of a rabbi, was a world-famous escapologist.

Born Ehrich Weiss in Hungary, he and his four brothers had to find work when their father proved unpopular with his congregation.

Houdini, aged 14, cut linings for neckties, but pursued his fascination with magic. At 17, he adapted the name of a Parisian magician named Houdin, (simply adding an i" to become Houdini) and became apprenticed to an escapologist. He was outstandingly successful, particularly in undertaking dangerous stunts.

Impresario Martin Beck suggested that he concentrate on spectacular escapes after being handcuffed and otherwise restrained.

When Houdini, on tour, would arrive in a city he would challenge the police department to try to shackle him in a way that he could not free himself. The magician knew more about locks than most locksmiths.

William Lindsay Gresham, who wrote *Houdini*, declared "he was no master manipulator of cards and coins, in spite of his ambition to be remembered as a wizard of dexterity. But he did manipulate life and circumstance and the imagination of men."

He suffered what proved to be fatal injuries, in Montreal, when a student unexpectedly punched Houdini in the stomach three times. The blows ruptured the magician's appendix and he died a few days later from poison released into his bloodstream. He died on Halloween, October 31, 1926.

In his will, Houdini specified that his massive collection of professional secrets as a magician be destroyed.

Many asked how he could escape successfully when chained and locked in a trunk. Houdini once explained he could escape because of his great strength and the fact that he was bowlegged !

LEONARD COHEN (1934-   ) is a novelist, composer, poet, and musician.

Born in Montreal, he was educated at McGill University. His professor, poet Louis Dudek, stopped him in a corridor one day and ordered the puzzled student to kneel. Dudek rolled up his newspaper and tapped Cohen on each shoulder, then commanded "rise, poet."

As a young man, he felt privileged to join other, older, more recognized personalities in the "poets corner" of Ben's Delicatessen in downtown Montreal. The corner remains, decorated with the autographed portraits of some outstanding poets.

His two novels are *The Favorite Game* and *Beautiful Losers*. He has also published six volumes of poetry. *Beautiful Losers* has been particularly successful; hundreds of thousands of copies have been sold.

As a songwriter, his classic composition was *Suzanne*.

Leonard Cohen is multi-talented, but is best known for his poetry and recorded songs.

JOEL GREY (1932-   ) played minor roles for years until his portrayal of the master-of-ceremonies in *Cabaret* made him a star. He is an actor, singer, and dancer.

Joel Katz was born in Cleveland, Ohio to parents who were members of a Yiddish vaudeville troupe. Naturally, he learned to sing and dance as part of growing up in a theatrical family. His first professional performance was at age 10, when he played Pud, in *On Borrowed Time*, at the Cleveland Playhouse.

He changed his name to Kaye and then to Grey and began performing in nightclubs.

He impressed Eddie Cantor, in a Miami nightspot, and Cantor hired him for several guest spots on his television show. However, in the clubs, on stage or television, he didn't make it big until he was cast in *Cabaret* in 1966.

He was also hailed for his portrayal of George M. Cohan in *George M*, playing the lead role in the Broadway musical in 1969, and in a television adaptation a year later.

Joel Grey's career peaked with his portrayal of the *m.c.* in *Cabaret*.

Oscar Levant combined musicianship with acerbic humor.

OSCAR LEVANT (1906-1972) was a pianist, actor, and wit. He said of himself "I am the world's oldest child prodigy."

Levant first focused on classical music. He studied music in New York, beginning at 16, and in a few years, he was renowned as a concert pianist, composer, teacher, and band leader. His life changed completely when he met George Gershwin. Levant idolized Gershwin and became one of the greatest interpreters of the composer's works.

Gershwin remarked to him one day—-"If you had to do it all over again, would you fall in love with yourself ?"

Levant responded—"Play us a medley of your hit."

Following Gershwin's death, Levant became a personality—appearing on the *Information Please* radio program, and playing character roles in movies. Particularly noteworthy were *Rhapsody in Blue* and *An American in Paris*, recalling his close ties with Gershwin.

He was noted for his biting wit. He described himself like this:

"In some moments I was difficult, in odd moments impossible, in rare moments loathsome, but at my best unapproachably great."

In his *Memoirs of an Amnesiac*, he wrote: "My behavior has been impeccable; I've been unconscious for the last six months."

S.N. Behrman, in an introduction to Levant's *A Smattering of Ignorance*, declared Levant was "a character who, if he did not exist, could not be imagined."

For one year and one month he declared my house his house. For one year and one month he ate my food, played my piano, ran up my phone bill, burned cigarette holes in my landlady's furniture, monopolized my record player and my coffeepot, gave his guests the run of the joint, insulted my guests and never stopped complaining. He was an insomniac. He was an egomaniac. He was a leech and a lunatic...but I loved the guy.
Harpo Marx on Oscar Levant in his
Harpo Speaks

AL JOLSON (1886-1950) is best known for his role in the first talking movie The Jazz Singer, and for such songs as Swanee, My Mammy, Toot, Toot, Tootsie, Goodbye, California Here I Come, and April Showers.

He was born in Lithuania. His family emigrated to the United States when he was seven. They settled in Washington.

Asa Yoelson (his real name) was the son of a rabbi and cantor who wanted Al to follow in his footsteps . But Jolson was stage-struck. He ran away from home, and performed in small parts in vaudeville. In 1909, in blackface, he sang "My Mammy", in San Francisco. The crowd applauded his performance wildly, convincing Jolson he should keep the number in his repertoire for the rest of his life.

One of his memorable lines, which he kept as a signature was "You ain't heard nothing yet."

He excited his audiences. Critic Gilbert Seldes wrote: "I have heard Jolson in a second-rate show before an audience, listless or hostile, sing (an) outdated and forgotten song ... saw also the tremendous leap in vitality and happiness which took possession of the audience as he sang it."

Jolson himself had no doubts about his talent. He called himself "The World's Greatest Entertainer."

Many agreed with him. Eddie Cantor, in his *Take My Life*, wrote about Jolson: "There was something electric about him that sent a thrill up your spine. He sang and talked; but he was more than just a singer or an actor—he was an experience."

The entertainer's fans included Charlie Chaplin, who stated "Al Jolson was a great instinctive artist with magic and vitality...he personified the poetry of Broadway, its vitality and vulgarity, its aims and dreams."

Al Jolson surged into popularity once more in the mid-1940s when Larry Parks played him (with Jolson's voice on the sound track) in two biographical movies—-*The Jolson Story* and *Jolson Sings Again*. Remarkably his old hits became million sellers once more.

The veteran entertainer died in a San Francisco hotel room shortly after returning from Korea where he had performed for US troops. 25,000 attended his funeral.

Al Jolson was one of the greatest entertainers of all time. He appeared in the first "talkie", *The Jazz Singer*.

MARCEL MARCEAU (1923-   ) is the greatest mime of all time.

He was born Marcel Mangel in Strasbourg, France, and his father, a butcher, was murdered by Nazis in the Auschwitz concentration camp. Marcel and his brother joined the French underground and saved a number of lives—-smuggling Jewish children into Switzerland.

He changed his name to fool the Nazis.

After the war, he went to drama school—particularly studying mime. His performances have been so imaginative over the past half century that mimes the world over copy his routines.

Stan Laurel and Red Skelton were fascinated by his work and

Marcel Marceau is the greatest mime of all time.

Barbra Streisand remains a super-star after decades on Broadway, in movies and on television.

It's true that I have a very healthy ego; anybody who creates does.
Barbra Streisand

arranged a visit to the United States.

He has spoken only once in his life during a performance. Appearing in Mel Brooks' *Silent Movie,* Marceau spoke the only line in the production.

I prefer silence," he told an interviewer, "because it leaves the door open to the whole imagination."

He was awarded the French Legion of Honour.

BARBRA STREISAND (1942-   ) is one of the living legends of American show business—singer, actress, director, and producer.

She started singing in small Manhattan nightclubs, made it big on Broadway by age 20 and soared to stardom playing Fanny Brice in the musical comedy *Funny Girl.* Her performance in the movie version of *Funny Girl* won her an Oscar in 1969. That film was her ticket to Hollywood.

She made her debut as a director in *Yentl* in 1983. And her 1991 presentation, *The Prince of Tides,* was nominated for seven Academy Awards, including one for best picture.

Barbara (she shortened it to Barbra on entering the world of entertainment) Joan Streisand was born in Brooklyn. Her father, a high school teacher, died when she was only 15 months old.

Diana Streisand, with Barbara and her brother Sheldon to support, took a job as a secretary but found it tough sledding. "I slept in my mother's bed, my brother slept on a cot," Streisand recalled in a 1991 interview with the *Chicago Tribune.*

The multi-talented Streisand says her mother never understood her. "By her not understanding me, she's responsible for my success. I had to prove to my mother that you don't have to be beautiful to be a movie star," she told a *Vanity Fair* interviewer in 1991.

Her many awards include an Emmy in 1964 for "outstanding individual achievement."

CHAPTER TWENTY-FOUR

THE COMEDIANS

"What a troupe they were in their heyday! What a wild yap of wit and super burst of song came surging out of the Jewish slums of the twenties! The Marx Brothers, Al Jolson, George Jessel, Fanny Brice, Eddie Cantor, Jack Benny, Jack Pearl, Benny Fields, Lou Holtz, Ed Wynn, Joe Laurie, the Howard Brothers, Julius Tannen, Phil Baker, Phil Silvers, Milton Berle, Belle Baker, Harry Richman, Ben Bernie, the Ritz Brothers, Smith and Dale, Ben Welch, Harry Green, Ray Samuels, Jackie Osterman, George Burns——these are some of them ... in their presence Jewishness was not Jewishness. It was a fascinating Americanism."

Ben Hecht, Journalist, author, and playwright

Jack Benny was a star comic on stage and screen for some 60 years – but always claimed he was 39!

JACK BENNY (1894-1974) was one of America's best-loved comedians—starring on stage, radio, television, and in the movies.

He joked, throughout his long stage, radio, television, and movie career that he was only 39. He gave every child in his home town of Waukegan, Illinois $39 invested in trust funds—not to be cashed until they were 39! The nickname for the Jack Benny High High School students and graduates, in Waukegan, is the 39'ers. (Jack Benny himself, in Irving A. Fein's *Jack Benny* claimed, "I was born in Waukegan a long, long time ago. As a matter of fact, our rabbi was an Indian...he used a tomahawk...I was eight days old....what did I know?")

Benny (Benny Kubelsky) was born in Chicago but raised in Waukegan, seriously studied the violin and played in vaudeville. He was offered the job of accompanist to the Marx Brothers in an early phase of their career but his parents convinced him not to accept the offer.

While serving in the US Coast Guard, he entertained his fellow sailors by playing his violin and, between numbers, telling jokes. Gradually he was encouraged to switch from music to comedy. He left vaudeville in 1932 when he was given his own radio show and assembled a cast including Mary Livingstone (he had married her in 1927), announcer Don Wilson, band leader Phil Harris, and Eddie "Rochester" Anderson. He remained on radio, with his group largely intact, until 1955.

He appeared on television for a further 15-year spell—from 1950 until 1965. And he continued to make occasional guest appearances and specials, working into his eighties.

Part of his act involved jokes about his violin playing, but in his later years Benny (who was a very generous individual, although on the show he pretended to be a penny-pincher) teamed up with violinist Isaac Stern to play duets benefiting various symphony orchestras.

President Ford, in a tribute on the comedian's death, wrote:

"If laughter is the music of the soul, Jack and his violin and his good humor have made life better for all men."

Benny's best friend was fellow comedian George Burns, who wrote about his pal in his book *All My Best Friends* (1989):

"This was some great act this guy had: Jack Benny carried a violin he didn't play, a cigar he didn't smoke, and he was funniest when he said nothing."

The morning after Benny's death, his widow, Mary, received a single long-stemmed rose. There was no card. When Mary checked with the florist, he explained that Benny had made a provision in his will that, after his death, his widow would receive every day "one perfect red rose for the rest of Mary's life."

SHELLEY BERMAN's (1926-　　) act featured telephone humor.

Born in Chicago, Berman's goal was to be an actor and his monologues are often said to resemble one-act plays.

He froze during an audition in New York, but managed to pick up work as a writer for Steve Allen. However, after a time, he retreated to Chicago where he worked as a cabbie and, later, managed a drugstore. But he kept his hand in by acting in summer stock.

In 1955, he joined Chicago's Compass Players improvisational group and created his first solo routine. It involved a man, on the telephone, engaged in an embarrassing call to his host of the drunken night before. He called it "The Morning After the Night Before":

"How did I break a window? I see. Were you very fond of that cat? It's lucky the only thing I threw out the window was a cat!

Oh...she's a very good sport, your mother....."

Berman developed the telephone routine to its ultimate. In one of his greatest, entitled "The Hotel Room," a guest finds himself in a pitch-black room in which he cannot find either windows or doors to escape.

Berman's popularity began to decline in the 60s, in part due to competition from Bob Newhart and Woody Allen.

He has kept busy in relatively minor roles on television and on stage.

Shelley Berman made his mark with mock telephone calls.

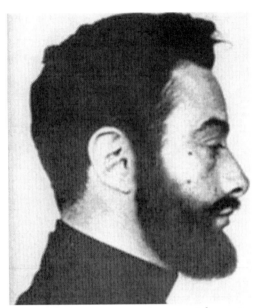

Lenny Bruce was a controversial comic, often jailed.

LENNY BRUCE (1925-1966) broke new ground in nightclub comedy, with bold use of sexual and ethnic material.

The veteran of World War Two began his career in cheap strip-tease joints in the 50s. Often accused of obscenity, and jailed, he made no secret of his intention of living life to the fullest, no matter what the cost. In an interview in 1953, when he was 28, he told a reporter:

"You only have 65 years to live. Before you're 20, you can't enjoy anything because you don't know what's going on. After you're 50, you can't enjoy it either, because you don't have the physical energies. So you have around 25 years to swing. In those 25 years, I'm going to swing."

He lived another 13 years, dying at age 40 from a drug overdose.

His final years were dark for him. His reputation for obscene performances resulted in a constant monitoring of his shows by police, and nightclub owners were wary of hiring him—fearing they would be arrested too.

A year before he died, the performer was declared bankrupt.

George Burns had been booked into the London Palladium to celebrate his 100th birthay, but didn't quite make it.

GEORGE BURNS (1896-1996) continued to be a featured performer into his 100th year.

He began performing at age five, dancing in the streets accompanied by an organ grinder.

He was born Nathan Birnbaum, in New York. He was seven when his father died and George immediately had to go to work—selling newspapers, shining shoes, anything to help maintain the family. He left school in the fourth grade.

He formed a musical group with three friends called the "Peewee Quartet." When the group won an amateur contest in a Presbyterian Church, Burns told his mother he wanted to convert. Asked why, he explained: "Well, I've been a Jew for seven years and never got anything. I was a Presbyterian for one day and I got a watch." The watch stopped and Burns remained Jewish.

His early years in vaudeville were so unsuccessful that he kept changing his name so he could be hired again. His luck changed when he met 17-year-old Grace Ethel Cecile Rosalie Allen. They teamed up, but it quickly became apparent that the audience was laughing at Gracie and not him. George and Gracie were married in 1926.

A typical exchange:

George—"Did the nurse ever drop you as a baby?"

Gracie—"Don't be ridiculous. We were too poor to have a nurse. My mother had to do it."

And, at the end of every show, George would suggest—"Say goodnight, Gracie," and the comedienne would respond "Good night, Gracie."

They were a hit on stage, on the radio, and television.

Gracie died of a heart attack in 1964. And Burns virtually stopped performing.

However, in 1975, Burns was asked to appear in *The Sunshine Boys* with Walter Matthau. His closest friend, Jack Benny, had been slated to play the part but died before production began.

Burns won an Academy Award as best supporting actor. He appeared in other movies, most notably *Oh, God*, where he played the title role.

He writes, in his autobiography *The Third Time Around*, how he was puzzled by the fact that he was being asked to play God. "Then I realized it made a little sense. I was the closest one to His age. Since Moses wasn't around, I suppose I was next in line."

He had been booked into the London Palladium on his 100th birthday but didn't quite make it.

EDDIE CANTOR (1892-1964) was a vaudeville star who made a successful transition to radio and screen—in both movies and television.

In fact, the saucer-eyed singer/comedian hand-clapped and joked his way to success in every medium he tried.

He was born Isidor Iskowitch, on New York's Lower East Side, and never finished elementary school. When he was 15, he won an amateur contest conducted in a music hall. He then began touring with a blackface comedy act. His animated performances drew large audiences and he became a vaudeville star who broke attendance records at many theatres where he appeared.

What made him so great on stage? The *New York Times* described him as "prancing about, clapping his hands, rolling his eyes ..." Sheer energy made him entertaining. He was one of the top stars of the Zeigfield Follies.

An autographed Eddie Cantor portrait.

Cantor began working in films in the 1920s and, in 1923, he was featured on Broadway in *Kid Boots*, a musical that ran for three years. Eddie Cantor originated the idea of the March of Dimes while chatting with President Franklin Delano Roosevelt, a victim of poliomyelitis. The President said a donation of a million dollars for polio was needed to fund research.

Cantor responded that it would be difficult to find someone rich enough, during the Great Depression, to come up with such a large sum, but—he continued—the money could be raised if 10,000,000 people each gave a dime (10 cents). And the idea of the March of Dimes was born.

In a 1963 interview with *The New York Times*, Eddie Cantor suggested:

"It takes twenty years to make an overnight success."

Cantor always closed his radio show, singing "I love to spend this hour with you, as friend to friend, I'm sorry it's through."

BUDDY HACKETT's (1924-2003) wild style of comedy was unique and was intended to shock with its vulgarity.

"When I was 14, I used to go with some other kids to the Star Burlesque in Brooklyn. They went to see the strippers, and the only thing I saw were the comedians."

In his later teens, Buddy (born Leonard Hacker) boxed for a living, calling himself "Butch Hacker."

He also found work in the Catskills, the mountainous resort area where many Jewish comedians got their start. He was hired as a busboy and waiter, but then began performing. He filled in when scheduled comedians did not show up.

After appearing on Broadway, he played a zany newsstand operator in the 50s situation comedy *Stanley*.

With his goofy grin and raspy Brooklyn accent, he began appearing in the movies and on stage, and was a particular favorite of Johnny Carson on the *Tonight Show*.

Once described as looking like a baked potato out for a stroll, he claims he couldn't help but make people laugh. "If I say something serious, it comes out funny anyway."

Buddy Hackett shocked his audiences with vulgarity.

RODNEY DANGERFIELD (1921-   ) made a career out of his claim that no one respected him.

Typically, he told an audience on one occasion: "I told my psychiatrist that everyone hates me. He said I was being ridiculous; everyone hasn't met me yet."

Born Jacob Cohen, his first years in Babylon, New York, were tough. His parents were separated, and there were money problems. He was embarrassed because he had to deliver groceries to homes of fellow students. He drove a laundry truck after graduating from high school.

His first try at comedy flopped and he became a salesman. However, he still wanted to get into show business. Booked for a gig in a nightclub, the owner suggested a new name: Rodney Dangerfield. That's when he ventured, successfully, into his new persona—"I don't get no respect."

Example: "I broke up with my psychiatrist. When I admitted I had suicidal tendencies, he told me from now on I had to pay in advance."

Rodney Dangerfield made a success about not deserving respect.

ALAN KING (1926-   ) was a drummer and a boxer before he became a comedian.

Born Irwin Alan Kniberg, he was one of nine children—eight boys and a girl. He grew up in a tough neighborhood, on the lower east side of Manhattan, and in Brooklyn.

His family was poor. "We went on relief when I was three years old and for nine years my father couldn't get a job." He tried playing the traps and boxing before he became, first, a musician and finally a comedian, in the Catskills. "We got ten bucks a week and all the borscht we could drink." He became a regular on the night club circuit, and then was picked up by Ed Sullivan for his highly-rated television variety show.

"It's a funny world we live in," says King. "If we didn't laugh about it, we'd cry."

King's humor often focused on wife and family. He claimed his wife was a fanatic about neatness. "How would you like to get up at 5 a.m. to go to the bathroom, and when you come back, the bed is made?"

Alan King tried drumming and boxing before making it big in comedy. He often chairs sessions of the College of Comedy Faculty.

Beatrice Arthur triumped as *Maude* and a Golden Girl.

BEATRICE ARTHUR (1923-   ) was voted the "funniest girl" in her high school class and made her reputation largely in two TV situation comedies *Maude* and *The Golden Girls*.

Born Bernice Frankel, Bea Arthur grew up in Cambridge, Maryland. She graduated from the Franklin Institute of Sciences and Art, in Philadelphia, and after World War Two (she served in the US Marines) moved to New York to study acting.

Bea Arthur, a statuesque five foot ten, had an up and down acting career for years and—even after winning a Tony Award for her performance in *Mame*, in 1966, was not well known.

In fact, with an ailing husband, Arthur became the breadwinner of the family by playing Yente the Matchmaker in *Fiddler on the Roof*, for years.

She became a star when Norman Lear cast her in the lead in *Maude* after the director discussed Arthur with her husband, Gene Saks.

"Gene told him what he loved about me and what he hated about me, and that's how Maude was born."

Her next success was the series *The Golden Girls*, in which Bea was the dominant figure among four older women—including Betty White, Rue McLanahan and Estelle Getty.

Responding to stories alleging feuds among the quartet, Bea Arthur stated: "We really do get along. We don't socialize of course ... but we are professionals who respect one another."

Arthur dropped out of the show in 1992; her character married. She felt that was a graceful way of retiring from the series. "It's better than having me killed off in a car wreck."

———

Woody Allen launched his career at age 15 – selling gags to TV stars.

WOODY ALLEN (1935-   ) moved from gigs in nightclubs to a highly successful career producing movies. He started selling jokes to newpaper columnists when he was 15.

Woody (real name Allen Konigsberg) was born in New York City and assumed the pseudonym "Woody Allen" when selling jokes to newspaper columnists.

After graduating from high school, in 1952, he became a comedy writer on the *Sid Caesar Television Show*. He also wrote material for

Art Carney, Jack Paar and Gary Moore. While working, he occasionally attended university classes but was expelled for failing grades and poor attendance.

In 1961, he left his job with the *Gary Moore Show* (which paid him a handsome $1,700 a week), to speculate on his ability to be a standup comedian. It took him more than a year to find the right formula.

Intrigued by Hollywood, he became a producer—inevitably starring himself in lead roles. In fact, some believe his films are semi-autobiographical.

In July, 2003, *Time* Magazine reported that "six of his movies have grossed more than $35 million."

JOHNNY WAYNE (1918-1990) and FRANK SCHUSTER (1917-2002) were showcased repeatedly on *The Ed Sullivan Show* and had a long run with their antics on the Canadian Broadcasting Corporation (CBC).

The two Torontonians studied English literature at the University of Toronto, wrote for The Varsity student newspaper, and performed in the U of T's *University College Follies*.

Before going off to War, they managed to wangle their own comedy show, called *Wife Preservers* on CFRB Toronto. Their comedy routines went over well with the troops and, when they returned from military service, they were given their own national CBC show and, in 1954 moved successfully into television.

They appeared on *The Ed Sullivan Show* a record 67 times, and twice were chosen as the best comedy team in North America.

Former U of T drama professor David Gardner stated "what I think was unique about their comedy was that it was very literary. They wrote and performed parodies on such topics as the Trojan War, Julius Caesar, and Shakespeare."

The Wit of Woody Allen

The lion and the calf shall lie down together but the calf won't get much sleep.
From a quote in The New Republic, 1974.

If only God would give me some clear sign! Like making a large deposit in my name in a Swiss Bank.
From an article in The New Yorker, 1973

It's not that I'm afraid to die. I just don't want to be there when it happens.
From his 1975 film Love and Death

I think crime pays. The hours are good, you travel a lot.

Not only is there no God, but try getting a plumber on weekends.

Wayne and Schuster were the Canadian comics who were repeatedly featured on the Ed Sullivan Show.

Peter Sellers began acting at 14.

PETER SELLERS (1925-1980) was a direct descendent of the British boxing champion Daniel Mendoza and began his long stage and film career at 14.

Born in Portsmouth, Sellers as a boy knew what he wanted to do in life. And his family reluctantly allowed him to drop out of school at age 14 to work in a theater owned by his uncle.

He served in the Royal Air Force in World War Two and then broke into radio using his ability to impersonate other people. He telephoned BBC producer Roy Speer, and pretending to be two different radio stars, recommended that the producer audition their "discovery."

In the early 50s, Sellers teamed up with Harry Secombe and writer Spike Milligan for a ten year run of *The Goon Show*, an outrageous comedy series.

By the late 50s, Sellers was one of Britain's most popular film stars. In Hollywood, in the early 60s, he starred in *Lolita* and *Dr. Strangelove* and then he created the role of French Inspector Clouseau in *The Pink Panther*.

He won an Academy Award nomination for his performance as Chance the gardener in *Being There*.

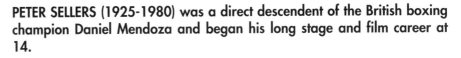

Danny Kaye started his comedy career in the Borscht Belt.

DANNY KAYE (1913-1987), one of the entertainment world's most popular comics, was a high school dropout who worked for a time as a soda jerk.

Daniel David Kominski was born in Brooklyn and loved to entertain people. His first public performance, at age 5 $\frac{1}{2}$, was in an elementary school minstrel show; he played a watermelon seed. He dropped out of high school and worked at a variety of jobs, including time in an ice cream parlour.

However, for four years—beginning in 1929—he worked as a "toomler" (Yiddish for noisemaker), entertaining guests in the "Borscht Belt," the mountain vacation area where many Jewish comedians got their start.

Kaye worked up his pantomime techniques while touring the Orient for two years, playing to audiences who did not speak English.

Back in the states, he met a young songwriter named Sylvia Fine at a summer camp for professionals in Pennsylvania. Using her material,

Kaye was a smash hit when he appeared in the *Straw Hat Review* on Broadway in 1939.

Appearing in Moss Hart's *Lady in the Dark*, he rattled off the names of 54 Russian composers in 38 seconds.

During the 40s and 50s, Kaye perfected his rapid-fire delivery—appearing in a number of movies. His first film, *Up in Arms* in 1944, was followed by *Kid From Brooklyn, The Secret Life of Walter Mitty, A Song is Born, Inspector General, Hans Christian Anderson, Knock on Wood, Me and the Colonel*, and others.

He had his own television production *The Danny Kaye Show* for four years and won an Emmy in 1963 and a George Foster Peabody Award.

He toured the world for UNICEF, entertaining thousands of children.

JOAN RIVERS (1935-   ) wrote comedy material for Phyllis Diller before getting her big break—appearing on the Johnny Carson *Tonight Show*.

She was born in Brooklyn, raised in Larchmont and, at 19, graduated Phi Betta Kappa from Barnard College.

She wanted to go into the theater, but her family wouldn't hear of it. She became a fashion coordinator (for Bond Stores), married —for six months—and recalls that "marriage gave me courage to go into show business." Rivers was an extra in the film *Mr. Universe* when she was 18.

She tried everything to build a reputation—working clubs for free, spent some time in the Borscht Belt, and even dreamed up ideas for *Candid Camera*. She began writing jokes for Zsa Zsa Gabor and Phyllis Diller. And she worked, 1961-1962, with the Chicago improvisational troupe Second City, where she honed her skills as a comedienne. More nightclub shows followed and then, in 1965, Johnny Carson learned that here, indeed, was a funny lady. An appearance on his *The Tonight Show* put her on the show business map.

She made her debut in Las Vegas in 1969. And she was snapped up for a variety of television appearances. She was a regular guest host on *The Tonight Show*.

In 1990, she won a Daytime Emmy Award.

Joan Rivers wrote material for Phyllis Diller before becoming a star herself.

Milton Berle was TV's first Superstar.

MILTON BERLE (1908-2002), television's first superstar, won a Charlie Chaplin look-alike contest when he was five.

The beginning of television, in 1948, brought the comedian into the homes of millions of people as the wise-cracking host of the *Texaco Star Theatre.*

He was born Milton Berlinger and was raised in a Jewish working class district of New York. His family was desperately poor. He recalls how, at age four, he and his brothers went through an entire day with nothing to eat. When, after nightfall, his mother returned "all she had was four bagels which she'd gotten for two cents because they were leftovers...We all went to bed and cried, because we were so hungry and miserable."

His mother entered him in a Chaplin lookalike contest when he was five. He won—and, to his stagestruck mother, her little son was a future star. He kept winning the Chaplin contests, and peddled the $2 silver loving cups he won for 25 cents spending money.

Milton went into vaudeville, and his mother—who worked for a time as a store detective—performed with him ("Milton and Mom").

He began appearing in silent movies (Miltie claimed he was the baby Marie Dressler was holding in the early film *Tillie's Punctured Romance*), then radio and back on film.

He became master of ceremonies at the Palace in New York—the leading vaudeville house in the US—and then starred in both the *Earl Carroll Vanities* and *The Zeigfield Follies*. But television, with his vaudeville background, beginning in 1948, saw him wow audiences with his frantic, non-stop routines.

His Tuesday night show was so popular that some nightclubs and restaurants remained closed that evening.

Known as "Uncle Miltie" or "Mr. Television," his show lasted seven seasons. He picked on latecomers trying to reach their seats. "You can sit down madam. We saw the dress." And, to an embarrassed woman with a feather in her hat:

"That looks like the feather that signed the Declaration of Independence. And the guy with her looks like he signed it!"

In 1951, Berle signed a contract with NBC guaranteeing him $200,000 a year for 30 years. And he lived to collect every dime. In 1985 he underwent heart surgery and told everyone:

"I went to an honest doctor. He would never operate on someone unless he needed the money."

In his autobiography, Berle wrote:

"It took me 35 years in show business to become a star overnight."

After his show folded, Berle continued to perform in clubs, in a few films and even on stage, but the magic was gone.

SID CAESAR (1922-   ) was a classical musician who switched to comedy and reached the peak of his career in the early television period with his legendary *Your Show of Shows* (1950-1954) and *Caesar's Hour* (1954-1957).

Half a century later, in 2000, a 50th anniversary collection of his comedy routines was still being snapped up by young people.

The day after his 79th birthday, he made a guest appearance on *The Drew Carey Show*.

Actually, Caesar was trained as a classical musician. He studied at Juilliard and played both the saxophone and clarinet. However, he switched to comedy while serving in the Coast Guard in World War Two.

A major slice of his routine centered on his ability to mimic dialects and accents, an ability picked up while working in his father's luncheonette. Most of the patrons were from Russia, Poland, and Italy.

He made his comedy debut at the Copa in 1947. Later he received enthusiastic reviews about his work in the Broadway revue *Make Mine Manhattan*.

Sid Caesar's *Your Show of Shows* topped the ratings in the early days of television. He had an incredible team of writers working on the show, including Mel Brooks, Neil Simon, Carl Reiner and Larry Gelbart—who created the *M*A*S*H* series. When asked why so many of the writers were Jewish, Gelbart responded:

"It was probably because all our parents were old and Jewish."

Nevertheless, despite all the talent, Caesar states "I worked on every line with the writers every day before each show went on the air."

Sid Caesar was one of the greatest comedy stars of early television.

FANNY BRICE (1891-1951) starred on stage and radio, using a pronounced Yiddish accent; on radio she played a seven year old brat named "Baby Snooks."

Her original name was Fanny Borach.

She began her career at age 14 singing in an amateur show in Brooklyn's Keeney Theatre. Her prize was $10. But, in addition, members of the audience tossed coins onto the stage which Brice

Fanny Brice starred on stage and radio.

scrambled to collect. Furthermore, owner Frank Keeney was so impressed by her performance that he hired her, at a handsome $60 a week, to perform in two other theaters he owned.

She was popular in both vaudeville and burlesque, using a Jewish dialect.

Florenz Zeigfeld hired her, at 18, for his *Follies of 1910,* and she appeared in many editions of the show. For her first number, Fanny Brice donned an Indian costume and belted out "I'm an Indian," with a Yiddish accent!

She learned to dance with the help of chorus girls, and paid for her lessons with lingerie stolen from her mother's dresser.

She began playing "Baby Snooks" in 1936, her baby talk stemming possibly because she had a problem with her dentures.

Fanny married and divorced three times. Her most scandalous husband was a confidence man named Nicky Arnstein, who went to jail for bilking Wall Street of $5,000,000. When Fanny sadly sang the ballad "My Man", the audience knew she was still devoted to Nicky.

Nevertheless, a year after divorcing Nicky—in 1927—she married showman Billy Rose. That marriage lasted only a year. Fanny knew she was falling for the wrong kind of man, saying "I've been singing about this bum for 15 years under different (song) titles. He's always the same lowlife, always doing me dirt but I keep loving him just the same."

Her most memorable song was "Second Hand Rose".

Brice had a huge nose and, in 1923, tired of being kidded about it, she had plastic surgery. Dorothy Parker quipped that Fanny had "cut off her nose to spite her race."

Brice talked about repressed emotions in an interview with Darryl Lyman (published in his *Jewish Comedy Catalog,* 1989):

"Being a funny person does an awful lot of things to you. You feel you must never get serious with people. They don't expect it from you. You are not entitled to be serious. You are a clown. And maybe that is what made me dislike emotion."

A musical on Fanny Brice's life, *Funny Girl,* was produced on Broadway in 1964 and a movie with the same name was released four years later. Barbra Streisand played the role of Brice. And a sequel, *Funny Lady,* hit the screens in 1975.

I never did a Jewish routine that would offend my race, because I depended on my race for the laughs. In anything Jewish I ever did, I wasn't standing apart making fun. I was the race, and what happened to me on stage is what could happen to my people. They identified with me, which made it all right to get a laugh, because they were laughing at me as much as at themselves.
Fanny Brice quoted in Great Jewish Women, 1994

FRAN DRESCHER's (1957-   ) great break came with her portrayal of the "Nanny" in the situation comedy of that name.

Born in Flushing, N.Y., Drescher was eager to act, beginning in high school, where she performed in such plays as *"Our Town"* and *"The Trojan Woman."*

"I really always had a very clear picture of what I wanted to do with my life," she told *New York Magazine*. "When everybody else was taking driver's ed in high school, I said I'd rather use the $150 to get myself a (picture) portfolio."

When she found Queens College was difficult to break into because "the acting classes were so crowded," she switched to a hair-dressing school.

However, after a few modeling assignments, she won a small part in *Saturday Night Fever*, and after that, in part because of her pronounced accent, she won character roles.

She came up with the idea of *The Nanny* during a visit to her friend, Twiggy, who had teenaged children. CBS liked the idea. Drescher played Fran Fine, a door-to-door salesperson of cosmetics. But Broadway producer Maxwell Sheffield, answering the door, hires her as nanny for his three children.

Fran Drescher as Nanny Fine on *The Nanny*.

HENNY YOUNGMAN (1906-1998) was famed for his "one-liners," pleading with his audiences: "Take my wife........please."

In one act, he told his audience: "I once wanted to become an atheist, but I gave up...they have no holidays."

Youngman's parents encouraged him to study the violin; they hoped their son would be another Heifetz. But, as was the case with Jack Benny, the violin became only a prop.

"I was a lousy fiddler," he states. "People used to laugh at me when I played. So I became a comedian."

He was born in England but his parents moved to Brooklyn when he was a youngster.

Youngman first did a few routines in speakeasies (illegal drinking spots during Prohibition), but he began to attract attention while performing at Manhattan's old Yacht Club.

Singer Kate Smith liked his style, and featured him on her radio show in the 1930s.

Henry Youngman was the King of the One-liners.

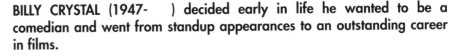

Billy Crystal (the short one) in the movie My Giant.

His patient wife, Sadie Cohen, was often the butt of his jokes. "My wife asked me to take her somewhere she'd never been, so I took her to the kitchen."

He claimed his brother-in-law crossed a parrot with a tiger. "They don't know what it is, but when it talks, everybody listens!"

———

BILLY CRYSTAL (1947-   ) decided early in life he wanted to be a comedian and went from standup appearances to an outstanding career in films.

He came from a show-business family. His grandfather was a Yiddish actor; an uncle founded Commodore Records and his father promoted jazz concerts.

From age eight, Billy performed for his family. He studied drama at New York University, and teamed up with friends Dave Hawthorne and Al Finelli to appear in nightclubs. Urged by his agents to go it alone, Crystal worked up a 20-minute routine at an NYU fraternity party. The crowd responded so enthusiastically he kept performing for a full hour.

Still, Crystal did not do so well in nightclub appearances. His wife, Janice, had to work as a secretary to help when he was "at liberty."

But through movies and television, Billy Crystal established himself as a topflight comedian. And, after appearing in one episode of *All In The Family*, he became friends with Bob Reiner ("Meathead") who later fitted him into productions Reiner directed.

Crystal has been the master of ceremonies for the Academy Awards six times—-1990-1993 and in 1997 and 2000.

A lifelong New York Yankees' fan, he paid $239,000 for Mickey Mantle's baseball glove in 1999.

———

JERRY SEINFELD (1954-   ) began his career in comedy clubs and returned to standup after an outstanding nine year run with the TV situation comedy *Seinfeld*.

Seinfeld was remarkably successful and totally different from other sitcoms. The show was built around the interplay among the four central characters in the show. The series was witty, rather than built on normal comedy interchanges.

Seinfeld was born in Brooklyn, and claims his inspiration for becoming a comic was his father. The comedian told *People* in a 1988 interview, Kalman Seinfeld "was always making people laugh. I watched the effect he would have on people, and I thought that was for me."

At Queen's College, in Flushing, N.Y., he was a dean's list student with a double major in theatre and communications. But when he took his first stab at stand-up comedy—during an open mike night at "Catch a Rising Star," a Manhattan comedy club—"the bright lights hit my face and I froze solid."

However, his next attempt brought a good response from the audience, and he began appearing in New York comedy clubs, earning so little he had to take odd jobs. And he chose jobs he liked the least, hoping he would be motivated to do better as a comic.

His big break came when a talent scout for the *Tonight Show* heard him in a Los Angeles club. That appearance with host Johnny Carson was the first of many for Seinfeld.

In 1988, now with a national reputation, NBC/Castle Rock Entertainment approached him an idea for a TV show in which he would play himself. The rest of the cast included Julia Louis-Dreyfus, as a former girl friend, Jason Alexander as his best friend and Michael Richards as Kramer, Seinfeld's wild and unpredictable neighbour.

"I love everything about being famous," he wrote in an article for GQ in1991. "You hear so many celebrities talk about the price of fame. As I see it, there is no price. It's all free."

In the fall of 2002, Seinfeld published his first children's book, *Halloween*.

Jerry Seinfeld had an outstanding nine year run on TV with his program *Seinfeld* – and then went back to stand-up, by choice.

JERRY LEWIS (1926-   ), a popular comedian on both sides of the Atlantic, began his performing career at age five singing "Brother Can You Spare a Dime?"

Joseph Levich was born in Newark, New Jersey, the son of vaudeville performers Danny and Mona Levich. It was only family tradition that made Lewis a performer. His first appearance, at 5, was

Jerry Lewis has been a success on both sides of the Atlantic.

on stage at a Borscht Belt hotel in the Catskills where countless Jewish comedians got their start.

In high school, he was nicknamed "Id" for "idiot." He dropped out of school in the tenth grade and began performing in hotels where his parents—also using the stage name "Lewis"— had appeared. His frantic clowning made him a living at 19.

In 1946, Lewis teamed up with Italian singer, Dean Martin—a strange combination of a buffoon and a straight man. That interplay brought them instant success and, for a decade, they were one of the most popular comedy teams in the United States—appearing in nightclubs, on television, and 16 movies produced by Paramount.

They split up in 1956, but both continued to be successes for a time. By the late 60s, Lewis' popularity was fading. His most prominent annual appearance was on television to raise money in support of muscular dystrophy. He began that effort in 1953 and has collected tens of millions of dollars for MD research.

One of the places where Lewis is still wildly popular is France, where the comic's wild antics and pantomime hurdle the language barrier.

DON RICKLES (1926-   ) barged into show business while still a teenager and made it all the way to the top with his abrasive style.

Still in high school, he was hired as entertainment director for a resort in the Catskills. "I played bingo with the guests ... if it rained, I was supposed to go out and make it stop."

He served in the US Navy in World War Two "I grew up in the Navy ... it was better than summer camp."

At first, his nightclub act was a failure, but in the late 1950s, he joined the ranks of popular comedians with his insulting style of humor. His biggest break, however, came when Johnny Carson gave him a spot on *The Tonight Show*.

"Hello Dummy," was his oft-repeated opener. "My style is to rib people I like. If there is anger in it, it isn't funny."

JACKIE MASON's (1931-   ) first career was as a rabbi—but he switched to comedy after the death of his father in 1957.

Mason (real name Yacovf Moshe Maza) was born in Sheboygan, Wisconsin, but—as his accent testifies—he was brought up on New York's lower east side.

He started performing in the Borscht Belt—those summer hotels where many entertainers got their start, while continuing his rabbinical studies. He worked as social director and lifeguard at one hotel in the Catskills, "But I can't swim," Mason told the manager. "That's alright. Just don't tell the guests."

He moved on to nightclubs but, in 1960, Steve Allen gave him a guest shot on *The Tonight Show* and that brought him offers from better night clubs and television.

Despite his rabbinical background, Mason was very much a new wave comic.

"Ask in any country, 'where's the American Embassy?' They'll tell you it's only a stone's throw away."

"President Kennedy rides around in a $12,000 car. How does he know I want to buy him such a fancy car? Special car made to order with an open top so he can stand up. If he wants to stand up he don't need a car, let him take a bus!"

Mason's career was derailed for years when he had a falling out with TV host Ed Sullivan, who misunderstood a hand gesture, and Mason had to start from the bottom. In fact, in 1983 he went bankrupt.

One-man shows on Broadway—*The World According to Me*—were a big success for him starting in 1986, and he took his show on the road.

One writer called his routines a "Talmudic argument with life."

In 1990, Oxford University established a Jackie Mason Visiting Fellowship for the study of Hebrew.

Mason's career dipped when he had a falling out with TV host Ed Sullivan, but he roared back with a solo show on Broadway. (William Morris Agency)

ZERO MOSTEL (1915-1977) won a Tony in 1965 as the original 'Tevye' in *Fiddler on the Roof*.

Born in Brooklyn (real name Samuel Joel Mostel), he graduated near the bottom of his class at Seward Park High School, hence the moniker "Zero."

Zero Mostel won a Tony for his Tevye in *Fiddler on the Roof*.

The freedom of any society varies proportionately with the volume of its laughter.

Zero Mostel

His father wanted him to be a rabbi; his mother wanted him to be an artist. Instead, in 1936, he dropped out of New York University and spent ten years wandering around the country, working in factories, on docks, and in mines.

Oddly enough, he then became a popular and humorous lecturer on art at the Metropolitan Museum of Art and the Frick Museum. To earn extra income, he began to do stand-up comedy, earning five dollars a night doing comedy routines at private parties.

However, after he made his professional stage debut, he was quickly signed up for appearances on radio and vaudeville. In the space of one year, his weekly salary rose from $40 to $4,000. "It didn't go to my head, it went to my waistline."

In the early 1950s, Mostel was blacklisted for being associated with groups alleged to be communist fronts.

However, back in New York and on the stage, he did well.

In 1961, he won a Tony for his acting in Ionesco's *Rhinoceros*. In 1963, he starred in *A Funny Thing Happened on the Way to the Forum*, (another Tony) and a year later he played "Tevye" in *Fiddler on the Roof*.

He died in Philadelphia while rehearsing a new show.

SOPHIE TUCKER (1884-1966) called herself the"last of the Red Hot Mamas" and was an entertainer for 62 years.

She was born Sophie Abuza in Russian Poland while her mother and brother were en route to the United States to reunite the family. She was raised in an orthodox Jewish, Yiddish-speaking home in Hartford, Connecticut.

The family operated a kosher restaurant (meals were no more than 50 cents) and a rooming house. As a child, Sophie would be up before dawn to prepare lunches for workers.

She sang in school and at outdoor concerts in Riverside Park. A hefty person, even as a teenager, she belted out songs and won prizes. She also performed in the family restaurant for tips, while her mother cooked and the father gambled, disastrously, in a back room.

Sophie changed her last name to Tucker and with her lifesavings of $100, moved to New York where she managed to get a break—singing

Sophie Tucker called herself the "last of the red hot mamas."

in the Cafe Monopol. She knew that, to be a success, she had to become a recognizable personality, so she appeared on stage encrusted with cheap, gaudy jewelry, singing lustily.

One of her most famous songs was "My Yiddishe Mama" and in 1911, she adopted "Some of These Days" as a signature tune. Three years later (after bombing out in the *Zeigfield Follies* because her voice drowned out that of the star!) she made a sensational appearance at the Palace Theater in New York, the number one vaudeville house in the nation.

Sophie Tucker never forgot her youthful poverty. " I've been rich and I've been poor," she declared. "Rich is better."

A highlight of her career was a royal command performance at the London Palladium on behalf of the King George V Memorial Fund, in 1934. On stage, she nodded her head towards King Edward VIII, seated in the Royal Box, and yelled "Hi yah, King."

Tucker had her own brand of wisdom. "From birth to age eighteen, a girl needs good parents," she said. "From eighteen to thirty-five she needs good looks. From thirty-five to fifty-five, she needs a good personality. From fifty-five on, she needs good cash." And she added brightly: "I'm saving my money !"

On her 80th birthday, January 13, 1964, she was asked about the secret of longevity. "Keep breathing," she responded.

THE MARX BROTHERS were a zany troupe who starred on stage in vaudeville, and in movies which have become classics.

The brothers were Chico (real name Leonard/1891-1961), Harpo (Arthur/1893-1964), Groucho (Julius/1895-1977), Gummo (Milton/1892-1977) and Zeppo (Herbert/1901-1979) who left the act in 1935.

Legend has it that they were given their odd names by an entertainer named Art Fisher during a poker game in Galesburg, Indiana. In 1924, they formally adopted the nicknames as their professional monikers.

Was there any basis for the names? Groucho was so-named because he carried the family "grouch bag" or money bag; Harpo, because he played the harp; Chico, because he chased the "chicks"; Gummo because he wore rubber-soled shoes (i.e. gumshoes) and

The Marx Brothers' movies are still classics after 70 years!

Groucho Marx was the best comedian this country ever produced...(He) combined a totally original physical conception that was hilarious with a matchless verbal delivery.
Woody Allen in Darryl Lyman's Jewish Comedy Catalog, 1989

Zeppo, apparently named after another vaudeville act, "Zippo," the chimp.

In the wake of a wildly-successful career in vaudeville and in the movies, the only one of the brothers to continue prominently in show business was Groucho.

First on radio, and then more successfully on television, he hosted the quiz show *You Bet Your Life*. He won an Emmy in 1951 for the show.

In 1972, he was a rousing success at Carnegie Hall in *An Evening with Groucho,* and that same year, he journeyed to the Cannes Film Festival to receive a special award.

Before departing, he told reporters:

"I have two French phrases I'm working on. 'Voulez-vous couchez avec moi?' and 'Vive le beaujolais.'"

Brothers Gummo and Zeppo made it to his 85th birthday party, and other stars in attendance included Bob Hope, Carl Reiner and Jack Lemmon.

Peter Sellers, another guest, remarked:

"Just to sit there and realize that you are in the same room with Groucho Marx is a delightful experience."

Harpo Marx pretended to be a mute in his performances, but was a remarkable personality. He was taken into the Algonquin round table group, one of the most intellectual gatherings in New York in the 1920s.

Harpo himself marvelled at the experience. "I've been a member of the two most famous round tables since the days of King Arthur...sitting with the finest creative minds of the 1920s at the Algonquin in New York, and with Hollywood's sharpest professional wits at the Hillcrest....

"The truth is, I had no business doing any of these things. I couldn't read a note of music. I never finished second grade. But I was having too much fun to recognize myself as an ignorant upstart." (From his autobiography *Harpo Speaks*.)

The Algonquin group spent some summers on a small Vermont Island, where they played sophisticated games. In one, it was instantly apparent that Harpo was the "murderer" when the victim found the words "you're ded" written on a roll of toilet paper.

CHAPTER TWENTY-FIVE

THE ISRAELI DIMENSION

"In a generation haunted by doubt, fear and ideological confusion, the revival of Israel has a significance beyond its material dimensions. Land and people throb in vitality and homecoming ... The Negev Desert is being watered; the Hula swamps have become fertile land; the City of Jerusalem, Israel's capital and fountainhead of lasting inspiration, is being rebuilt; the hills and valleys are covered with hundreds and hundreds of settlements; great academies of learning—religious, secular and scientific—are flourishing. There has evolved a democratic society that has withstood the test of external threats, economic difficulties and all attempts at communal diffusion."

Yaavoc Herzog, Israeli diplomat and scholar speaking in Boston
December 13, 1959

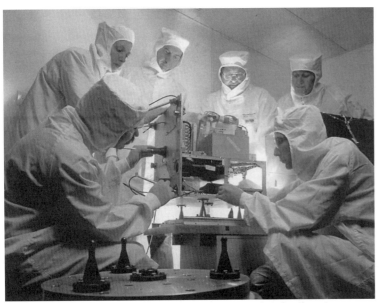

Israel's Technion is a world leader in science and technology.

WORLD LEADER IN EDUCATION

Israel leads the world in the proportion of scientists and technicians in its work force: 145 per 1,000—compared with 85 in the United States, 70 in Japan, and less than 60 in Germany.

Newsweek, (April 8, 1996) commenting on the tremendous growth of high-tech in the Jewish state, declared: "the land of milk and honey has become a land of tech and money" The magazine added: "Silicon Valley really has only one rival outside the United States — Israel."

Tiny Israel—about the size of New Jersey—has nevertheless managed to attract some of the biggest names in industry, including Intel, IBM (which has established at Haifa University the most advanced computer technology center in the world outside of the US), Digital, Amdex and others.

Israel exports a hefty 22.5 billion dollars in goods annually, and about 70% contain high-tech components.

The Israel Information Center says the country "has more start-up companies in absolute terms (somewhere between 1,500 and 2,000) than any other country in the world except the US."

Onetime Industry and Trade Minister, Natan Sharansky, once stated Israel "boasts more high-tech start-ups than all the countries in Western Europe put together."

The range of products is immense—and the response of world markets is remarkable. Its high-tech industries develop and manufacture computer software, highly-sophisticated medical equipment, communications devices, and biotechnology products.

The Russians are coming

Israel, from its rebirth in 1948, emphasized higher education, and research and development. Prime Minister David Ben-Gurion, in 1962, put it this way:

The imposing tower of Haifa University, serving all of northern Israel wih the most advanced computer technology in the world outside of the United States.

"Scientific research and its achievements are no longer merely an abstract intellectual pursuit ... but a central factor ... in the life of every civilized people."

At the beginning of the 1990s, high-tech comprised 23% of all Israeli industrial exports. But the arrival in the state of more than one million Jews from the Soviet Union included more than 10,000 scientists and engineers.

The state geared itself up to take advantage of a pool of expertise.

By 1997, civilian research and development expenditures reached 2.2% of gross domestic product—-the fifth highest percentage in the world. And, from this immense R&D effort came, in software alone, $3 billion in sales in 1999, $2 billion of which was exported.

Some key points:

—-The cell phone was developed in Israel by Motorola, which has its largest development center in Israel;

—-Most of the Windows NT operating system was developed by Microsoft Israel;

—-The Pentium MMX Chip technology was designed at Intel Israel.

—-Voice mail technology was developed in Israel.

—-Both Microsoft and Cisco built their only R&D facilities, outside the US, in Israel.

—-Four young Israelis developed the technology for the AOL Instant Messenger in 1996.

—-The first PC anti-virus software was developed in Israel in 1979.

Some recent Israeli research breakthroughs in medicine:

The Weizmann Institute has succeeded in growing human kidney tissue inside the bodies of mice, potentially giving a new lease on life to thousands awaiting kidney transplants.

Researchers have developed a cardiac device to open arteries.

A laser technique to improve in-vitro fertilization success ratios has been created.

A new bone marrow transplant technique may eliminate the need for chemotherapy.

Hebrew University has developed an advanced microsurgical tool for corrective eye surgery.

Professor Ari Orenstein specializes in a novel cancer therapy that exploits characteristics of tumor cells to destroy them.

An experimental program of megadose stem cell therapy could help correct blood disorders, eliminate enzyme deficiencies, create a new immune system to aid in organ transplants, and use cell therapy to fight cancer.

Israeli bioengineers have produced one of the most important cardiological devices of recent years—the "NIR" stint, a device that could drastically reduce the need for coronary bypass surgery.

Many of Israel's research facilities are seeking to unlock the secrets behind genetic diseases. Among others, they have identified the gene that causes mucolipidosis (ML.4) Researchers are well along in their search to identify the gene causing deafness. (This has been undertaken by a joint Israeli-Palestinian team.)

Working with Johns Hopkins University, Israeli scientists are creating products from soy beans to bring pain relief.

Malaria was eliminated in Israel many years ago; Nevertheless, the Weizmann Institute is developing new and improved anti-malaria drugs.

Israeli scientists have found a chemical process that removes cholesterol from the body.

A new vaccine, developed at the Weizmann Institute, is effective in preventing a type of diabetes that can cause blindness and kidney damage, even when treated with insulin.

Dr. Michael Aviram has identified a powerful antioxidant in the pomegranate that is more effective in fighting heart disease than those in tomatoes and red wine.

Shela Gorinstein's research team at the Hebrew University Medical School has found that downing a beer a day alters the structure of fibrinogen, a blood protein active in clotting. It apppears to diminish the risk of heart attacks and stroke.

Israel's largest pharmaceutical company, Yeva, has begun marketing in the US (with FDA approval) its new tablet for relieving pain, especially among older people.

Scientists from Israel's IDgene Pharmaceuticals have discovered a gene that plays a significant role in the development of schizophrenia.

Israeli virologist Dr. Madeleine Mumcouglu has developed an extract from European black elderberry that has been clinically shown to shorten the duration of influenza types A and B and reduce their symptoms. The extract is called Sambucol and is being marketed in Israel, the US, and Canada.

Jews developed medical services in the early part of the 20th century. The ruling Turks had provided none. Here is the Misgav Ladach Hospital in 1915.

WORLD-CLASS MEDICAL SCHOOLS

Israel has four world-class medical schools, all engaged in research along with the country's 30 hospitals. The Israel Medical Association has a membership of 15,000 physicians. Nearly half of all medical research in the country is undertaken at the two Hadassah University hospitals. Israel's high standard of health services, coupled with medical resources and research plus modern hospital facilities have resulted in a low infant mortality rate - 7.5 per 1,000 live births (against 6.3 in the US); long life expectancy - 78.61 (76.2 in the US)

When Jews began to return to the Holy Land in substantial numbers, they found a backward and neglected part of the dying Ottoman Empire, in which such diseases as dysentery, malaria, typhus and trachoma were rampant.

Jews established clinics (Bikur Holim in 1843; Misgav Ladach, 1888; Shaare Zedek , 1902; Hadassah, 1913) which evolved into modern hospitals with networks of medical services and schools of medicine, nursing, and pharmacology. These facilities were open to, and used by, all elements in the population.

One of the greatest gifts the Jewish people gave to the Arabs living in Palestine was better health. Interestingly, the United States has adopted some Israeli health care procedures.

The Lavi fighter – capable of reaching twice the speed of sound. Israel is one of a handful of countries capable of designing and building such a complex aircraft.

ADVANCED TECHNOLOGY

Some examples of cutting edge scientific and technological achievements in Israel:

—-A tiny computer from DNA has been developed; they are so tiny, a trillion can be fitted into a test tube.

—-Israel, one of only eight nations to develop, construct, and launch its own satellites, is working on the smallest microsatellite of its kind. (Israel launched its first satellite —the Ofek I in 1988; Ofek 2 in 1989; Ofek 3 in 1995.)

—Professor Eviatar Nevo of Haifa University has pioneered studies on wheat and barley that could lead to a second Green Revolution.

—-A new microchip is the first to combine elements of cellular telephones and handheld computers.

—-A Hebrew University research team is working with the US Defense Department on a process whereby toxic tests light up contaminated water—a process to counter bioterrorism.

—-Professor Stuart Licht of the Technion has developed a super-iron battery that will last 50% longer than a conventional manganese dioxide one. The battery received the 1999 Technology of the Year Award from *Industry Week* magazine.

THE MILITARY DIMENSION

While hungry for peace, Israel has been attacked nine times by its neighbors in little more than half a century. Accordingly, the nation has been compelled to devote a considerable amount of its resources to the design and development of advanced weapons.

Israel's cutting edge technology is of value to the entire world. The Giga Information Group, a leading global advisory service, recently stated, in a Wall Street publication:

"Without Israeli technology, the West will not develop. Many organizations throughout the world, including the American national infrastructure, will not survive for long without constant support from the revolutionary technology coming from Israel."

Giga adds:

"Israeli technology has the greatest influence on the modern world, since it is leading both conceptually and technologically."

Furthermore, the Journal of Information Science (vol. 8, 1984), declared:

"There are select areas in which Israel's scientific performance matches or exceeds the most advanced science superpower."

"In just 55 years, Israel has built a thriving democracy; an economy whose per capita gross national product exceeds the combined total of its four contiguous neighbors — Lebanon, Syria, Jordan, and Egypt; eight universities that contribute to advancing the world's frontiers of knowledge; a life expectancy that places it among the healthiest nations; a prolific culture utilizing an ancient language rendered contemporary; and an agricultural sector that has shown the world how to conquer an arid land."

David A. Harris. Forward, May 9, 2003

Israel's own tank design – Merkava.

SOME 21ST CENTURY DEALS MADE BY ISRAELI FIRMS INCLUDE:

The upgrade of 110 Romanian Air Force Mig-21s (now called Lancers) with Elbit Systems as systems integrator.

An upgrade program for the Mig-29 (renamed the Sniper) with Elbit systems handling avionics development.

Israel Aircraft Industries is upgrading Mig-21s (renamed the 2000) for the Cambodian Air Force.

Israel Aircraft Industries has upgraded the Russian-built Mil 17 tactical assault helicopter with a potential contract with the Indian Air Force for 200 choppers.

Israel Aircraft Industries is working with Poland's military aviation plant on upgrading the Su-22M4 for the Polish Air Force.

Two Israeli firms—Elbit, for systems integration, and Elgad, as a project partner—have upgraded the Su-25KM (now called the Scorpion) for the Georgian Air Force.

Israel Aircraft Industries, Elbit and Singapore Technologies are upgrading 48 F-5 aircraft for the Turkish Air Force.

An Israeli unmanned aerial vehicle – UAV. The United States is among many customers for UAVs from the Jewish State. This is the Hunter, deployed by the US in its war against Iraq in 2002.

Israel is a world leader in many fields, including unmanned aerial vehicles (which it pioneered 20 years ago), missiles, aircraft, tanks, etc. The Jewish State sells military equipment to some of the most advanced industrialized countries in the world, including the United States, Sweden, and Italy. It works on joint weapons programs in partnership with a number of countries, including Russia.

One area in which Israel is a world leader involves upgrading Russian fighter aircraft. The purchase of the new generation of fighter aircraft, whether constructed by the US, Russia, Sweden, Britain or France, involves astronomical sums. Therefore, the upgrading of fighters, especially thousands of Russian Migs worldwide, has become a huge industry. Israeli success in acquiring contracts has been so great that Russian aircraft manufacturers have publicly criticized countries such as Romania and Georgia for making deals with Israeli systems manufacturers.

SOME OTHER RECENT DEVELOPMENTS IN MILITARY TERMS

The United States, in its invasion of Iraq, used several Israeli-developed weapons, including the Army's Hunter drones, the Litening targeting systems of the Marines' Harrier jets, the fuel tanks on the F-15 Eagle fighters, Popeye air-to-surface missiles (called AGM-142) dropped from B-52 bombers, the Marines' unmanned aerial vehicle, the Pioneer, on-board computers on the Army's Bradley Fighting Vehicles.

MERKAVA

When Israel battled for its independence in the late 1940s, she had to use whatever weapons she could acquire, including American and

British tanks battered by use in World War II. However, after decades of modifying and upgrading foreign-made tanks, Israel designed and built its own Main Battle Tank (MBT) the Merkava. The current version in service is the Merkava 4 which, in addition to regular tank fighting assignments, can carry eight infantrymen. Its main armament is an Israeli-designed 120mm smooth bore weapon, mounted in an all-electric turret. In addition, the tank carries 7.62 mm machine guns, and a 60mm mortar system. Its fire control system allows the Markava to acquire and lock on to moving targets while the tank itself continues to move. Israel sells the Markava 3 to other countries, but—for the time being—the Mark 4 is for domestic deployment only.

A Russian-built T-72 tank; Israel has won huge contracts to upgrade the armored vehicle for a number of European countries.

THIRD LARGEST EXPORTER OF ARMS

Israel is the third largest exporter of arms and military services—even ahead of Russia. The United States and Britain are first and second. *Jane's Defense Weekly* estimates Israel's arms sales in 2002 at more than $3.5 billion. The International Institute for Strategic Studies in London rates Israel as the world's fifth largest arms exporter. India has become an increasingly important partner with Israel in arms sales and development. The Jewish state's sales to India were running at a billion dollar a year pace. Israel built unattended ground sensors for India, sold New Delhi its Green Pine radar system for $250 million and the Indians bought $400 million worth of Israel's Barak anti-missile system. A contract for $200 million worth of unmanned drones was signed two years ago. Magal security systems won $4.7 millions in contracts to protect communications facilities throughout India.

In 2003, Israel was negotiating with India for the sale of three Phalcon early warning command and control aircraft worth $1 billion, but, as with a similar deal with China, the US pressured the Israelis to cancel the contract although aircraft were ready for delivery. Ties with India, one of the most populous countries in the world, have become so close that Israel sold the Asians $20 million worth of the new Tavor rifle, at a time when it was being issued only to the Israeli Defense Forces.

Another field with great potential in which Israel is a world leader is the design and construction of unmanned aerial vehicles (UAVs). Israel introduced the UAV in Lebanon in 1982 and has sold its equipment to many countries. Some of the products are secret.

In 2003, Israel completed development of a new system to target the flight of an incoming missile, and determine precisely where the weapon would hit. The system, called "Roman Temple," would allow authorities to move quickly with rescue teams should a missile be fired at Israel.

However, it is known that the country has three main centers for developing UAVs—the Malat Division of Israel Aircraft Industries, a division of Elbit Systems called Silver Arrow, and a division of Israeli Military Industries. UAVs are increasingly used for reconnaissance and delivery of weapons.

Conceivably, in a few years, the most advanced nations will have no humans aboard their combat aircraft. Obviously, Israel is in the front ranks of this kind of development. Flight International (February 3, 2003) quoted Israel Aircraft Industries as saying "in 15-20 years most advanced air forces will operate UAVs carrying out air-to-ground and air-to-air missions."

THE SECURITY DIMENSION

In addition to all-out war, Israelis from the moment their country was reborn, in 1948, have had to battle terrorism. The result is that Israelis are in all likelihood the most security-minded people in the world. And, in addition to a continuing exchange of intelligence information, the Jewish State provides expertise to many countries, particularly the United States, on countering terrorism.

One example: the American FBI now uses Israeli technology, in the form of the "ClearForest" system. The system powers the FBI's counter-terrorist data system.

Another interesting development is a technique for making fingerprints visible. It is a joint Israel-US research program. Researchers from the Hebrew University's Casali Institute of Applied Chemistry, work in cooperation with the Israel Police's Division of Identification and Forensic Science, the University of Pennsylvania's Chemistry Department, and the US Secret Service laboratories in Washington.

They have developed a new chemical reagent causing fingerprints to become visible under special lighting. Using this system, the Israeli police were able to identify one of the men suspected of assassinating Israeli Tourism Minister Rehavam Ze'evi.

THE AMERICANS SEEK ISRAELI GUIDANCE

Israelis, compelled to innovate security techniques and equipment to combat Arab terrorism, are now marketing their expertise. Israel's

Shin Bet security service, for example, provided a course for members of the New York Police Department on how to deal with suicide bombers.

Officials from the Los Angeles Police Department and the State of Georgia, visited Israel for lectures, seminars, and visits with Israeli paramilitary border police units. Israeli police superintendent Shlomo Aharanishky met in Washington with Police Chief Charles Ramsey, and FBI agents on handling suicide bombers. Israeli Police spokesman, Gil Kleinman, stated "No other law enforcement agency has the experience we have in dealing with terrorism within the constraints of a Western system of law and court systems."

No one knows how many Israelis have gone into the security business in America or elsewhere, but even the names of clients are not revealed by those providing security guidance. A popular t-shirt in Israel, on sale for many years, reads: "Don't worry America, Israel is behind you."

Searching for the past. Archaelogists from Haifa University (Israel) and the University of Cagliari (Sardinia) in a dig to uncover the history of the Northern Sea Peoples, known to have been living on the northern coast of Canaan in the 12th century BCE.

CHAPTER TWENTY-SIX

HITLER'S GIFT TO AMERICA

"The study of the history of Europe during the past centuries teaches us one uniform lesson: That the nations which have received and in any way dealt fairly and mercifully with the Jew have prospered; and that the nations that have tortured and oppressed him have written their own curse."
Olive Schreiner (1855-1920), author and feminist

The attainment of power in Germany of Adolf Hitler, in 1933, triggered a sharp and immediate decline in the quality of intellectual life.

THE TYRANTS EMERGE

In the early 1930s, as the world was gripped by the Great Depression, murderous dictators arose in a number of European countries. To seize and retain power, they needed an "enemy" to vanquish and in the minds of people such as Adolf Hitler, Jews were ready-made victims.

Their numbers were small and there were enough anti-Semites in Germany to easily strengthen his hand.

Hitler never counted nor understood the cost. When a German journalist had the temerity to ask him what Germany would do for brains when a multitude of intellectuals were being driven out of the country, the dictator responded "I'll be the brains."

Albert Einstein was one of the first to recognize the handwriting on the wall. Leaving for a lecture tour of the United States in late 1932, the scientist told his wife as they stepped off the porch of their home in Caputh, Germany: "Turn around, you will never see it again."

Princeton University welcomed the great physicist.

IGNORING INTERNATIONAL CONDEMNATION

The Nazis ignored the widespread outcry in reaction to their brutality. Onetime U. S. President Herbert Hoover, in a broadcast on November 14, 1936, declared:

"These indviduals are taking Germany back 450 years in civilization to Torquemada's expulsion of the Jews from Spain."

Laura Fermi, wife of the great nuclear scientist, wrote in her book *Illustrious Immigrants*, (1968):

"The main weapon of modern dictators against the intellegentsia was anti-Semitism. The European intellgentsia was especially vulnerable because a large part of it was Jewish."

Jews made up 1% of the German population when the Nazis seized power but they were 12% of university professors. When the exodus came, a variety of second- and third- rate scholars were only too willing to take over. Before Hitler assumed power, Germany was the foremost scientific nation in the world. Up until 1932, 100 Nobel Prizes were awarded to scientists who were either German or working in Germany. Although Jews were only, as stated above, 1% of the population of the country, one quarter of the German Laureates were Jews or of Jewish descent.

Only six prizes had gone to the United States in the years leading up to the dictator's assumption of power. With the flow of intelligentsia from Europe to the US, the situation was reversed.

German concentration camps (this is the entrance to Auschwitz) swallowed millions, including six-million Jews. How many Einsteins did the Nazis murder?

FLEEING TO THE NEW BABYLON

Hitler's first anti-Jewish law was promulgated in April, 1933, and all "non- Aryan" academics were dismissed. This law shut out of the classrooms one quarter of all the physicists in Germany. These included eleven who had been or would be Nobel laureates.

While precise statistics are not available, there were about 525,000 Jews, by religion, in Germany when Hitler became dictator. About 300,000 managed to emigrate from Germany and Austria in the mid- to late-1930s. A large proportion of these people—132,000—found sanctuary in the United States.

The Germans themselves estimate that more than 3,000 university employees alone migrated.

Alan D. Beyerchen, in his *Scientists under Hitler* states:

"By 1935, approximately one out of five scientists had been driven from their positions. The total among physicists was even higher— about one out of four."

American Men of Science indicated that 20 Nobel Laureates left their positions in Germany in the period 1933-1945. Of these, 18 were Jewish. The other two had Jewish wives. Britain absorbed more scientists than any other country, but didn't have the financial resources to keep them. Most went to the US

MORE THAN 100 PHYSICISTS AND THE BOMB

An American Emergency Committee reported that 30 scientists and scholars reached the United States in 1933; 32 more came in 1934;15 in 1935; 43 in 1938; 97 in 1939; 59 in 1940; and 50 in 1941.

The Nazis' Minister of Propaganda, Joseph Goebbels, almost immediately called for a boycott of Jewish business.

The Nazis burn books.

Approximately 100 of these scientists were physicists. Many were recruited for the Manhattan Project, and helped create the atomic bomb.

Max Dimont wrote in *The Jews in America*—"Between 1933 and 1939 the Johnson Act provisions were waived to permit 157,000 Jewish refugees from Hitler's Europe to enter the United States." Another 60,000, who applied for sanctuary, were unable to emigrate to the US, because of bureaucratic difficulties. The group absorbed by the US was to exert an immense influence on American life, as it represented a large segment of Germany's intellectual elite—world-renowned academic leaders and scientists—symbolized by Albert Einstein. Their entry marked the transfer of the world's intellectual leadership from Europe to America, as evidenced by the dramatic increase in the number of Nobel Prizes awarded to Americans."

MORE THAN 3,500 PROFESSORS AND TEACHERS

The United States listed among immigrants from Germany and Austria, for the 1933-1944 period, 1,500 musicians, 3,569 professors or teachers, 1,900 scientists and literary people, and 702 sculptors or artists!

Fermi, in *Illustrious Immigrants,* noted that Jews comprised 33.6% of the total immigration 1933-1944. "Among the intellectuals, " she wrote, "the proportion of Jews may have been slightly higher than in other groups."

Studies show the extent of the damage caused to the German educational system. 1,684 scholars were dismissed. Of these, 800 were professors or lecturers. Actor Marlon Brando, recalling the New York of the 1940s, told the *New York Post* (Oct. 3, 1994):

"The extraordinary European Jews (who immigrated to New York) were enriching the City's intellectual life with an intensity that has probably never been equaled anywhere during a comparable period of time. I was raised largely by these Jews. I lived in a world of Jews. They were my teachers; they were my employers; they were my friends. They introduced me to a world of books and ideas that I didn't know existed."

After 1937, changed German currency regulations permitted emigrants to take only ten marks out of the country, ensuring that the new arrivals in the US and other countries would arrive penniless. The immigrants, most of whom had been prosperous in the Old Country, had expensive wardrobes, but had to accept menial work.

The Nobel Laureates who escaped from Germany in the period 1933-1945

Name	Year of departure	Year of Nobel Prize	Discipline
Albert Einstein	1933	1921	Physics
James Franck	1933	1925	Physics
Erwin Schrodinger	1933	1933	Physics
Otto Stern	1933	1943	Physics
Felix Bloch	1933	1952	Physics
Max Born	1933	1954	Physics
Eugene Wigner	1933	1963	Physics
Hans Bethe	1933	1967	Physics
Dennis Gabor	1933	1971	Physics
Fritz Haber	1933	1918	Chemistry
George de Hevesy	1934	1943	Chemistry
Otto Meyerhof	1938	1918	Medicine
Otto Loew	1938	1936	Medicine
Boris Chain (Sir)	1933	1945	Medicine
Hans A. Krebs	1933	1953	Medicine

THE JEWISH CONTRIBUTION

"Of the lucky ones who escaped," wrote Jarrell C. Jackman and Carla M. Borden, " about one hundred physicists found refuge and a new productive life in the United States between 1933 and 1941." They continue:

"In the physical sciences, the influx of refugees from Germany, and later from the fascist tyranny in Italy and Austria, provided the necessary critical infusion of high talent that helped turn the United States rather suddenly into the world's pre-eminent country for the pursuit of frontier research."

A Committee "for the Study of Recent Immigration from Europe," in its 1947 report, stated "the total number of physicians and dentists, including medical students and non-practitioners, admitted to the United States from all countries in the period July 1, 1933, to June 30, 1944, was 6,426."

The Committee reported that 83% of respondents to its questionnaire were Jewish, 10%, Protestant; 5% Roman Catholics; and

The dictatorial sickness spread from Germany to other countries in central Europe. Here Hungarian Jews are forced to wear yellow badges, making them a target for anti-Semites.

2% of other faiths or with no religious affiliation. "Nearly 90% were licensed physicians," the Committee stated. The Report noted that of 707 refugee professors then in the US the most important groups were in Law—74; Physics—71; Medical Science—71; Language and Literature—65; Chemistry—63; Economics—60; Mathematics—53; History—45; Philosophy—44; Art and Archaeology—33; and Psychology—25.

DISTINGUISHED REFUGEES

The 1946 Report concluded with nine pages of "distinguished refugees," headed by 12 Nobel Prize winners. The immense contribution of the newcomers was further acknowledged with long lists of those mentioned in *Who's Who* and *American Men of Science*.

In 1958, chemist Hans Clarke reported, in connection with his research program:

"Among the many benefits which accrued to Columbia University from the racial policy adopted by the Germans under the Third Reich was the arrival in our laboratory of various European-trained biochemists....The scientific achievements subsequently made by these men are so well-known that their enumeration is unnecessary."

Eight of the refugee chemists were Nobel laureates.

THE UNITED STATES ENRICHED

In sum, the United States was markedly enriched by the arrival of intellectuals driven out of their European countries by dictators. And, similarly, Europe was proportionately impoverished by the loss of these exceptional people. The change was apparent in citations in the five leading journals of Germany, England, France, and America. In 1897, Germans had 64% of the citations. America had only 3%.

By 1933, with the influx of German (and overwhelmingly Jewish) scientists into the US, the figures were quite different: 36% were German and 33%, American.

Ellis Island, where millions of immigrants had their first glimpse of America – and freedom.

MORE THAN SCIENTISTS

There were many other fields represented among the refugees.

Milton Plesur, in his *Jewish Life in Twentieth Century America* noted:

"The cultural life led by this group (of German refugees) was cosmopolitan. Kurt Weill, the composer; Emil Ludwig, the biographer; Max Reinhardt of the theater; Dr. Theodor Reik, the psychoanalyst; and, of course, Albert Einstein, originator of the theory of relativity, were all examples of the intellectual eminence that Hitler drove to these shores."

Two generations earlier, Joseph Ernest Renan had written in his *Recollections of Infancy and Youth,"* (1883):

"Germany, after devoting herself entirely to military life, would have had no talent left if it were not for the Jews, to whom she has been so ungrateful."

Renan wrote those lines more than half a century before Hitler and the Nazis began a long-planned effort to wipe out European Jewry.

Bibliography

Arieti, Silvano, *Creativity; The Magic Synthesis*, Basic Books, 1976

Bermant, Chaim, *The Jews*, Sphere Books, 1977

Beyerchen, Alan D., *Scientists Under Hitler*, Yale University Press, 1977

Brody, Seymour, *Jewish Heroes of America*, Shapolsky Publishers, 1991

Bullock, Alan, Hitler: *A Study In Tyranny*, Harper & Row, 1962

Canning, John, *100 Great Modern Lives*, Souvenir Press, 1972.

Champlin, Charles, *Flicks*, Ward Ritchie Press, 1977

Clark, Ronald, *Works of Man*, Century Publishing, 1985

Comay, Joan, *Who's Who in Jewish History*, Routledge, 2002

Davie, Maurice R., *Refugees in America*, Harper and Brothers Publishers, 1947

Dimont, Max I., *Jews, God and History*, A Mentor Book, 1994

Dippel, John V.H., *Bound upon a wheel of fire*, Basic Books - 1994

Downs, Robert B., Flanan, John T., Westcott, Harold, *Memorable Americans*, Libraries Unlimited - 1983

Drennan, Robert E., *The Algonquin Wits*, The Citadel Press, 1975

Eban, Abba, *Heritage: Civilization and the Jews*, Summit Books - 1984

Feingold, Henry L. *Zion in America*, Twayne Publishers - 1974

Feingold, Laura *Illustrious Immigrant*s, University of Chicago Press, 1968

Flood, Charles Bracelen, *Hitler: The Path To Power*, Houghton Mifflin - 1989

Forbes, Malcolm with Jeff Bloch: *They Went That-a-way...*, Balantine Books - 1988

Friedlander, Saul, *Nazi Germany and the Jews*, HarperCollins - 1997

Gaines, James R., *Wit's End*, Harcourt Brace Jovanovich -1977

Gay, Ruth, *Jews in America; A Short History*, Basic Books - 1965

Gilbert, Sir Martin, *The Jews in the Twentieth Century*, Key Porter Books - 2001

Goldberg, M. Hirsh, *The Jewish Connection*, Stein and Day - 1976

Goldscheider, Calvin, *Jewish Continuity and Change; Emerging Patterns in America*, Indiana University Press - 1986

Gruen, John, *Close Up*, The Viking Press - 1968

Gutstein, Linda, *History of the Jews in Americ*a, Chartwell Books - 1988

Hertz, Rabbi Joseph Herman, *A Book of Jewish Thoughts*, Bloch Publishing Co. - 1937

Higham, Charles, *Celebrity Circus*, Delacorte Press - 1979

Hoyt, Jr., Edwin P., *The Guggenheims and the American Dream*, Funk and Wagnalls - 1967

Jackman, Jarrell C. and Borden, Carla M., *The Muses Flee Hitler*, Smithsonian Institution Press - 1983

Jaffe, Bernard, *Men of Science in America*, Simon and Schuster - 1946

Johnson Paul, *A History of the American People*, Phoenix Giant - 1997

Johnson, Paul, *A History of the Jews*, Phoenix Giant - 1987

Keylin, Arleen, *Great Lives of the Century*, Times Books - 1977

King, Joe, Mr. *Profile*, Canadian Friends of Tel Aviv University - 1984

Koppman, Lionel and Postal, Bernard, *"Guess Who's Jewish in American History,"* New American Library, 1978.

Kruif, Paul de, *Microbe Hunters*, Harcourt Brace & Co., 1926

Lamb, Brian, *Booknotes; Life Stories*, Random House, 1999

Leithauser, Joachim G., *Inventors of Our World*, Weidenfeld and Nicolson - 1954

Levy. Joel, *Really Useful*, Firefly Books - 2002

Lyman, Darryl, *Great Jewish Families*, Jonathan David Publishers - 1997

Mendes-Flohr, Paul & Reinharz, Jehuda, *The Jew and the Modern World*, - 1995

Morris, Desmond, *The Book of Ages*, Jonathan Cape - 1984

Mumford, Lewis, *Technics and Civilization*, Harcourt, Brace & World - 1962

Patai, Raphael, *The Jewish Mind* Charles Scribner's Sons - 1977

Plesur, Milton, *Jewish Life in Twentieth Century America*, Nelson-Hall - 1982

Polner, Murray, *Jewish Profiles*, Jason Aronson Inc. - 1991

Shapiro, Michael, *The Jewish 100*, Citadel Press - 1995

Shipman, David, *The Great Movie Stars*, A & W Visual Library - 1973

Silverman, Stephen M., *Where There's a Will ...*, Harper Collins - 1991

Smith, Godfrey, *1000 Makers of the 20th Century* - 1971

Thomas, Henry and Dana Lee, *50 Great Modern Lives*, Hanover House - 1956

Tynan, Kenneth, *Profiles*, Harper Perennial - 1989

Untermeyer, Louis, *Makers of the Modern World*, Simon and Schuster - 1955

Wallechinsky, David, *The Twentieth Century*, The Overlook Press - 1999

Wittke, Carl, *We Who Built America*; The Saga of the Immigrant, The Press of Western Reserve University - 1939

ENCYLOPEDIAE:

Asimov's Biographical Encyclopedia of Science and Technology by Isaac Asimov, Doubleday & Company - 1982

Biographical Encyclopedia of the World, Institute for Research in Biography - 1940

Dunlop Illustrated Encyclopedia of Facts, Dreghorn Publications - 1969

Encyclopedia Brittanica, 15th Edition - 1993

Encyclopedia of Jewish Knowledge, edited by Jacob de Haas, Benjamin's Book House - 1934

Encyclopedia of the Third Reich, Edited by Christian Zentner and Friedemann Bedurftig, MacMillan Publishing - 1991

Encyclopedia of World Biography, Gale - 1998

Grolier Academic Encyclopedia - 1983 edition

Harvard Encyclopedia of American Ethnic Groups, Stephen Thernstrom, Editor, Harvard University Press - 1980

The Hutchison Encyclopedia, Helicon Publishing - 1995 edition

The Illustrated Encyclopedia of Astronomy and Space, Ian Redpath, Editor, Thomas Y. Crowell - 1979
Jewish-American History and Culture, An Encyclopedia, edited by Jack Fischel and Sanford Pinsker, Garland Publishing Inc. - 1992
The New Standard Jewish Encyclopedia, Geoffrey Wigidor, Editor in Chief, Facts on File - 1992 (7th edition)
Pears Cyclopedia, Edited by Christopher Cook, Penguin - 2001-2002
The Shengold Jewish Encyclopedia, Edited by Mordecai Shengold, Shengold Publications - 2001

REFERENCE BOOKS:

100 Most Important Women of the 20th Century, author Kevin Markey, Ladies Home Journal Books - 1998
American Jewish Biographies, Lakeville Press - 1982
American Jewish Year Books - various years
American Jewish Desk Reference, American Jewish Historical Society - 1999
The Annual Obituary, Louise Mooney, Editor, St. James Press - various years
Asimov's Chronology of Science and Discovery, Isaac Asimov, Harper & Row -1989
Baker's Biographical Dictionary of Musicians, 8th edition, Maxwell MacMillan Canada - 1992
The Biographical Dictionary of World War Two, Mark M. Boatner III, Presidio - 1996
The Blackwell Companion to Jewish Culture, Edited by Glenda Abramson, Blackwell Reference - 1989
The Book of Jewish Lists, Ron Landau, Stein and Day - 1984
Calendar of Creative Man, John Paxton and Sheila Fairfield, Facts on File - 1979
The Cambridge Dictionary of Scientists, David, Ian, John and Margaret Millar, Cambridge University Press - 1996
Canadian Aircraft since 1909, K.M. Molson and H.A. Taylor - 1982
Celebrity Register, Simon and Schuster - 1973
Chambers Biographical Dictionary, Magnus Magnusson, General Editor, Chambers -1990
The Dictionary of Biographical Quotation, edited by Richard Kenin and Justin Wintle, Alfred A. Knopf - 1978
Dictionary of Jewish Biography, by Geoffrey Wigidor, Simon and Schuster - 1991
A Dictionary of Military History, edited by Andre Corvisier, Blackwell Reference - 1994
A Dictionary of Twentieth Century Quotations," Nigel Rees, Fontana/Collins - 1987
A Dictionary of Twentieth Century World Biography, Editor Asa Briggs, Oxford University Press - 1992
Famous First Facts, Joseph Nathan Kane, H.W. Wilson Company - 1997
The First of Everything, Dennis Sanders, Delacorte Press - 1981
Great Jewish Men, Elinor and Robert Slater, Jonathan David Publishers - 1996
Great Jewish Women, Elinor and Robert Slater, Jonathan David Publishers - 1994
Great Lives of the 20th Century, Edited by Arleen Keylin, Time Books - 1988
The Grove Dictionary of Opera, edited by Stanley Sadie - 1992
The International Opera Guide, F.M. Stockdale and M.R. Dreyer, MacLelland and Stewart - 1990
Inventions and Discoveries, editors Valerie-Anne Giscard d'Estaing and Mark Young, Facts on File - 1993
Inventors of Our World, Widenfeld and Nicolson - 1954
Israel Yearbook and Almanac, various years
Jane's All the World's Aircraft, Mark Lambert Editor-in-chief, Jane's Data Division 1992-1993
The Jewish Lists, Martin H. Greenberg, Schocken Books -1979

Jews in the World of Science; a Biographical Dictionary, Monde Publishers - 1956.

Larousse Dictionary of Scientists, Hazel Muir, Editor - 1994

Larousse Dictionary of Women, Melanie Parry, Editor - 1997

The Little, Brown Book of Anecdotes, Clifton Fadiman, general editor, Little Brown and Company - 1985

Makers of the Twentieth Century, General Editor Alan Bullock - 1981

Milestones in Science and Technology, by Ellis Mount and Barbara A. List, Oryx Press - 1987

Modern Men of Science, McGraw-Hill - 1968

The New Penguin Dictionary of Modern Quotations, Robert Andrews, Editor, Penguin - 2000

Newsmakers, Geri Koeppel, Gale Group - 2000, 2001, 2002, 2003

New Statesman Profiles, Phoenix House - 1957

The New York Public Library Science Desk Reference, Stonesong Press - 1995

The New York Times 2003 Almanac, editor John W. Wright - 2002

Nobel Prize Winners, an H.W. Wilson Biographical Dictionary, H.W. Wilson Company - 1987

The Oxford Companion to World War II, I.C.B. Dear, General Editor, Oxford University Press - 1995

A People that Dwells Alone, edited by Misha Louvish, Sanhedrin Press - 1975

The Shell Book of Firsts, by Patrick Robertson, Eloury Press and Michael Joseph -1974

Stories Behind Everyday Things, The Reader's Digest Association - 1980

They Made History; A Biographical Dictionary," Simon and Schuster - 1993

Thinkers of the Twentieth Century, Gale Research Company - 1983

Time Almanac, various years

A Treasury of Jewish Anecdotes, Lawrence J. Epstein, Jason Aronson Inc. - 1995

A Treasury of Jewish Quotations, edited by Joseph L. Baron, Crown Publishers - 1956

Who's Who in Comedy, Ronald L. Smith, Facts on File -

Who's Who in Frontiers of Science and Technology, 2nd edition, Marquis

Who's Who - 1985

Who's Who in Modern History 1860-1980 by Alan Palmer, George Weidenfeld and Nicolson - 1980

Who's Who in World Jewry, editor Judith Turk Rosenblatt, Who's Who In World Jewry - 1987

World of Invention, editor Bridget Travers, Gale Research - 1994

JOURNALS:

Air Forces Monthly
Air International
Business 2.0
Canadian Jewish News
Christian Science Monitor
Current Biography
Discover
Fortune
Gazette (Montreal)
International Herald-Tribune (Paris)
The Jewish Press (New York)
Jerusalem Post International
The Jerusalem Reporter
Lifestyles
Maclean's
New York Times
New Yorker
People
Science News
Scientific American
Times of London

LIBRARIES UTILIZED:

Atwater Library, Montreal
Dawson College Library, Montreal
Dollard des Ormeaux Public Library,
    Dollard des Ormeaux, Que
Eleanor London Public Library, Cote
    Saint-Luc, Quebec
Fraser-Hickson Institute, Montreal
McGill University
Ottawa Public Library
Reginald Dawson Public Library, Town
    of Mount Royal, Quebec
Toronto Reference Library
Westmount Public Library

WEBSITES:

Airship Image Library
Aviation-history
Carnegie Library of Pittsburgh
Carnegie Museum of Natural History
The Emile Durkheim Archive (L. Joe Dunman)
GNUPedia
Hebrew History Federation Ltd.
Idavette
Imperial College, London
Institut fur Psychologie
Invent/hall of fame
Jet Propulsion Laboratory,
California Institute of Technology
Jewhoo !
Jewish American Hall of Fame

JewishGen
Jewish Virtual Library
Masssachusetts Institute of Technology
Museum of the Jewish People
National Academic Press
National Aeronautics and Space
    Administration
The Nobel Prize Internet Archive
Realcart University
Rensselaer Alumni Hall of Fame
Retrocom
Science Women
The University of Chicago hospitals
    scienceworld.wolfram.com
Vanderbilt Medical Center

Index

Publications Committee

Professor Lawrence M. Bessner, F.C.A.   Hy Adelman
Co-Chairs

Sylvain Abitbol   Monty Berger   Joseph Paperman
Vice-Chairs

Honorary Editorial Committee

Honorable Sheila Abbey-Finestone, P.C.
Sara Bedzow
Rita Briansky
Melvyn A. Dobrin
Leonard Ellen, LL.D. (Honorary)
Marc Gold
Victor C. Goldbloom, C.C., O.Q., U.D., Litt. D, D.U., M.D.
Mildred B. Lande, C.M.
Judge Barbara Seal, C.M.
Bernard J. Shapiro, O.C., B.A., M.A.T., Ed. D., LL.D. (Honorary)

Dr. Charles Bedzow
Honorable Lawrence S. Bergman, M.N.A.
Rita Cohen, S.C.A.
Bina Ellen
Nathan Finkelstein
Nancy Gold

Stanley K. Plotnick
Donald W. Seal, Q.C.

The Author

Joe King is a veteran journalist and broadcaster whose career began with The Canadian Press News Agency in Toronto and has spanned some 60 years in radio, television and newspapers.

During that busy six decades he focussed on news and public affairs, largely on radio and television.

He travelled widely—nineteen trips to the Middle East alone. And interviewed or reported on some of the greatest figures in modern history. He travelled for half a day with Charles de Gaulle. He wrote and produced a television documentary with Yuri Gagarin, the first man in space. He relaxed on a spot in Israel with David Ben Gurion, who told him how he would be buried there—beside his "beloved wife Paula" and look out on the Negev desert "for eternity."

He feels quite honored that, during his career, he has come under fire on several occasions—in the Syrian City of Kuneitra in 1967 when sniper bullets whizzed by his head, in the Bar Lev Line in 1973 when Egyptian artillery shells pounded the fortifications, and in 1982 when he observed, from the steps of the Lebanese President's Palace in Beirut the final Israeli aerial assault on Palestinian terrorists' positions.

A pilot officer with the Royal Canadian Air Force in World War Two, he did extensive post-war television reporting on NATO activities—working from submerged submarines, patrol bombers, carrier-launched aircraft and in the field, from German tank units to British commandos training in Canada

He interviewed and often profiled some of the leading figures in Canadian history, from Lester Bowles Pearson to the colorful Pierre Trudeau.

In 1999, "retired" for ten years, he was commissioned to write a "popular, illustrated history" of the Montreal Jewish Community. The result was *From the Ghetto to the Main*," now in its third edition.

Two years later, angered by a statement by the Grand Mufti of Jerusalem that "there's not a Jewish stone in Jerusalem. The story of the Temple is a myth," he researched and wrote *The Case for Israel*.

Along the way, he has collected more than 30 awards, including the Liberty Television News Documentary Award for a program on Adolf Eichman, two Radio and Television News Directors' radio documentaries and Dalhousie University's prestigious gold "D" for a program he wrote and produced on the Nova Scotia university. Most writers are poor speakers; most orators are weak in writing style. But Joe King is rather unusual that he, if anything, articulates more effectively than he writes. He is a passionate speaker. And his calendar generally includes about 30 speaking engagements a year.

Married, for 55 years, to Shandle Lipkus King, with three children—all with partners—and four grandchildren, the author still finds time to remain involved with the Montreal Print Collectors Society, which he founded 20 years ago, and is active seven days a week.

Printed in Canada